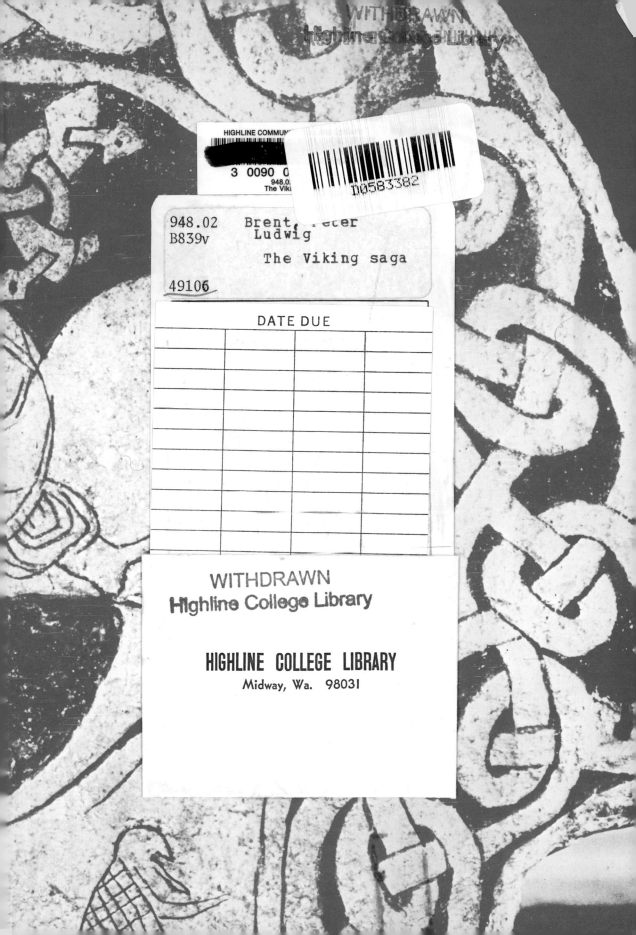

THE
VIKING
SAGA

THE VIKING SAGA

PETER BRENT

WEIDENFELD AND NICOLSON
LONDON

PREVIOUS PAGE Silver cross in Slav-Byzantine
style from Norsberg, Botkyrka.

Designed by David Eldred for
George Weidenfeld and Nicolson
Limited, London
Filmset in Great Britain by
Keyspools Limited, Golborne, Lancashire
Printed by
Tinling (1973) Limited, Prescot, Merseyside
ISBN 0 297 76935 9

CONTENTS

ACKNOWLEDGMENTS

The author and publisher would like to thank the following museums, institutions and photographers for supplying the illustrations reproduced on the pages listed below:

Antikvarisk-Topografiska Arkivet, Stockholm title page, 44, 54 (top), 132, 142, 147, 160, 163, 169 (right), 180, 181, 217 (left), 223, 233; British Museum 40, 67, 72, 89, 97, 102; British Tourist Authority 104–5; C. M. Dixon 122; Department of the Environment, Edinburgh 126; Françoise Foliot 39; Gävle Museum, Sweden 169 (left); Guildhall Museum 64–5; Michael Holford Library *81, 82, 99, 100, 133, 151*; London Museum 71; Manx Museum 125; Nationalmuseet, Copenhagen 150, 205, 213 (right), 217 (right), 218 (top), 229, 235; National Museum of Iceland, Reykjavik 147 (bottom), 196, 198, 200, 203; National Museum of Ireland 107, 110, 111, 115, 116; Österreichische Nationalbibliothek 36; Radio Times Hulton Picture Library 60, 88, 174, 226, 230–1, 238–9; Scala 50; Service de Documentation Photographiques, Paris 35; Universitetets Oldsaksamling, Oslo 10, 12, 16, 20 (left), 21 (right), *134,* 164–5; Utrecht University Library 32–3; H. Roger Viollet 46–7; Werner Forman Archive 2, 8, 17, 43, 128–9, 137, 144, 145, *152,* 157, 172, 177, 206, 210, 213 (left), 214–15, 242, 243, 247.

Numbers in italics refer to colour illustrations.

Picture research by Pat Hodgson.

The maps on pages 24–5, 42, 79, 167, 191 and 249 were drawn by Jennifer Johnson.

FAROES

TROMS

NORWAY

Nordland

NORRLAND

FINLAND

Vatnsfjord

Trondheim

Tröndelag

Nordfjord

Sogn

Hedemark

SWEDEN

Dalarna

Bergen

Ringerike

Västmanland

Uppsala

Rogaland

Vestfold

Sigtuna

Stavanger

Oslofjord

Birka

Stockholm

Vest Agder

Helgö

ESTONIA

Västergötland

Östergötland

Småland

Gotland

LATVIA

Jutland

Århus

Hälsingborg

Copenhagen

Skåne

Ribe

Fyn

Zealand

Lund

Bornholm

BALTIC SEA

DENMARK

Schleswig

Hedeby

Wendland

Scandinavia

8

A fifth-century picture stone from Martebo,
Gotland, Sweden. It is the earliest one known,
and depicts hunting scenes and whorls
symbolizing the sun.

INTRODUCTION

The ship sings. It thrums to the wind, to the tensions of its wide sail. The water darkens the carvings on its prow; the salt lies in their intricacies, outlining fanged skull and dragon tail. Gape-jawed, the ship's head stoops and stretches above the spray, unafraid of the horizon's recession.

The *langskip*, dark in the grey water, striding relentlessly over the broken crests of these northern seas – the dragon-ship, its maw hungry for plunder. It is a twenty-bencher, clinker-built, low above the waves. It runs as the wind runs, its woollen sail taut before its single mast. In the stern, a man stands braced against the pull and tug of the wide paddle-rudder slung over the starboard quarter. When he looks forward, he can see the full shape of the ship he steers. That head, held so high, so menacingly, is some seventy feet from where he stands; it bumps towards the sky, then bows again in momentary meekness. The timbers moan softly, creak, sigh and settle; below the long keel the water hisses, hisses. . . . Behind the steersman where he balances upon the loose planks of the short deck, cloak flapping and hands firm on the tiller, the tail of the dragon-ship rises and curls, carved, frisking and bobbing above the waves. Under the stern a white wake bubbles, then dies.

Beside the steersman sits the expedition's leader. He is in his thirties, perhaps, fair-haired, long-headed, bearded. His father, almost certainly, is an aristocrat, a *jarl* – and so will his elder brother be, when the father is dead. Land and high birth press him, and time. Or it may be that he has left behind him not the security of an established house but defeat and disgrace, a failed attempt at usurpation, a blood-feud. In his homelands, there are many such, many men in flight as a result and all hungry for new fortune and recovered honour. Whatever his reasons, he must make his own history. The wind tugs at his green tunic, at his rough, cowled cloak. He peers forward, over the heads of his men, beyond the dragon-head, at the waiting realization of his dreams. He thinks of fat cattle, plump women, of green lands and great deeds. In his head he hears the voice of the *skáld*, the poet, the singer of praise, adding his name to the long catalogue of heroes. For that most of all he has chosen the sea-ways, has gone *i víking*.

In the wide body of the longship, the men wait, his men, free men who have taken his way for their own share of the plunder. They sit on their dark sea-chests. Kept from the corrosive sea their weapons lie – sword, axe, spear. Their shields hang outboard, wooden shields, painted, metal-rimmed, each shield-boss a glaring Cyclops's eye. Some of the men have bows, and arrows in cylindrical quivers.

ABOVE The burial ship of a Viking princess, excavated at Oseberg in South Norway in 1904. The wood carving on it and on objects found in it are typical of the best in Viking art.

LEFT The reconstructed prow of the Oseberg ship is decorated with animals and, at the tip, a serpent's head.

Perhaps these are Norsemen from Norway, that long country of black water and grey rock, whose bowmen are famous. They sit, staring out over jagged waves whose tops lift higher than their heads; they feel at one with these waves, with the motion and weight of the sea; they can feel the sea through the oak timbers of their ship, their *kölfågeln* or keel-bird, as Swedes might call it, their *havsbocken*, their sea-goat.

How do they know where they are on that wide sea? Perhaps by something close to instinct. The ship-master knows these ways, the winds and currents of these waters, as though they flowed through his own body. He knows that – like his body – they can betray him, overturn and kill. Nevertheless, they are a part of him; he responds, then masters, like a skilful rider on a thoroughbred. The world he moves through is a dictionary, its clouds and smells and drifting weeds the words which fill it. He can define each one; from each one he learns another phrase of his geography. The sun and the stars are his constants, the winds and the birds which sail on them the variables which give depth and a new precision to his knowledge. Perhaps, too, he has instruments – a bearing-dial of wood, notched for the points of the compass; it may be even the light-polarizing *sólarsteinn*, which, by gathering the light into a single direction, will offer the sun's guidance even when the sun itself cannot be seen.

In the distance, low-lying clouds coagulate, become the blue outline of a coast. Landfall! A look-out calls the news. Someone laughs, another sings a snatch of song. All gather weapons, check their keenness. Swords are hefted, spears weighed in the hand. The son of the *jarl*, the leader, looks out to his right. Two more ships leap there, marked by the white foam, shaded by sails. He smiles. In his own ship, men are already at the mast. The sail diminishes, collapses. Already the bungs have been taken from the holes along the sides, already the first oars are in the water. Twenty-eight men, bent on their sea-chests, stretch for the first short stroke. The oars dig and hold, the men grunt with effort. The shore is dragged closer. There are huts under a hillside, sheep on pasture, smoke from hearths still for the moment peaceful. The men drive their ship forward. To the right and a little behind, their companions hammer out the same direction. The men struggle to keep the honour of bringing the first ship to the shore. Their leader, standing now, has put on a *hringskyrta*, a shirt of chain-mail; on his head there is a conical helmet, made sinister by its attached nose-guard and protection for the eyes. He stares out at the unfolding world of his new fortune. Its beaches, its headlands and green hills are now very close.

The keel scrapes, strikes, scrapes again. Already, the first men are over the bows, wading ashore. Others drag the ship higher. The second ship is at the beach now, its crew wading to land. They shout, to gather up courage, to pinion the enemy with fear. The third ship reaches the land. Already, the leading men of the first crew are on the path that will bring them to the village under the hill. As they reach the top of the low bluffs, distantly a shout arises, then a cacophony of screams. Laughing, the Vikings run towards their prey. . . .

Part of the reconstructed mid-ninth-century
tapestry from the Oseberg ship burial. It was
woven in a long strip about 23 centimetres
wide, and illustrated mythological scenes
probably associated with the cult of the dead.

1 BREAK-OUT

Lindisfarne: even today the name carries a remote echo of shock and outrage. Alcuin, spreading Christ's word to the followers of Charlemagne, felt its first resonance and wrote that 'never before in Britain has such a terror appeared as this we have now suffered at the hands of the heathen.' Norsemen were known, of course, in that turbulent eighth century; some were known as pirates. Until that time, however, most of their vigour had been used up in the knifings and ambuscades, the sudden raids and vicious battles of their own endless, fragmented struggles for personal power.

All the same, the *Anglo-Saxon Chronicle*'s entry for the year 787, telling of the reign of Beohtric, gives the ominous information, 'And in his days came for the first time three ships of Norwegians from Hordaland, and then the king's reeve rode thither and tried to make them go to the royal manor, for he did not know who or what they were, and with that they killed him.' Written with glum hindsight, that 'came for the first time' shows a recognition of what this single visitation portended. For the chroniclers, writing in Alfred's day, there was no surprise that the king's reeve, a man named Beaduheard, should have been killed out of hand, riding down from Dorchester to the three ships, perhaps with a hand raised in greeting, some question, only half-suspicious, on his lips, something about their cargo or their purpose, only to be abruptly and mercilessly cut down. What was important was that these had been 'the first ships of the Danes to come to England' – and if there was confusion about the raiders' origins, there was none about their identity or purpose.

But Alcuin, a civilized man, a learned and religious man, and one faced directly with events he could hardly comprehend so heinous did they seem, was thrown back after Lindisfarne in horrified confusion. Lindisfarne was holy ground, the monastery there famous and well-regarded, the island a place of peace, an abode dedicated to those dedicated to God. For these men to be slaughtered, for these walls to be affronted by their screams of pain, for their blood to flow and their gold – God's gold – to be taken, seemed to contemporaries an act of inexplicable savagery. Alcuin could not understand, either, how it had happened – 'Nor was it thought possible that such an inroad from the sea could be made.' It had been made, however, and would be made again, at Lindisfarne and a hundred other places.

In 794, it was the monastery at Jarrow, on that same north-eastern coast of

Britain, which felt the violence of Viking greed, for in this year 'the heathens ravaged in Northumbria.' The island of Iona, off Scotland's west coast, a widely known centre of faith, a monastery like that of Lindisfarne, intended for a continuing idyll between man and God, was plundered and partly destroyed in 795. In the same year, so the old stories say, the Vikings fell upon what is now Glamorganshire, but were hewn down or thrown back by the men of Morgannwg, determined then as now to maintain their integrity. And, still in that same active year, the Norsemen sailed westward from the Western Isles and robbed a church on the isle of Lambey, north of Dublin, and burned it down. Four years later, they had reached the Bay of Biscay and were harrying, in the same bloody fashion, islands off the coast of Aquitaine. By the end of that last decade of the eighth century, much of Europe must have begun to realize that a new force had sprung up, vicious, unpredictable, striking with abrupt ferocity, taking what it could carry off, destroying what it could not. The true years of the Viking had begun.

There was never, of course, a Viking nation; indeed, for a long time there were no nations of any kind in Scandinavia. There were groupings, mostly tribal, dominated by leaders who arose, ruled and were struck down in a constant confusion of warfare, regicide, rebellion and catastrophe. There were strong men who rose above this welter and left a recognizable mark on history. In Denmark at about this time, Godfred came to the throne and, with an inventive audacity, struck at the threatening power of Charlemagne. In Norway, Østland, centred on the long hook of the Oslofjord, was the nucleus of power, a conglomeration of chieftaincies, petty kingdoms and embryonic commonwealths enriched by the good land which they divided and by the trade their own wealth drew to them. In the north lay Trøndelag, the land there rich too, the high slopes heavy with grazing for cattle and sheep. Westward lay the dark fjords and scanty pastures upon which generations of hardy men grew sinewy and perhaps bitter with poverty. It was there that Hordaland lay, identified by the Saxon chroniclers, with whatever truth, as the place from which those first raiders had come to plunder, and in the process to kill the king's representative. They were right to think it likely; these were the Viking settlements, bleak places from which the rest of the world, away to the south and west, looked very rich.

Sweden is dark, its political structure unresolved. It was in slow ferment, but we, eleven centuries later, cannot make out the details. The Suiones described by Tacitus in the first century AD still retained their cohesion: the Svea of the year 800 grew rich on trade. They looked eastward for their exchange of goods, dealing with the people of the further Baltic shore, with the settlements which lined the upper Volga. Stockholm stretches out now near where those rich market towns – Birka, Helgö – used to stand. Their wealth gave the Swedes (and their neighbours, followers and allies, the Gauts) the means to reach out for greater power; the eastern focus of their attention gave them a different direction in which to seek it. It was to Russia that they looked, and to Byzantium beyond it.

Nevertheless, if there was not a Viking nation, there was a Viking culture.

Carved objects from the Oseberg ship burial:
OPPOSITE A cart (bottom), with a detail from
one of the panels (above). RIGHT Part of the
runner of a sledge, decorated by the master
craftsman known as the 'Academician'. On its
corners are beautifully carved
animal-head posts.

Variations were regional, deviations from a discernible norm. Two main factors
made for unity – language and religion. Old Norse seems to have been spoken by
all these sea-traders and marauders; runic inscriptions from many points of north-
west Europe give evidence of that. The first of these date from around the year 200,
and although by the end of the millennium discrete languages were beginning to
emerge from the original common form, they are still to this day immediately
recognizable as belonging to a single linguistic family.

The Viking nations remained a northern, pagan bloc two centuries after even
the Saxons had succumbed to Christian rhetoric and Frankish swords. Recognizing
common gods, they recognized each other as fellow-worshippers. The legends
which embroidered their religion gave them a stock of images and references
which, held in common, unified their literatures. Not only was this religious unity
a positive one, based on what all believed; it was as powerfully a negative one,
based on what all did not believe. As non-Christians in a Christian world, their
isolation reinforced their comradeship. Rejecting Jesus, clinging to Odin and to
Thor, clustered in the shadow of Yggdrasil – called by Snorri Sturluson, the
thirteenth-century Icelandic poet, 'Of all trees the hugest and most stately' – the
world tree, the holy root and centre of the universe, the Vikings were ready (and,
as it turned out, able) to defy the world.

The way in which society was organized was also recognizably the same in all
the lands from which the Vikings sailed. There were districts, each with its *thing*,
its assembly of free householders, which discussed issues, tried cases and took
decisions. There were often provinces not so much ruled as overseen by noblemen.
And there were sometimes kings, the most firmly established during the ninth
century being probably the king of Denmark and the king of the Swedes, enthroned in Old Uppsala. Although a Viking throne was passed through the
generations on a broadly hereditary principle, the man each time destined to sit on
it had also to face an election. It was in the power of free men in those countries to
choose who should rule them, although their choice was more or less limited by
blood. (And in more ways than one, of course, if one remembers the many
crowned heads brought low by treachery, warfare and abrupt revenge.)

Their system of justice, which gave them their rights and imposed their
penalties, also linked the Vikings. For them, free men and householders, the law
meant judgment by their peers. It was the *thing*, whether local or provincial, or

even, on a representative basis, national, which tried their cases, the members signalling assent or hostility by a lifting and clashing of weapons, the *vápnatak*. When cases were difficult, the men (and women) of the North were asked to submit to trial by ordeal; or men might, if challenged or wronged, take on their adversaries not with rhetoric but with arms, duelling to establish right and wrong. As the Viking years passed, however, these ancient customs faded; judges appeared, and therefore men skilled in the law; kings appointed representatives; to an extent, the ancient liberties were eroded by the apparatus of a more sophisticated state. But it was as men stubbornly equal, in law as well as self-esteem, that the Vikings first came boiling out of their crags and pastures and narrow, cliff-bound harbours.

Their weapons, and the clasps which held their cloaks, were witness to another kind of unity, the unity of art. In their decorations, they developed a stylized elaboration, based largely on animal forms, an intricate, almost baroque turning and tumbling of twisted, elongated shapes, legs thinning into complex curlicues, wings stretching into endless ramifications and fantastications, tendrils looping and knotting all about, the whole as abundant in energy as the Viking raiders themselves. The figureheads of their ships, the stems which held the figureheads, the sterns, the rudders, the tillers which directed the rudders – all seem to crawl and quiver with a strange, vibrating, only just petrified animal life. It was not as uncouth and bewildered barbarians that they set out in blood-thirst and ambition, but as men confident in the beauty as well as the utility of what they made.

What linked the Vikings above all, however, was their ships and the skill they showed in sailing them. The Viking ship had been brought to perfection by the centuries-long need to circumvent the gales and distances of the North. Communities in Norway cut off from each other by the razor-backed ridges between fjords, in Sweden by the endless rivers and lakes, the long inlets, the island-heavy coast, in Denmark by the sea itself which washed deep into the flats of the sandy mainland or bordered the large island-provinces – all needed to learn the skills and techniques of the water-borne in order to survive. As a result, the Viking ship had had a long development – the boat-shaped graves of Bronze Age Scandinavia, placed over a thousand years before, already had the high prow and stern which would develop into that dreaded dragon shape, the hallmark of the Northmen.

The foundations of the Viking world were what might be called its middle class – the broad mass of free farmers, owning inherited land, under their chosen king the equal of any man, each with the right to speak and to vote in the *thing*, each with the right to judge his peers and to be judged by them, each entitled to the full protection of land law and criminal law. Above these – in so far as they accepted that anyone was above them – stood the aristocrats, the *jarls* and princes and kings who ruled their provinces and kingdoms and jousted endlessly for power; below them – and that they would admit – were the freedmen and the slaves. But it was the sons of this middle layer of Viking society who manned the *langskips* and took to the open sea in search of new territories, booty, women and the gargantuan adventures which would place their names, too, in the timeless record of the sagas. They were not invincible; later, when they began to challenge the armies of established peoples, they would be defeated. What they knew was the sea and its hidden routes; what they understood was the swift landing, the unmerciful wielding of the axe, the terror inspired by surprise and a limitless cruelty.

Was it really something so mundane as an ever-increasing population jostling within the intractable boundaries of arable land which led the Vikings out into the unknown seas, to plunder or to colonize? Nobody now knows, although it seems likely: there were those younger sons. There were also the men, determined leaders, who had been defeated in dynastic battles; and there were those with wealth enough to learn a new ambition. Behind them, the Vikings had a long tradition of restlessness. They had learned the skills of war during the centuries-long, bloody arguments over who ruled whom. They knew the sea-ways, and at some time between 600 and 750, they had perfected the ships which could best use them. As always, it was a concentration of circumstances which, knotting together, altered the endless rope of history. What is certain is that when the free men of the North cut down that king's reeve in 793, they let loose a cascade, a cataract, of bloodshed which would take three centuries to dry up. Once the break-out from Scandinavia began, the rest of the Western world had to endure it, until northern energies ran out at last and even the helmeted, axe-swinging Viking was glad to rest.

All through the early years of the ninth century, the Viking raids continued. The Northmen landed, questing and exultant, on the shores of Frisia, England, Scotland, Aquitaine and Ireland, killing, raping, taking some into slavery, leaving others bereaved or maimed, then burning what stood, before slipping swiftly into their ships again and making off. They would then make the long, triumphant journey home, or, often, would strike again and again at coastal towns and monasteries which, always vigilant, were never ready. A time was coming, however, when the Vikings were no longer prepared to make such lightning-like assaults on the rich countries they plundered, carving out what they immediately needed, or could reach, then retreating and leaving the rest. What was left was fatter than what was taken and it looked as easy to annex; it must have seemed more and more distressing for men who knew they could take it, not to make the necessary, enjoyably violent moves to do so. Silently, therefore, as far as history is concerned, Viking settlements grew up in many small places; one knows they were there only when some new force has consolidated them into coherence and thus into power.

Ireland was a place of seven kingdoms, with a High King enthroned at Tara. Often there was peace, but in the thirties of the ninth century there was not, an arrogant and sacrilegious tumult having been raised by the king of Munster. Perhaps for this reason the time seemed ripe for the Vikings to strike; more precisely, perhaps, because they had found a leader in the Norwegian Turgeis. No one

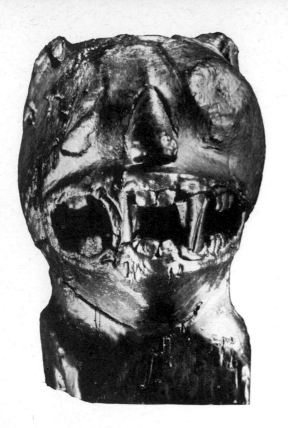 

is certain now when exactly he landed in Ireland; in his as in so many other cases, legend obscures history. But he was probably of royal descent and certainly a man of vigour and great ambition. First he claimed to speak for all foreign settlers in Ireland, within a short while had captured Armagh, a little later stood supreme in Ulster. He raided Connaught and Meath, he sacked monasteries, desecrating some – it is said that at Clonmacnois his wife Ota stood as pagan priestess by the erstwhile Christian altar. He made the power of the Viking felt – and felt as one of the contending powers within Ireland. This was in part because Turgeis offered an alternative focus to the traditional ones for disaffected Irishmen, thus gathering under his banner the Gall-Gaedhil, men newly returned to heathendom and happy to fight shoulder-to-shoulder with these ferocious anti-Christians from the North.

The power of Turgeis, however, was to be transitory. His Irish (or Norse-Erse) allies proved troublesome, the Irish themselves more sinewy in their own defence as his depredations made them increasingly desperate. The thought of their lives under Norwegian suzerainty became more than they could bear. Meath arose in arms, but it was by trickery that Turgeis was brought down. (Was he the Torgils of whom Snorri Sturluson wrote that he 'was a long time king over Dublin, until he fell into a snare of the Irish, and was killed'?) He was drowned at last, in Lough Owel, a death by water, but not the sort Vikings might look for.

In mid-century, the Danes arrived; soon they were at the throats of their Norwegian predecessors, massacring them in what had been their own stronghold of Dublin. By now, Vikings, mainly Norwegians, held the harbours — Waterford,

A group of carved animal-heads: they were
possibly used to ward off evil spirits and protect
those using the sledge or bed they were
carved on. FAR LEFT A head from a sledge in
the Oseberg ship. CENTRE A monster from
another sledge, found in the Oseberg ship.
LEFT A horse's head carved on a bed post, from
the ship found at Gokstad, Vestfold, in Norway.
There are distinctive whisker-lines on
the muzzle.

Wicklow, Wexford, Limerick (or, as they knew these last three, Vikingaló,
Veigsfjördr, Hlymrekr), as well as Dublin. Near another such, Anagassan, Danes
and Norwegians fought a cumbersome battle, three days of bitter axe-work and
arrow-flight, before the Danes won again. For the Irish, although they favoured
the Danes, it hardly mattered; even in this irrelevant preference, however, they
were to be disappointed, for in 853 Norwegian reinforcements came roiling in
under an Olaf never certainly identified, but showing signs of vigour and battle-
hungry ambition which seem to mark him as a kinsman of Turgeis. Soon he was
established in Dublin, with both Danes and Norwegians accepting his leadership,
and the Irish his domination. His regal jurisdiction stretched, it may be, across the
Irish Sea, although certainly it was often challenged. He cemented it by marriage,
taking three wives, one the daughter of an Irish king, one the daughter of the
McAlpin who had in the decade before forged union between Picts and Scots,
the third named Aud the Deep-minded, whose father held Viking sway in the
Hebrides. Northumbria, however, by now in the hands of the Danes, recoiled
from Dublin's new importance. Was that the rivalry of two centres of power, York
and Dublin, or a continuation of the old struggle between two strains of Vikings?

Olaf died fighting, some think in his native land, others in Scotland, a few that it
happened in the Ireland he had made partly his own. His son, Eystein, had to face
a Northumbrian invasion, led by Halfdan, himself the son, it is said, of a legendary
leader, Ragnar Lodbrok. But the High King of Ireland moved to preserve his
Norwegian neighbours' peace (accepted now in their burgeoning settlements,
trade frequent, inter-marriage increasing) and Halfdan died by Strangford Lough.

In this way, the Vikings struck roots in Ireland. As time passed, the brooding disagreement with York became more and more dynastic; it was cousins who faced each other, with unity their intention and who should rule that unity their disagreement. The Irish, with Celtic fecklessness or Christian resignation, appeared to accept them, their resentment deep and not yet to be displayed. It seemed as though the Northmen would always be in Ireland. In one direction, they had broken for ever out of their ancient borders of rock and sea.

Halfdan had come from Northumbria to die beside an Irish lough. As Viking colonies settled in Ireland, so similar kingdoms were being founded in England. Again, it was the thirties of the ninth century which saw the beginning of the story, with raids in force upon the isle of Sheppey, on the coast of Dorset – thirty-five ships in this, and battle nearby, with an English king, Ecgbert, worsted – and then in Cornwall, where Vikings allied to rebel Cornishmen were put down by that same previously unlucky monarch. The next decade saw a constant flaring of battle about the south-eastern corner of England, a flickering, darting warfare of swift, bloody incident, with the whole coastline painfully on watch for Viking fleets now often nearly forty ships strong. If the seaward sentries thought they were living through the worst that could befall, they were to learn they had mistaken comfort for insecurity.

In 850 a horde of Danes in some 350 ships came thundering in on the isle of Thanet, raided – and stayed. One wonders with what dismay the southern English saw this ferocious band (if they had thirty men to every ship, there would have been over ten thousand of them, though that is certainly a vast over-estimate) settle down for the winter of that year, with what terror they saw them in the following spring march on Canterbury, and then London. Both fell; to the south of the Thames the West Saxons prepared themselves. Under Æthelwulf, a king unlucky in his claims to greatness because overshadowed by a greater father, Ecgbert, and a son, Alfred, more famous than either, they faced the Danish invaders and broke them. There were other defeats for the raiders in that year, but one bad year could do no more than check the break-out from the North. The raids continued, the unending and apparently unendable battle clamoured, all steel-sparks and screamed defiance, about the English coast. In 865, however, it ceased at last to be a sporadic sequence of violent incidents but settled into the steady pressure of true war: the Northmen had invaded the island.

They landed in East Anglia, led by the three sons – or so it was said – of the legendary Ragnar Lodbrok, come to avenge – or so it was said – the latter's death at York; he had been thrown into a pitful of adders, to die slowly of their poison. So northward moved the Danes, following this filial triumvirate of Ivar called the Boneless, Ubbi and that Halfdan later to rush so ruinously across the Irish Sea. Northumbria was in turmoil; a king had been replaced by another, both had followers, there was confrontation and treachery – and while factions fought, what Roger of Wendover called 'the abominable army of the Danes' took York.

Astonished, then united in dismay, the two Northumbrian monarchs marched, but the situation was beyond retrieval and in 867 both kings died. (One, we are told, by having his back opened and his lungs laid out like wings upon his shoulder-blades – this the 'blood-eagle', witness to a precision of cruelty which, whether ritualistic in intention or not, remains hard to accept.)

Southward to Nottingham marched the Danes, to winter there, to stand a siege and then accept a bribe to leave; England was proving soft for these invaders. Based on York, they moved southward again, this time into East Anglia. The king of that country, Edmund, brought his army against them; his only victory was posthumous, for he was put to death in so horrifying a manner that, although we do not know exactly what it was, the recoil of detestation with which the rest of the world reacted to it is pressed deeply into the historical record. Edmund, martyred and sanctified, thus defeated the Vikings at a level mere sword-play could never have reached, for much of the hatred with which they were regarded stemmed from his death.

So East Anglia fell, and Wessex prepared. In 870 Halfdan moved south. 'During the year nine pitched battles were fought against the host,' the Saxon chroniclers tell us. Busy in this clamour was Alfred, brother to the new King, Æthelred, riding on forays, rallying his West Saxons, skilfully retrieving one defeat after another. It was because of the skill and energy he displayed that Alfred was made king when, in 871, his elder brother died. He should not have been; there were two infant sons in the direct line of succession. But it was Alfred and not his tiny nephews who led the Saxon fighting men and, with the Danes loose in England, it was this that counted. The fighting continued, the Danes generally victorious, but never decisively so. Each battle they fought only led them to another; each victory had to be paid for. At length even they could see that a succession of such victories would eventually add up to an enormous defeat, for their resources were not limitless; a truce was arranged, they crossed to the northern shore of the Thames – and turned to savage the Mercians. Tribute kept them at bay for a year, but then the towns of England's central kingdom began to fall to the Danish advance: Nottingham again, Leicester and Lichfield, Tamworth – by 874, Mercia was under Danish control, Halfdan setting on its throne an English satrap named Ceolwulf.

He turned north now, conquering, then consolidating conquests into the realm he had carved out for his Danes and which he was determined should be permanent. Comprising Deira in the north-east, Mercia and Bernicia in the centre and East Anglia in the east, it was a vast segment of England which he now ruled. In all these lands, it was Danish law which prevailed, for Danes and English alike. Lincoln, Stamford, Nottingham, Derby and Leicester were fortified and made centres for Viking defence. In each, a Danish *jarl* ruled over his appointed province. In this way, Halfdan laid down the structure of the Danelaw, that part of the island which would henceforth be under Danish domination. The flaxen-haired children of England's east coast bear witness to how long it has lasted. With the

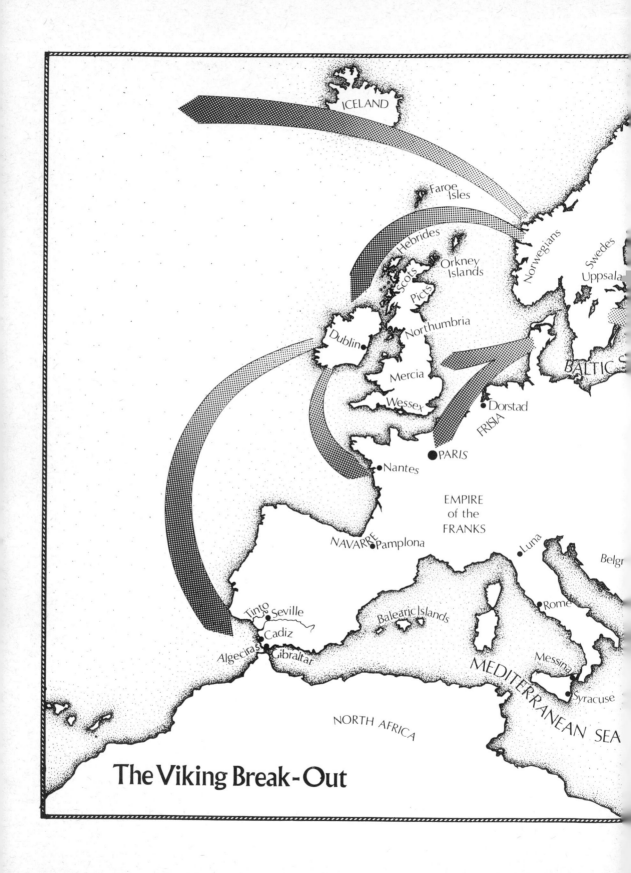

The Viking Break-Out

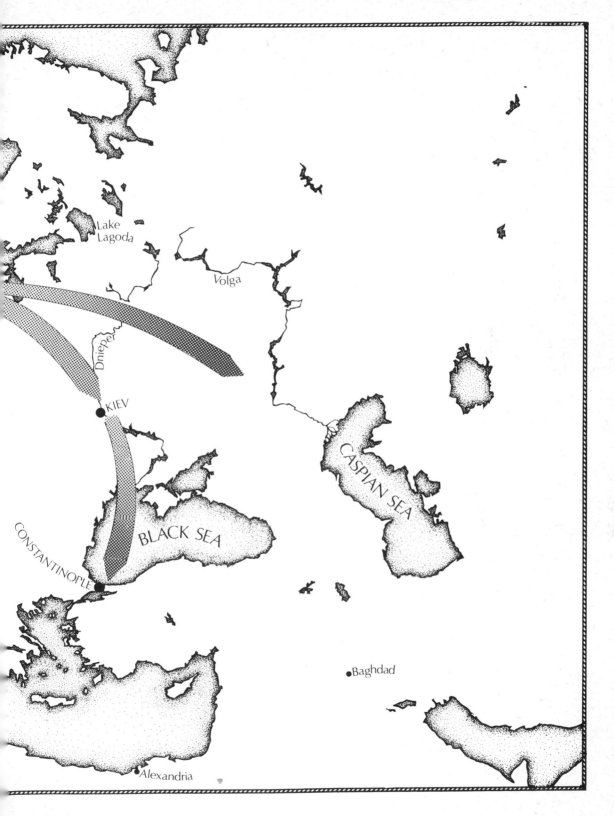

Lake Lagoda

Volga

Dnieper

KIEV

CASPIAN SEA

CONSTANTINOPLE

BLACK SEA

Baghdad

Alexandria

Danes secure and ready to make a new attempt on Wessex, it is clear that another thrust in the great Viking break-out had been successful.

The Nordreys and the Sudreys, island groups we know as the Orkneys and the Hebrides, fell early to the Vikings. The Scottish mainland, on which for a long time no kingdom was supreme, nor any true union likely, presented perhaps a less easily inviting prospect. Welsh in the south-west, Picts, Celtish Scots, Angles in the Lowlands: these had Scotland to themselves, raiders apart. But as the ninth century progressed, neither remoteness nor force of arms preserved immunity. With the Vikings in Ireland, Scotland's west coast lay open, and Olaf, once settled in Dublin, seems to have thought of it as within his fief. In 866 and again four years later he moved violently across that narrow sea, returning each time with booty and, one can assume, a sense of having created a proper respect for his authority.

In Norway, during the second half of the century, Harald Fairhair was establishing himself as supreme king. He was, Snorri Sturluson tells us, 'a stout, strong, and comely man, and withal prudent and manly', and he was perhaps fortunate to achieve this condition in such turbulent times, for he had been left fatherless at the age of ten. His father, Halfdan called the Black, had achieved some power, a condition which always brought danger to those who inherited it. First because he needed to defend himself, then upon the secure base this defence had created, finally out of simple ambition, Harald Fairhair extended the power he had been born to. However important this was to him personally and to Norway as a whole, it had perhaps its greatest significance in the impetus it gave to the Viking break-out. Many men of vigour and independence refused to accept Harald's overlordship, but found that such refusal left them with no role to play at home. In their hundreds, these men took to the seas, to live by piracy and raiding, or to found new homesteads in lands beyond Harald's control. This had immediate consequences in Scotland, the nearest available country to Norway.

The Vikings who settled in the Orkneys and Hebrides felt themselves as free to attack ships within Harald Fairhair's authority as they did those owing any other allegiance. Indeed, there were aspects of civil war in the stand they took – had Norway been a modern state, they would have been classified as rebels. To thwart them, Harald placed a viceroy on the Hebrides, a Viking who had made his reputation by being as energetically destructive as the worst of those he now had been enjoined to curb. And curb them he did – indeed, Ketil Flatneb (father to Olaf's deep-minded Aud) neglected only one of his new duties, but that one in Harald's eyes perhaps the most important: he omitted to pay tribute to the Norwegian king. Harald sequestrated his lands in Norway and almost took him, but he was able to flee, settling in the Hebrides for the rest of his life.

Other picturesque characters moved through the onslaughts and defences, the sudden ambushes and diplomatic *détentes* of these decades. Önund named Tree-Foot – at least after he had lost one leg in battle against Harald – who dominated the islands for a while; Eyvind, called the Eastman because of his Swedish ancestry, who carried the authority of his father-in-law, the Irish King Cearbhall, through these waters; his son-in-law, Thorstein the Red, who drove onto the mainland, annexing Caithness; and Thorstein's friend and partner in conquest, Sigurd, first *jarl* of the Orkneys, who carved this new kingdom out with him. There was Hallad, sent to bring order to this bloody chaos, but harried back to Norway, his charge unfulfilled; and there was Turf-Einar, his successor, who settled more firmly the authority of the Orkney earldom – only to have it wrested from him by Halfdan Halegg, rebel and murderous son of Harald Fairhair, who made himself king of the islands until Turf-Einar returned from the mainland with a new army, took him and killed him. (Later, Einar paid Harald, only conventionally irritated by this summary execution, the whole of the fine the Norwegian king imposed on the Orkneys, receiving in return their freehold from those who lived on them, thus, in a sense, becoming the islands' owner as reward for having killed the prince.)

It was Harald Fairhair himself who had founded the Orkney earldom and set Sigurd up as his first ennobled representative. It was probably already in the early decades of the tenth century that he arranged this, sailing himself in punitive wrath against the Vikings who had set up their headquarters in the islands, from there harassing their homeland. These he slaughtered wherever he found them, rounding the northern capes and isles and descending into the western waters as far as, some insist, the Isle of Man. There, according to Snorri, 'the report of his exploits on the land had gone before him . . . and the island was left entirely bare both of people and goods, so that King Harald and his men made no booty when they landed.' In this way, a calm at last descended on the Western Isles, which Sigurd, as we have seen, exploited, with Thorstein the Red subjugating Caithness and, it may be, taking the borders of what he commanded even further, into Sutherland and Ross, to build himself a fastness at last on the Moray Firth itself. (Sigurd came to a bizarre end, as the *Heimskringla* tells; he had 'killed Melbridge-Tooth, a Scotch earl, and hung his head to his stirrup-leather; but the calf of his leg was scratched by the teeth . . . and the wound caused inflammation in his leg, of which the earl died. . . .')

With an earl in the Orkneys, the land there his own and the Viking power stretching across the north of the mainland, the invaders had thus struck roots in Scotland. If they owed allegiance to Norway, it was nominal and personal to Harald, for the moment hardly surviving his death, though later revived often enough. On the west coast, too, there was Galloway, perhaps founded by those mixed Gall-Gædhil who had earlier fought both their native and their foreign cousins in Ireland, and had now established their own belligerent community. Although elsewhere the remnants of McAlpin's kingdom remained, in Scotland, too, the break-out had been consolidated and the Vikings, with their usual investment of blood, had taken a stake in a new homeland.

The Swedes looked eastward. In Snorri Sturluson's *Ynglinga Saga*, it was to Finland, Great Svíthiod (which is Russia) and Turkland that, as often as not, the legendary Swedish kings and heroes travelled, there to meet bewitchment and magical, unpleasant deaths. But it seems to have been the case that Swedes, with their southern neighbours the Gotlanders as (probably inferior) partners, early made themselves the lords of settlements in modern Latvia, and a little later controlled trading settlements elsewhere on the eastern Baltic.

In 859, the Swedes moved further. In what is called the *Nestor Chronicle*, or more accurately the *Primary Chronicle*, an early attempt to set down the details of Russian history, the entry for that year speaks of 'Varangians from beyond the sea', who imposed tribute upon a number of peoples, among them the Slavs. In Old Norse, *várar* means an oath or pledge, *væringi* 'a sworn brotherhood', and from the mouth of the Volga to Byzantium, Varangian came to mean Northman. These early invaders were largely unsuccessful, and at some time between 860 and 862, 'The tributaries of the Varangians drove them back beyond the sea.' Freedom, however, brought its problems, 'and they began to war one against another'. Wisely, they decided to call in an outsider to rule them and keep them in peace. 'They accordingly went overseas to the Varangian Russes,' and brought back with them three brothers who, say the chroniclers, 'took with them all the Russes and migrated. The oldest, Rurik, located himself in Novgorod; the second, Sineus, at Beloozero; and the third, Truvor, in Izborsk.' It is not clear exactly which 'Varangians' these Russes were, but the Finns, who inhabited the shores of Lake Lagoda, called Sweden *Ruotsi* then as they do now; moving eastward themselves, it is probable that they took the word with them, used it to name the newcomers and so spread it among their Slavonic neighbours, who were now to be their fellow-vassals.

It seems likely that there were movements eastwards earlier than this by Swedish traders and adventurers; around Lake Lagoda there is evidence that Scandinavians lived, formed communities and died there a hundred years before. The waterways of the Volga and the Dnieper, for centuries the major trading routes to the borders of Asia, would have drawn some of them further. It is clear that by the end of that busy ninth century, Swedes were travelling to the Caspian and beyond, trading as they went, sending back exotic wares from Persia, Arabia and even China; later, in their homeland, these would lie as unintended testimony to their energetic voyaging in the elaborate graves of the mighty.

This penetration was repeated along the Dnieper as it curved its way across central Russia towards the Black Sea. Based on Lake Lagoda, then established in Novgorod, the Vikings pushed on, through Smolensk and Chernigov, to settle in great strength at Kiev. In 860, they made what, knowing the Viking nature, seems almost inevitable: an attempt on Constantinople itself.

Two hundred ships sailed southward, crossed the Black Sea and, on 18 June, appeared before the great city. The Byzantines, actively at war on other fronts, were caught in defenceless astonishment. The Patriarch Photius, preaching in St Sophia cathedral, asked, 'What is this? What is this grievous and heavy blow and wrath. . . . A people has crept down from the North . . . the people is fierce and has no mercy; its voice is as the roaring sea.' It was a description many others, on a dozen far-distant coastlines, might ruefully have recognized. In the end, the raiders – it is unlikely that they thought themselves would-be invaders, unless they had been much misinformed about the city's actual size – were defeated by an emperor forced to hurry back in defence of his capital. They had, however, made their mark in a faraway and exotic place – the same mark, it will be seen, as that they had made in other, more mundane localities.

Towards the end of the century, the Scandinavian settlements along the Dnieper were united, as usual by force. A ruler named Oleg, about whom history, wreathed with legends, can be only half-believed, marched from Novgorod to Kiev. This city he made his capital, and from it he ruled over a vast and increasing tract of land, and a number of various peoples. His strength lay not only in his position but in the energy with which he held it, and the way he used it to protect those sailing with merchandise towards Byzantium from piratical intervention. Every year a vast convoy set out from his city, made its way through hostile territories and a series of cataracts, past which goods and boats had both to be transported, to reach the estuary of the Dnieper at last. There they had to run the gauntlet of the Pechenegs, coastal pirates ready to snap up any wayward or disabled ship, before heading in comparative safety for Constantinople.

In 907, given cause by who knows what insult or disagreement, Oleg, with an enormous force, himself appeared before Constantinople. Was it a Viking ambition to take at last that fabled 'Mikligard', the name by which their poets knew the Byzantine capital? Perhaps the Byzantines thought so; certainly they threw a protective chain across the harbour. Men who had circumvented the cataracts of the Dnieper, however, were not to be turned away by a chain. To the horror (and, say the chroniclers, the awe) of the defenders, Oleg put his ships on wheels and trundled them past the obstruction. Outlying churches were plundered, but with the city itself Oleg made an advantageous treaty. (He hung his shield on the city gates, later considered by the Byzantines an insult, but to the Vikings most probably a signal of peace.) Russian merchants were to profit from this, for the terms of the treaty gave them preferential treatment, both in the length and manner of their stay and in their exemption from customs duties. There was even a clause which allowed these visitors as many baths as they wished.

With the final signing of this treaty in September 911 (Oleg's fifteen emissaries all bore Viking names, doubtless in those days and places a sign of their trustworthiness), the continuing wealth of Kiev was guaranteed. More than wealth, however, was to pass through its defended gates. At a stroke, the ancient culture of Greece and Rome, and the complex embellishments added to it by Byzantium, were made available to Russia, not exactly for the first time, but more directly and easily than ever before. And not only Russia benefited – the route led back to Novgorod and Lagoda, and so across the Baltic to Sweden itself. In the east, too, the Viking break-out had in this way found fertile soil, put down alien roots and flourished.

Charlemagne died in 814, his empire vast and apparently secure. That it was his character which had given it unity was not discovered until his departure made it clear. Raiders terrorized its seaward flanks, Muslim in the South, pagan in the North. In the decade after the great emperor's death, Vikings were already snapping at France's Atlantic coast, sacking monasteries near Nantes and La Rochelle, burning and robbing on the coast of Flanders, seeking booty along the south Breton coast. The Danes, however, the most active in this, had a common border with the Franks and thought it prudent for a while to hold back from affronting them. The fact that the Danish king, Harald, used the help of Charlemagne's successor, Louis the Pious, in his own dynastic struggles, going so far to curry favour with that convinced churchgoer as to have himself baptized at Ingelheim Palace, may have had something to do with this lull. But Harald was finally deposed and, whether this was a factor or not, the Vikings were soon on the rampage once more.

Dorstad stands at a point where the Rhine, already splitting as it approaches its mazy mouth, sends an arm, the Kromme Rhine, wandering northwards towards the Zuider Zee while continuing westwards as the River Lek. It was a great centre of commerce, perhaps the most important in north Europe, minting a coinage of which copies circulated widely in Scandinavia. Although it was protected by moats and fortifications, as well as by the hypothetically enormous strength of the Carolingian Empire, it was a prize any ambitious raider might speculate about. In 834 Louis the Pious found himself in serious trouble in a dynastic struggle of his own, his rivals, successful for a time, being his sons; the Vikings, jackal-like in their awareness of when their prey had weakened enough to be attacked, chose that year to plunder Dorstad. They killed, enslaved, robbed and, leaving, burned; Frisia had learned a pattern of suffering which the following decades would see worked out to the last stain of blood.

In 836, Antwerp was plundered and burned, Dorstad attacked and laid waste again, while far away, on the Bay of Biscay, Vikings dug their fangs into another imperial flank at the monastery of Noirmoutier, near Nantes, which was abandoned in this year. The following year, the Vikings were again loose in Frisia, dark smoke rising through the moans of the dying and the screams of the bereaved, a signal which the Emperor could no longer disregard. But the army he sent to bring order to Frisia found the forces of disorder melted away; Vikings were not yet prepared to stand and fight land battles. Instead, they struck in what would become Normandy, crashing into Rouen with all their usual destructive violence; in 842, the following year, they plundered Quentovic, near today's Étapes (as well as London and Rochester on the other side of the Channel), a town which was a trading centre of great wealth and reputation.

In the same year, they were on the Loire, thrusting past abandoned Noirmoutier towards Nantes itself (invited in, some think, by a Count Lambert with covetous eyes on that city, and thus piloted safely through the river's intricate channels). It was a holy day, the day of St John, and high summer. When the Vikings –

Norwegians, this time – leaped from their ships, death struck everywhere. Not even the bishop in his cathedral was immune. Laden with booty, the longships straggled downriver at nightfall, reached the open sea safely, landed once more at stricken Noirmoutier and, contrary to Northern practice hitherto, settled there for the winter. (It was a custom others would soon copy, until at last they would cease going home altogether.)

Not departing in the usual manner was, in some ways, a mark of Viking intention. In 840, Louis the Pious had died, still clinging to his throne, still holding together the empire he had inherited from Charlemagne. After his death, however, his sons, earlier so anxious to rob him of his state, turned predictably on each other. For the men of the North, calculating in spotting opportunities, experienced in making use of them, the internal violence which followed was clearly as good as an invitation. Indeed, in some cases they were to receive an actual invitation, for the Frankish aristocracy, busily at each other's throats, was not above calling in Viking forces to redress the balance of their own. It had worked for Count Lambert in Nantes; it would work for others in the future. From this time on, what had been the Carolingian Empire became to some extent a Viking playground, and one they liked so much that, around the mouth of the Seine, they would eventually set up yet another of their colonies. In the empire of the Franks, too, the great break-out would fling down the seeds of new states, new societies. Before that happened, however, despair and bloodshed would order the lives of its people, as hungry Vikings combined with greedy lords (and proselytizing Muslims) in unravelling the life-work of that first, magnificent Charles.

A battle scene included in a religious allegory
from the Utrecht Psalter, of the school of Reims
(c.800). It is a good example of the style of
Carolingian illumination which flourished
under Charlemagne.

2 THE HARRYING OF THE FRANKS

Lothar, Charles the Bald, Louis the German – the three sons of Louis the Pious, tearing at each other and at the empire they all coveted. To the Danes, watching as always for a chance to strike, such fraternal rivalry must have been too tempting to resist. The empire's northern coastline lay open; in 845, under their king, Horik, they swarmed over it, engulfing Hamburg. They killed and plundered for two days; with church, school and library all destroyed, Anskar, famous for his missionary successes and now archbishop there, was forced to flee, his cathedral's most holy relics all he could save. (He would return, however, as Bremen's archbishop and play his part in the conversion of the North.)

In March, early enough to catch the Franks off-guard, another force of 120 ships sailed up the Seine, under a Ragnar powerful enough to have had his name intertwined with the royal Ragnar Lodbrok of legend. Hardly pausing at Rouen, the Vikings thrust towards Paris; Charles the Bald, coming to the city's defence, sent his forces marching down both banks, a classic error classically punished. Ragnar fell with all his undivided strength upon the smaller detachment; in the defeat that followed, 111 of the Franks were captured. These he hanged on an island in mid-Seine, thoughtfully before the eyes of the second Frankish force. Unsurprisingly, this group did not prolong its argument with the Vikings, and Ragnar stepped unopposed into Paris on 28 March – Easter Sunday.

Charles the Bald, cooped in the abbey at St Denis, his forces gone, could do nothing to prevent Ragnar's men from grabbing what might be removed of the city's valuables, both ecclesiastical and lay. It was not only Charles's forces that had vanished, however – his nerve too seems to have left him. Once reinforced and poised, in theory, to cut off the Viking retreat to the sea (now an unfamiliar two hundred miles away), he stood aside and let the Northmen pass. He did more – he paid them seven thousand silver pounds not to molest his domains again, thus initiating the many timid payments other monarchs would make to racketeering Vikings up and down the Western world. Only sickness, attacking Ragnar's men on their return journey, permits us to retain some belief in natural justice.

Franks elsewhere felt the flashing axeheads of these raiders, saw their wealth clawed seaward and their roofs collapse in sparking smoke. Settled in Noirmoutier, Vikings raided as they pleased along the Loire valley and across the rich fields of Aquitaine. Further north, they ranged along the Scheldt, sacking the Church's various establishments there, and once more levied their dreadful tribute from the

A ninth-century bronze statuette of
Charlemagne, who founded the Frankish
Empire, in an effort to realize the principles of
St Augustine's *City of God*. He has also been
called the 'Father of Europe'.

OPPOSITE Louis the Pious as defender of the
faith, from a ninth-century book of poems.
He had been made king of Aquitaine as an
infant and was consequently out of touch with
the Frankish magnates at the time of his
succession to the imperial title. He was not
gifted either as a statesman or as a military
leader, and would probably have preferred life
as a monk.

town of Dorstad. Again and again they fell upon Frisia, until the three Frankish
kings sent the Danes warning of impending joint action – words their fraternal
suspicions and rivalries robbed of all force. In Brittany, an army was defeated;
further along the Atlantic coast, Bordeaux was besieged, then taken.

The Garonne was penetrated by a Viking fleet perhaps in league with Pepin,
would-be king of Aquitaine, who might well have turned even to them in his
search for allies against Charles the Bald. The fleet did not, however, return home
after this raid, but continued down the coast of Spain and Portugal, battling sometimes to preserve itself, sometimes to prevent the self-preservation of others. The
high point of this perhaps impromptu expedition came when they sailed up the
Guadalquivir and for a week held all but the central citadel of Seville. Pleased with
their pickings, they set up their quarters on an island in the river's mouth and from
there raided the surrounding towns and villages with what must have seemed
impunity. But before two months had passed, the Moors, whose kingdom it was,
had rallied.

Thirty Viking ships were sunk in a sea-battle with them, but Northmen, even a
long way from home, did not easily lose heart, and their mauled fleet could not
resist the temptation to raid Niebla, up the Rio Tinto. Turned away there, they
sailed back past Cadiz once more to make an attempt on Sidonia. But now the
Emir, Abd al-Rahman, having hanged on the trees and gallows of Seville all the
Vikings he had captured during that first engagement and sent two hundred of
their heads in triumphant testimony to his Tangierian cousins, came looking for
them again. Clear at last that a good thing had come to an end, the raiders
withdrew, safeguarding their flight by exchanging the prisoners they had taken
for a guarantee of unhampered departure. Some of them were cast by storm on the
shores of Africa; the rest made their way, snapping up all available booty as they
went, along the coast of Spain, to come to rest finally in the fleet's rallying point
at the mouth of the Gironde.

This Moorish adventure having ended by diplomatic rather than military confrontation, its sequel was unexpectedly the sending by the Emir of an ambassador
to the Court of the Viking leader. The chosen emissary, a man named Al-Ghazal,
says that he travelled to a large island three days' journey out to sea. Water flowed
there, and gardens grew. The king of that place ruled not only there but also on
the mainland. More important personally to Al-Ghazal was the fact that he had a

Charles the Bald, from the Psalter of Charles
the Bald produced, possibly at St Denis,
between 842 and 869. The period of his rule
coincided with the decline of the
Carolingian Empire.

beautiful wife, who, he says, was named Noud. She seems to have been as pleased
with him as he was with her, finding occasion to point out that among her people
men were not jealous and women thus free to change them. Indeed, the one fact
we do not know about this relationship is the historically important one of where it
took place. Was 'Noud' actually Aud, the king Turgeis, the island Ireland? From
which part of what mainland did Al-Ghazal sail? Was it rather the Court of King
Horik in Denmark that he visited? (We do not know the name of Horik's wife.)
Most experts plump for the Danes, a larger, more settled community, a nation
already established, their Court a true nexus of Viking power. Yet the name of that
adaptable lady nags, and so does, a little, the appointed meeting-place for the
previous year's raid – the Gironde, ideally placed for the pull up the Breton coast
and the dash across to Ireland.

The Gironde, however, that long snag in the coast of France, was ideal in any
case for raiders. When Asgeir captured Bordeaux in 848, he demonstrated how
little was safe from the ferocious Viking greed. (He showed, too, what part outsiders of his kind were playing in Frankish politics, for the ineffectual sorties of
Charles the Bald against his invasion were matched in feebleness only by the total
inactivity of Pepin, uncertain perhaps of how to deal with what may once have
been his allies; the result was that the bad triumphed over the worse and Charles
was crowned king of Aquitaine.) The indifferent Vikings, however, had their
minds on other things than which king might or might not oppose them; they
pushed on to Perigueux, nearly another hundred miles inland, broke it open and
scraped it clean of wealth.

The second half of the ninth century continued this tale of Frankish calamity.
A force of theirs did manage to ambush a party of Vikings who, under the same
busy Asgeir, were on their way back from sacking Beauvais. Many Northmen
died, but not enough to discourage the remainder, who within the few months had
plundered the monastery of Fontanelle and destroyed it by fire. When they moved
back to the area of Asgeir's last great triumph, Bordeaux, a party of Danes succeeded them. Under two men named Sigtrygg and Godfred, they set up camp at a
placed called Givold's Fosse, their presence and the implied intention that it
should be a long one finally moving Charles and his brother Lothar to attempt
concerted action. Little but the attempt proved commendable, however; despite
having two armies with which to pincer the Vikings, the Franks, enfeebled by

Lothar, brother of Charles the Bald, from the
Lothar Psalter, 840–50. He was named sole
emperor in Louis the Pious' settlement of 817,
but was defeated by his brothers. Eventually
the empire was united under Charles the Bald.

either rivalry or congenital lack of resolution, stood back from battle and not only allowed the Danes to leave unmolested but in gratitude for this departure presented Godfred with a tract of Flanders to call his own.

It is true that in the sum of Frankish troubles the Vikings did not represent the greatest contributory amount, but crisis on one frontier does not excuse collusion with an enemy on another. A people looks to its rulers for protection, and such protection is not divisible, to be offered in one place and not another, against one danger and not another. Nor will robbers probing for weakness be discouraged by feebleness and an offered bribe. It is not surprising, therefore, that in 853 Nantes once again felt the weight of Viking greed, nor that in that year the Northmen set up camp on the Loire and, exchanging their ships for horseback, ranged the rich territories on either side of the river, sacking in the process Poitiers and Angers.

One forgets that the Vikings, great seamen, were also accomplished riders. Sitting high on their horses' backs, their wood-and-leather saddles just behind the necks of their small beasts, their feet in long and sometimes elaborately decorated stirrups, they covered the cool miles of their homelands, just as now they careered across the rich pastures and through the dusty village streets of the lower Loire. Late in the year they came to Tours. Two famous monasteries stood there, one in the town itself, the other just outside. The Vikings smashed into both, destroying relics, plundering gold, killing the unresisting monks – 126 of them in the outer establishment. Blois burned a few months later; soon Orleans was invested, although – perhaps foreshadowing the Maid to come – this town at first stood firm. Not for long, however – two years later the Viking torches kindled its roofs too, the Viking hands clutched at its gold and women, dragging both back to their new encampment on an island near Nantes. In 857, Poitiers, Blois and Tours once more bent under the force of Viking fury – it was as though these Northmen felt an exultant resentment against the warmer southern lands which nothing could assuage. The truth, however, was more mundane: born plunderers had found a people apparently born to be plundered. The people's kings and overlords struggled for obscure advantage – it was with Pepin's help, again, that Poitiers was sacked – and upon the defenceless, bereft of their leaders' proper attention, the Vikings fell with energy and promptitude and a terrible regularity. The bishop of Bayeux died, killed by the raiders still ranging along both sides of the Seine; the abbots of St Maux and St Denis had to be ransomed for vast sums; Chartres was

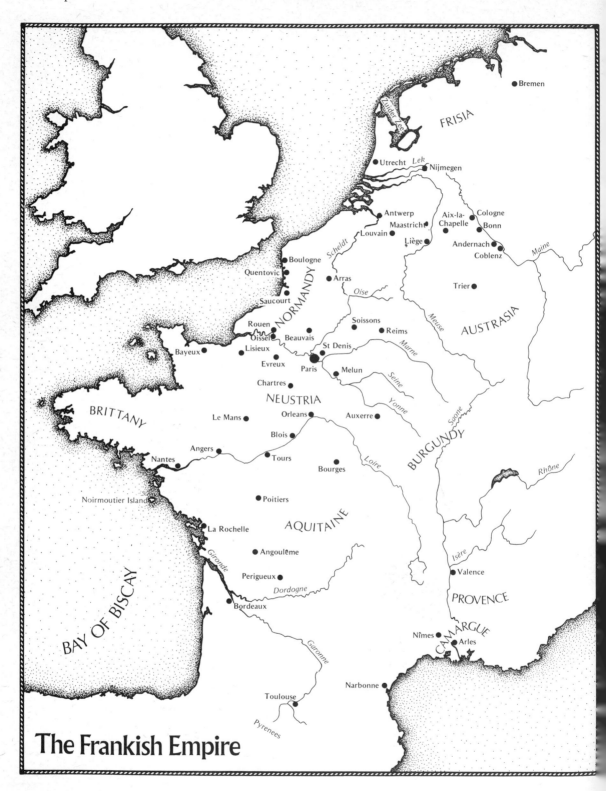

Bremen

FRISIA

Zuider Zee

Utrecht *Lek* Nijmegen

Antwerp Aix-la- Cologne
Maastricht Chapelle Bonn
Louvain Liège Andernach
Scheldt Coblenz

Boulogne *Maine*
Quentovic Arras
Saucourt *Oise* Trier

Rouen Soissons AUSTRASIA
Oissel Beauvais Reims
Bayeux Lisieux St Denis *Meuse*
Evreux Paris Melun *Marne*
Chartres *Seine*

NEUSTRIA *Yonne*

Le Mans Orleans Auxerre
BRITTANY *Saône*

Blois BURGUNDY
Angers Tours
Nantes Bourges *Loire* *Rhône*

Noirmoutier Island Poitiers

La Rochelle AQUITAINE *Isère*

Angoulême Valence

Perigueux *Dordogne* PROVENCE

BAY OF BISCAY Bordeaux *Garonne*

CAMARGUE
Nîmes Arles

Toulouse Narbonne

Pyrenees

The Frankish Empire

A glass vase, probably from the Rhineland, found in a Viking burial.

Coins discovered in Sweden, probably brought back from the German mainland by Viking raiders.

plundered, and Evreux; in Frisia, Utrecht was taken, robbed and totally destroyed.

Paris fell again, this time to another part-legendary hero, said too to be the son of legend – Björn Ironside, son of Ragnar Lodbrok. It was in 857 that he captured the city, falling ferociously upon its churches, only four of which he did not sack and burn. It was probably his band which took up quarters on the island of Oissel, in the Seine, where Charles, at last summoning his resolution, cooped them up and seriously besieged them. His army was supported by a fleet and his allies included even the slippery Pepin, his rival for Aquitaine. Would the Franks at last discover how to defeat their harassers and so serve notice on them that the easy days were over? For a while it looked like it, as week succeeded vicious week and Viking supplies ran low. But Charles fell ill; there was treachery, as always, among his noblemen; finally, the normal steadfast self-destructiveness of his family re-asserted itself and his brother Louis the German moved against him (using, how-ever, the ploy, still useful today, of insisting that he was coming to help, not hinder). The siege was raised after twelve weeks.

Unable to do the work himself, therefore, Charles resolved to pay someone else to do it, choosing as his mercenary a Dane named Weland. The sum agreed was three thousand pieces of silver; so harsh was the royal tax collection that Weland received in the end two thousand pieces more, a sum which still enabled Charles's exchequer to show a profit. The principle of setting a thief to catch a thief seems initially to have been successful – Weland invested the island of Oissel a second time, squeezing his fellow-Vikings there until they sued for terms. These, it turned out, meant their paying Weland a further six thousand pieces of silver to let them depart unharmed. So rich had they grown on their robberies, they paid this enormous sum quite cheerfully – though not as cheerfully, one may assume, as Weland accepted it. Thus the only result of all this expenditure of Frankish effort and money was that, by 862, two bands of marauders were scouring the Seine valley instead of one.

The first group, however, if it was commanded by Björn Ironside, would by then have become somewhat depleted, for Björn had decided to set off on an adventure of his own. With another Viking named Hastein, he led a fleet of sixty-two ships southwards towards the Mediterranean. At first, the expedition seems to have had small fortune, being driven from the coast of Galicia and beaten by a Moorish

OVERLEAF Charles the Bald and his court, from
a fourteenth-century French manuscript.

force at the mouth of the Guadalquivir (yet captured longships were found by the Moors to be laden with prisoners, gold and silver, so they must have had substantial successes somewhere). Thus set back, they probably did not attempt, as the earlier Viking fleet had done, to sack Seville; instead, they sailed on to plunder the more accessible Algeciras, as a change from purely ecclesiastical destruction burning down the mosque there.

Crossing to North Africa they defeated a feeble effort at defence and took advantage of the terror this struck to capture a number of prisoners; these, transported and enslaved, would eventually appear as *fir gorm*, or blue men, in early Irish records. After a week on the Moroccan coast, the Vikings returned to Spain, this time ravaging the peninsula's Mediterranean coast before putting in at the Balearics and plundering people who might have thought themselves safely out of the way of such north European scourges. Back on the mainland, on the Frankish side of the Pyrenees, they descended on Roussillon and, it may be, Narbonne.

At last even their energy had to be recharged. With winter coming, they found the islanded flatlands of the Camargue, on the Rhône delta, and set up their encampment there. They had a few wounds to lick, but knew they had done marvels. What they had captured had enriched them; what they had accomplished would enrich their reputations. Nothing now would hold them back – one senses their zest, their heedless conviction that only action, endless action, violence, the raw snatching of what they wanted from a world unable to keep it from them, would or could satisfy them. In this, they typify the swirl and sword-clash of the Viking break-out. It was as though somewhere there was a victory complete and overwhelming, a prize so rich that its wealth might be taken as absolute, and until these had been achieved nothing would induce them to rest.

These raiders now, in any case, had little thought of resting. They struck at Arles, at Nîmes, they travelled up the Rhône as far as Valence, where the Isère brings its waters from the Alps, a hundred miles from the coast. At last a force was gathered by the Franks and, being gathered, rallied its nerve and fought. The Vikings, not strategic fools, stood one defeat, then left. Turning eastward, they sailed along what we know as the Rivieras of France and Italy, a littoral of such warmth and beauty that it may well have astonished men used to bleaker coastlines.

After this, they drift away into legend and conjecture. They may have sacked

Pisa. It is said that, coming to the city of Luna, they mistook it for Rome. Having come so far, it would have been remiss not to attempt its sacking. The gates were shut, but the Vikings sent messengers – only the hazards of storm had brought them here, they said, their chieftain lay sick, they needed succour; within a day, the messages had changed – the chieftain now, they said, was dead, and before departing all they wanted was to bury him in the manner proper to a Christian. What Italian city could withstand such a plea? The gates were opened, the coffin brought in, the phalanx of the sorrowing behind it. Set down in the cemetery, abruptly the coffin lid swung open, an armed Hastein leaped out and the massacre had begun. When he discovered that his delight had been premature and it was not Rome which he had taken, Hastein set the city alight.

Perhaps after this they travelled on eastwards; it may be they whom the records speak of as having anchored as far away as Alexandria. Certainly by 861 they were back within the Moorish sphere of influence; near Gibraltar, a fleet came out to meet them and in the consequent battle they were defeated. Nothing could alter them now, however; landing on the coast of Navarre, they thrust inland to capture its capital, Pamplona, and its prince, then ransomed the latter for an enormous sum and sailed on, rejoicing. By the following year they had returned to the Loire, some twenty of the original ships left, four years of travelling behind them, heroes of one of the great naval exploits of the Viking years.

The situation in the Frankish Empire was little different from what it had been when they left. However, in this year Charles did at last inflict the kind of defeat on the Vikings which had always, probably, been within his power, but which his vacillation and his concentration on other issues had hitherto made unlikely. The fact that it was the Dane, Weland, whom he defeated may have had something to do with it – one can imagine the royal wrath when that avaricious mercenary, having taken money from both sides, let slip the Oissel Vikings he had been over-generously paid to destroy. Charles forced the Danish raiders to hand back the prisoners they had taken, and he barred them from the Seine valley, which he now – 'At last!' one can hear his people murmur – began to fortify. Parapeted bridges began to be built, to prevent the Viking ships from sailing with their previous impunity up-river. He appointed aristocratic lieutenants whose function would be to superintend defence against the marauders – the Count Adalhard along the Seine, and on the Loire the Marquess of Neustria, Robert the Strong, whose descendants a century later would be the Capetian kings of France.

Nothing now, however, seemed able to stop the relentless depredations of the Vikings, and though Robert in particular was wanting in neither ability nor energy, he could not prevent the sacking of both Poitiers and Angoulême during the first two years of his responsibility. Weakened by a Breton rebellion on his flanks, he was forced to see the Vikings thrust towards Toulouse, and smash their way through the defences of Orleans again, and of Poitiers a second time, and could not prevent their allying themselves with the insurgents in Brittany to form a combined force which attacked and plundered Le Mans. Yet he was able, by the

end of 865, to rally his forces, to put courage and order into them and so to out-face
the marauding Northmen. These, defeated several times, knew as always when the
easy harvests of their violence were over. They withdrew, not to return for more
than a year.

Adalhard, under Charles's orders, had meanwhile been building a great protective bridge at Pitres, to guard the higher reaches of the Seine. In this same year,
865, a Viking fleet reached it and at once began an attack upon it. Meanwhile, a
land-party rode on to Paris and once more savaged that city. Chartres, too, was
attacked, though here the raiders were repulsed. Pressure on the bridge at Pitres,
however, was sustained; probably it had not yet been completed, and one can see
the desperate thrust of spear and pike, the flash of axes and the rippling flight of
arrows among its rough and disconnected timbers. For Adalhard, it was a matter
of reputation. He had the ships below him, although it is probable that the
Vikings, swift on horseback, would at times invest either end of his long structure,
besieging his men within it, half-trapped in their awkward, rectangular fortress.
Sometimes, perhaps, these tables were turned, and it was the Franks who, racing
along the river bank, would threaten to cut off the ships from all hope of progress
or retreat.

In the end, as so often before, Frankish resolution proved no match for Viking
ferocity; the Northmen broke through, smashed their way further, reached St
Denis and for twenty days ranged those rich settlements, plundering, murdering,
raping and imprisoning, burning the many scenes of their violations, then
moving on to new ones. This time, Paris could not contain their lust; they thrust
further, to Melun, spreading the experience of their cruelty to areas hitherto
peaceful. Distracted, Charles switched Robert the Strong from Aquitaine and dismissed Adalhard, but if he thought that his new commander, for all his vigour,
would work some immediate miracle, he was disappointed. The Vikings were too
swift for the Franks, too elusive, perhaps too single-minded. As before, Charles
surrendered, the Viking price for departure being this time set at four thousand
pieces of silver. An enormous consignment of wine was added to this, suggesting an
unexpected level of connoisseurship in these northern marauders. It must, in any
case, have been to their taste, because for the next ten years the Seine was to be
free of them.

The Loire, however, was not to be so fortunate. It was beset by a new force, this
time under a Viking already deeply embedded in their history of plunder and
adventure – Hastein, who had sailed, it is said, to far-off Alexandria and who, for
one exultant morning, believed he had sacked Rome. Robert was immediately put
in the field against him – two men of high reputation, both setting these once more
in the bloody scales of battle. They met at Brissarthe, near Châteauneuf-sur-Sarthre,
and it was Robert who fell, a loss to Charles, who had used his resolution as a
bulwark for the feebleness of others.

Hastein now was loose and uncheckable on the lower Loire. He attacked
Bourges, he attacked Orleans. From the Breton point of view, these events were

A typical warrior nobleman of the Frankish
Empire: from a fresco in the Oratory of St
Benedict in Rome. Charlemagne's Frankish
counts, who combined fiscal, judicial, and
military power, formed the pattern for the
feudal nobility of Europe throughout the
middle ages.

very gratifying. They detested the Franks (a feeling which the intervening
centuries have not totally eroded) and were prepared to like those who seemed to
share this attitude. They had once worked successfully in alliance with the Vikings
and knew them well, or thought they did, having fought beside them and traded
with them. Now the Duke of Brittany, Salomon, made a formal treaty with them,
recognizing the Northmen's right to settle as neighbours of the Bretons. It is unlikely that those whose lands were more directly affected were as happy with this
arrangement as the Bretons may have been, but these were days when a sword bit
deeper than a title-deed.

For three years the Vikings lived in apparent calm, settling into their new
possessions. But the need to plunder was their disease, the leap for their ships its
symptom. In the spring of 872, it came upon them once more. They left their base,
an island on the Loire, and sailed up the river. When they came to the fork where
the Maine flows down from Angers, they turned north upon it. This news must
have been brought with the speed of terror to the citizens of that town; by the time
the Viking fleet reached Angers, its inhabitants had vanished, distributed and
cowering in the villages, hamlets, farms and woodlands of the surrounding
countryside.

It was now that the exuberant genius of Hastein showed itself. While the men
and women of Angers watched, waited for the flames to rise and then to die,
waited for the moment when they could repossess and, if necessary, rebuild their
town, the Vikings calmly closed the gates on them. Angers, abandoned and complete, had been taken over. For almost a year the town lay in Viking hands, a
fortified and comfortable headquarters from which they threatened Tours, Le
Mans and the countryside of central Brittany. Once more the harassed Charles
gathered an army and marched against them, this humiliation too great to over-
look. On the way, he gathered allies – the furious Salomon and his Breton cohorts,
distressed not only by Hastein's treachery but also by the threat the Vikings now
posed to their own domains.

With the cumbersome, elaborate techniques of the day, Charles's forces set
about their siege, sitting entrenched outside the fortifications, perhaps with some
version of the Roman *ballista*, the catapult, to hurl large stones at the defiant
Vikings within. The essence of siege, however, is blockade, and this complete
turning of the screw the Franks and Bretons were unable to achieve. Thus, despite

the building of great rams and towers, despite the tunnelling of mines and saps, despite the bombardment of stones and arrows, despite assault and constant challenge, the defending Northmen remained in comparative comfort, their ships occasionally scuttling up and down the river to bring in essential supplies, and to prove that, should the time of need arrive, escape was always possible. The year dragged on towards autumn; sickness attacked the besiegers and their fervour waned. Some master-stroke was needed now to bring this confrontation to its crisis.

Once the problem the Franks faced had been properly isolated, ingenuity could find a solution. And their problem was, of course, the river, the Vikings' chosen highway. With a display of intelligence one finds it hard to attribute to Charles, the Franks devised their counter: they would divert the waters of the Maine. They turned from Angers, they set to with pick and shovel, they built a great canal and they directed the river down it. For the Vikings, this *coup* brought disaster. The long ships, like landed fish, died on the mud. Their masts heeled over, they lay unwieldy on their clinkered sides, their proud heads bent low at last.

Hastein, a Viking in his understanding of defeat as much as in his zest for plunder, accepted the logic of this disaster and sued for peace. Once again, one might have thought, Charles had a Viking force at his mercy. Once again, however, instead of taking advantage of his victory and ridding his people of these strangers who had for so long unsteadied the foundations of their lives, the King allowed the Vikings to leave. He demanded, of course, some promise of good behaviour, and indeed received their word that they would leave his lands, but it was not this that his men had struggled for over the previous three bitter months. It has been suggested that Hastein bribed him and it is true that with the plunder of Angers to draw on, the Northmen had funds enough to buy off a hard-pressed king. Whatever the truth of that, the raiders withdrew after their exuberant year and settled once more in their previous base, their island low on the Loire; they did not, despite their promise, quit the kingdom.

From his efforts at Angers, crowned as they had been with indifferent success, Charles was drawn by other pressures to battle in the north. Immediately, another band of Vikings struck, thrusting up the Seine towards the much-harassed St Denis, the seventh prowling brotherhood to make that journey. Charles came hurrying back, paid up for peace for one last time, sending these Danes away richer by five thousand pounds of silver; a year later, he died, worn out, it may be, by his constant scuttling to and fro as this or that rival, this or that pirate, raider or invading enemy demanded his fretful and often ineffectual intervention.

To him goes the dubious credit for initiating the payments which, for a while, bought from the Vikings the safety which was in their gift, to permit or to withhold. As a result, ordinary people must have been hard put to it to choose between the depredations of the Northmen and those of the King's tax-gatherers. Since it was Charles's brothers who posed the greatest threat to his kingdom – or at least represented the greatest obstacle to his enlarging it – this painless way of ridding himself of his Viking visitors was not quite as feeble as it might seem at first sight.

The Vikings, on the whole, were robbers; they came and stole and went away. His brothers, and the rebels in Brittany and Aquitaine, menaced the very structure of his kingdom. When the Vikings, as at Angers or, earlier, around Paris, threatened to become a permanent factor in the internal strife of his state, he could and did move against them with some vigour. On such occasions, his demonstrations of force had some success.

Eighteen months after he died, his son Louis the Stammerer followed him to his Carolingian grave. With two young sons, and a third to be born posthumously, the situation was perfect for undoing what Charles had struggled all his life to preserve. Three years after Charles's death, his kingdom had been divided, Louis, now Louis III, becoming ruler of Neustria and Francia, while his brother Carloman received Aquitaine and Burgundy. The setting up of this arrangement not only involved all sorts of internecine disturbance, in which Louis of Saxony, a son of that far from avuncular figure Louis the German, was unpleasantly active, it also led to the loss of Provence, which became an independent kingdom under the rule of a vigorous usurper named Boso.

Louis the German having died, his eldest son, Charles the Fat, had succeeded him. Among his other griefs and riches, he inherited the Vikings. Danes had established themselves on the Scheldt, had survived a defeat by Louis of Saxony to burn Arras, Nijmegen and the more accessible areas of Saxony. The stripling Louis III had beaten them at Saucourt, but these Vikings were, apparently, men not easily discouraged. They made a new camp on the Meuse and by 882 had carved their predatory way through Maastricht, Liège, Aix, Cologne, Bonn and Trier, the last-named being held terror-struck for three whole days. It was therefore essential, if the newly-established Charles wished to prove he could preserve his kingdom, that these raiders should swiftly feel the keenness of his steel. Instead, in a manner reminiscent of his bald namesake and uncle, having marched an army up in apparent determination, he took to diplomacy rather than warfare. The three Danish leaders, Godfred, Sigfred and Orm, were paid nearly three thousand pounds of silver to depart; Godfred, baptized to prove his fitness, was even given a large tract of Frisian land, presumably in the supposition that gratitude would cure him of piracy for ever. That other land-hungry Vikings might take Godfred's reward as an example to be followed, could they only prove their case with a sufficient urgency, does not seem to have occurred to Charles the Fat. Indeed, the gift did not serve even to keep Godfred quiet.

Before this became apparent, however, Charles the Fat had achieved new and even greater power. Louis III had died in 882, making Carloman the sole inheritor of his grandfather's kingdom (with the continuing exception of Boso's Provence). In 884, however, Carloman died too, leaving the throne vacant, or at least filled by no one more portentous than the third, and baby, brother. The aristocracy, afraid of a new round of would-be usurpers, of rivalries and dynastic battles, turned to Charles. As a result, he succeeded to all the Frankish domains, thus gathering into his hands most of the empire his great-grandfather, Charlemagne, had once held.

Two Frankish ornaments: a gold three-tongued
mounting from a sword belt, found in a grave
at Hon near Oslo (top); mounts and a buckle
for a baldric, from Ostra Påboda (bottom).

The grasp, however, had noticeably weakened over the intervening generations.

It was at this point that Godfred, a man who seems to have been single-minded to the point of idiocy and having experienced one good thing could imagine nothing but that he should experience it again, fatally over-reached himself. He demanded a further grant of land, the vineyard-rich districts of Andernach and Coblenz. This time Charles dealt with him, although more like a Renaissance prince than a medieval king. He had Godfred assassinated by his agents. Leaderless and perhaps softened by the expectation of easy triumphs, the Danes could put no effective force into the field when Charles chose to come at them in a more conventional manner. In this way the Vikings lost their hold on Frisia, a territory which before their assaults had been rich and which, with cultivation, would be rich again, a territory which might have been their own, a Norse kingdom stretching into the Netherlands, but which through greed and ineptitude they had now thrown away for ever.

Meanwhile, Godfred's colleagues, Sigfred and Orm, had not been idle. Bought off by Carloman, they approached Charles for a similar bribe. Less amenable to blackmail than his cousin, he refused to pay. As a result, affairs between Viking and Frank, at tension for so long, now reached a sort of climax. This time the force gathered by the Danes was no mere raiding party but an army geared to full-scale invasion. Some seven hundred ships made up their fleet, suggesting a man-power well in excess of thirty thousand. In this massive manner they set themselves to smash their way up the Seine. They stormed and overran Rouen in July; by mid-November they had reached Paris. Here, however, they were checked, the fortifications stout, their defence resolute.

Paris in those days was no more than the Île de la Cité. On its island, it stood in the centre of the Seine, not yet anyone's capital, a city among others. It was clear, however, that if the invaders took it, they would be free to range south-east along the river, past Melun, or north-east across open country towards Reims, or eastward along the Marne, or even to strike towards Burgundy along the Yonne. Preventing this breakthrough were the city's fortifications, above all its two bridges. A stone bridge connected it to the Seine's north bank, a wooden one to the south. Both were defended by towers at each end, both were stout, solid bulwarks against invasion. Both were now set upon by the Danes. Within the city, commanding its defence, was the Abbot of St Germain, Joscelin, and Odo of Neustria, a blood-inheritor of the struggle against Northmen, for his father had been Robert the Strong. To continue the fight, they had under them not more than two hundred men-at-arms.

Sigfred began, perhaps uncharacteristically, with negotiation; he had after all learned already that Charles, and thus his lieutenants, might be amenable to the bribes and treaties of diplomacy, rather than the blood and steel of war. Contemptuously, Odo and Joscelin turned him down. They stood firm for Charles and the kingdom; Charles had ordered them to bar the Vikings' way, here they stood across the Seine to bar it and here they would remain.

On 26 November, the Vikings struck at the city's defences for the first time. The dark whine of arrows lay across the air, their shimmering canopy shredded at intervals by the heavier flight of catapulted stones. Shield-protected, the North-men came up under the walls, the towered parapets. From above, a lazy smoke arose, the smell of pitch, of oil – then, in a moment, the searing cataracts had plunged upon the attackers. Their flesh scalded, men ran, bent double, purple with burns. The battle concentrated on the right bank, the northernmost tower; here screams of defiance, of terror and of pain arose, here the bright Viking shields advanced, then scattered, turned away, only to advance again; here the insect-thrum of arrows was at its most vibrant. Dusk came, and nightfall. The tower had held fast; it stood now, its buttressed top outlined by Frankish watch fires.

In the morning, that top was closer to the clouds – overnight, its defenders had raised it by one storey. Below them, Vikings called the war-cries which had terrorized a thousand towns and villages, then made their thrust. Under arrow-fall and shield-wall, they ran a battering-ram at the tower's timbers. Beyond it, a great catapult now threw and threw again the destructive weight of larger stones. More subtly, sappers began to tunnel at the tower's foundations, while others laid bales of kindling to its wooden walls and lit them, in an attempt to burn a weakness in. But at this second nightfall, the tower still stood, its defenders still firm within it.

Now there was a lull of over a month. The Vikings dug trenches, they settled in for the winter, they clawed supplies for their army out of the surrounding country-side and, squirrel-like, hoarded them against the cold. It was the end of January before they struck at Paris again, this time dividing their advance, so that for the first time the bridge itself came under direct attack. Their assault now was at least as desperate as those of the first two days. This time, they tried to fill the moat which guarded the tower walls. They threw in straw and branches they had gathered. They slaughtered cattle and other animals, and threw their carcases in. They displayed their prisoners, then killed them and threw their bodies, too, into that inconvenient ditch. For two days the battle continued, dragged on into a third. The Danes piled wood and pitch into three ships, then fired them. Blazing, these swung and yawed their way down-river, each under its fragile tower of sparks, to lodge themselves against the bridge's wooden columns. Eagerly the Vikings watched, hoping for a transfer of flame, but the ships burned, staggered, collapsed upon themselves, sank clumsily. Scorched and blackened, the bridge remained, standing apparently as firmly as before.

Perhaps those timbers had been weakened after all, however; on 6 February winter flooded the rivers, the Seine rose and under the weight of its waters the southern bridge trembled, tottered and then, with a scream of tearing wood, swung away from the banks. Foam-flecked, the water thrust the wreckage aside. The way up-stream was open. The Danes stormed the now isolated tower on the southern bank, overwhelming the twelve men who had been left to defend it. Then they pushed on up the river, leaving the city still besieged by a force just large enough to coop up its garrison. Vikings now overran the fertile lands between

Seine and Loire, they sacked Evreux, they moved against Chartres and Le Mans.

Messages went desperately out from the city, demands for help and reinforcement. Charles, however, was far away, in Italy. Henry of Saxony did come marching down from Germany, but, after one clash with the waiting Danes, withdrew again. The besiegers moved their camp to a place of greater safety, on the left bank's St Germain-des-Prés (where intellectual Vikings of a later age would cause an equal consternation in the Western world), and to the defenders on their narrow island – with its long stem and stern itself like a Viking ship upon the river – it must have seemed as though all that had threatened for so long was about to overwhelm them.

Vikings, however, like other men, had the weaknesses of their strengths. If they were magnificent marauders, pirates of ingenuity and daring, they were not true strategists, long in patience, prepared to wait out the slow processes of attrition. Thus already they were becoming restive; Sigfred sufficiently so to allow himself to be persuaded, by the insignificant donation of sixty pounds of silver, to move away again towards the sea. As yet, however, not many of his colleagues were prepared to take their impatience to these improvident lengths; there had to be, they must have felt, better pickings for them after all the efforts they had made. In the second week of April, therefore, it was only his own men who followed Sigfred as he sailed off down the Seine. Inside the city, conditions became increasingly desperate. With Henry standing off and Charles far distant, it seemed as though no one would ever come to save them. And, in May, one prop of their long defence at last gave way – the Abbot, Joscelin, died. His was one death among many, for disease was now striking right and left, but it was the most disastrous, the most heavily mourned.

Desperate times demanded desperate measures. Odo crept from the invested city, almost alone, passed through the Danish lines and set out to spread the word of Paris's need among those who could help, the Frankish nobility. His message, and perhaps he himself, finally reached Charles. Provided with an escort, Odo returned and, to the incredulous delight of those beleaguered there, carved his way through the Danes and back into the city. He brought new and hopeful tidings – Charles, with a great army, was on his way to save Paris. And, in truth, before the end of summer, Charles was on the move.

The Frankish advance, however, was delayed by tragedy; Henry of Saxony, Charles's brother, died while patrolling far ahead of the main body of the army. For a while, Charles's resolution trembled. Eventually, however, he continued to move towards disease-ridden, half-starved Paris. The Danes, aware of this, roused themselves to attempt for a last time the one result which could stave off relief – their own success. Furiously they swarmed at the fortifications, their arrows once more dimming daylight, their greater engines hurling sporadic destruction. This time, however, the men within knew that there was a term to their agony; they would not at this stage hold less than firm. Once more, the Viking attacks recoiled.

Now tables were turned. The Vikings were defeated, driven before Charles's forces on the south bank. The Paris garrison was reinforced. Finally, the Danish camp was itself besieged. The main body of the Frankish army settled threateningly at the foot of Montmartre's bluffs, entrenching themselves, preparing, one might have thought, to deliver the *coup de grâce* which would finally rid the kingdom of these most stubborn scourges. Perhaps the army thought so too, and the watchful Danes. Perhaps it was only Charles himself who thought differently – but his was the thought that counted. Instead of making his last, decisive move and thrusting the Danes back once and for all, he sent them words, he suggested terms. Negotiations began, to arrive at conclusions which must have been as surprisingly bitter to the Parisian garrison as they were sweet to the Vikings. For a year now Odo and his men had tried to hold back the Viking sweep across Charles's kingdom. Many of them had died in this effort, of wounds or sickness. Joscelin had stood steadfast, then fallen. Loyalty, and the logic of national structure – a new logic, only recently learned, yet already beginning to be understood – had enthused them. They had been prepared to die themselves in order to hold the rest of the kingdom safe. This safety Charles, with breathtaking ingratitude, with an almost criminal heedlessness, had bargained away.

The Danes, he agreed, should have free passage up the Seine. They should, he added, be permitted to take up winter quarters in Burgundy. (Here he was not perhaps as feeble of will as he appeared – Burgundy was in revolt; the Danes would give the rebels something else to think about.) When the winter was over, he would pay them seven hundred pounds of silver, on condition that they would leave the kingdom for good.

The people of Paris, their dismay an oppressive thing, turned to Odo: should this treaty be honoured? Odo did not believe it should; soon, the city was preparing to dispute the Viking advance once more. So vigorous were they in their efforts that the Danes had to forsake the river, heaving their ships along the undefended banks until they were well past the fortifications before launching them again, to sail on upstream and carry out their – or, more accurately, Charles's – programme. In this, however, they proved as little steadfast as Charles himself had been; soon they had turned from Burgundy and it was Soissons and Bayeux which crumbled under their greedy assaults.

The siege of Paris had two results: it established that city as the key to the whole of central and northern France, and it caused the final unravelling of the old Carolingian Empire. Charles's deviousness had been too blatant, after all, too obvious in its cynicism. In 888, he was deposed and his great state parcelled out into new kingdoms. One of these was that of the West Franks; faced with the need to choose a king who could stand up to Vikings, they turned to the one obvious man, Odo, Marquess of Neustria.

At first, everything appeared to go well. In the Argonne, Odo defeated a large force of Vikings, leading his outnumbered forces against them with such energy that he was himself wounded. Danes approached Paris once more; Odo placed himself between them and the city, a manœuvre he had to repeat the following year when the Vikings advanced again. This time they came on with more serious intent, demanding the silver which the deposed Charles the Fat had promised them. If they did not get it, they said, they would smash their way past Paris into the rich lands beyond. Odo stood, as always, and fought; he pushed the Northmen back, but not far or decisively enough. The threat remained. Gauging his enemy's mood with nicety, Odo decided to honour Charles's promise – he paid the bribe. He had not miscalculated. When the Danes withdrew, it was for the last time. Their ships would never again come on their bleak errands up the Seine, nor would Viking axes knock peremptorily for entry on the gates of Paris. That city had won its safety and established its status.

Elsewhere, however, Viking gangs still criss-crossed the kingdom. Odo had to fight again on the Oise; Carloman's bastard son, Arnulf, now king of the East Franks, had similarly to ride out against a horde which had for almost a year burned and plundered their way along the Scheldt. These he defeated near Louvain, in 891, and mauled them sufficiently to make them hesitate. Famine came to add cogency to their doubts and in the following year they went off in search of simpler and more rewarding harvests, crossing the Channel from Boulogne to Kent. Theirs seems to have been a penetrating example, for in the same year the famous Hastein, defeated too by Odo and as always glad to withdraw when the going became difficult, set sail for the Thames estuary. A strange quiet descended upon the shallow river valleys and the huddled towns of the Franks. Monasteries could display their riches for the greater glory of God, roofs could settle on their timbers without danger of being overtaken by flame. For the first time in nearly half a century, there were no Viking raiders in the land. (It is more than likely, however, that encampments and wider settlements continued to give them shelter on the lower Seine, an area they had largely controlled for many years.)

Despite some minor expeditions, it was not until 910, nearly twenty years later, that another sizeable force of Vikings decided to repeat in their turn the profitable history in which their fathers had figured. Bourges was sacked that year, although the bishop of Auxerre, riding out armed and spurred in the fashion of the day's ecclesiastical cavaliers, had managed to defeat them. In the following year, Vikings laid siege to Chartres. Perhaps remembering Paris, and certainly their own embattled history, the citizens stood firm. Like Odo in Paris, they called for help and perhaps, like Odo, they received it. Certainly, despite their most thunderous efforts, the Northmen were held by the town's defences; eventually, they were forced to call off the attack. This fact, the massive losses which seem to have accompanied it and the hastiness of their flight immediately afterwards lead one to think that it was an outside force which raised the siege. Soon they were back once more on the lower reaches of the Seine, safely entrenched in what had become, *de facto*, Northmen's territory.

Their leader was a man named Rollo. Was he the *Heimskringla*'s Gange-Rolf

A nineteenth-century representation of Rollo,
who created the dukedom of Normandy after
Charles the Simple had granted the Norsemen
lands beside the mouth of the Seine.

who travelled 'over the sea to the West', coming at last to 'Valland', which was the Vikings' name for France? Was he in fact Norwegian, as this would suggest, or was he Danish, as most of the men who followed him were? The dispute over this has been long in the boil, but there are not the ingredients to bring it to a resolution. It has even been suggested that he was Swedish. What is certain is that he was there, established on Frankish soil, leader of a band of hungry men, but for the time being foiled in his efforts to gain for them the plunder they had come for.

What they gained in fact was not, one may suppose, what they had expected. The last of the three sons of Louis the Stammerer, the baby whose claims to the throne had earlier been superseded by those of Charles the Fat, had now grown old enough to take his rightful place (a factor Charles might have taken into consideration before beginning his self-interested manipulations of the kingdom). As the new king of the West Franks, Charles the Simple had to face the reality of the Northmen's presence. By one subtle concession, he turned the invaders into a buffer: he granted them the lands which they already held. In this way, he made sure that later raiders would meet men as ferocious as themselves, anxious to defend their new territories – the prize which, finally, they had left their overcrowded homelands to find and take. At St Clair-sur-Epte, in 911, Charles and Rollo signed their treaty.

Rouen, Lisieux, Evreux, all towns often sacked in the past, now became part of Rollo's fief. In addition, he was to be overlord of the lands between the Bresle and the Epte; it was even hinted that he might treat his Breton neighbours as he pleased – if he felt the itch to go *i viking*, he might go in that direction without censure. Clearly, Brittany had remained rebellious.

All that now had to be done was that Rollo should allow himself to be baptized – the Franks were, after all, a Christian people – and should pay formal homage to Charles as his sovereign. Such conditions might have been expected to stick in the craw of a rampaging Viking; surprisingly, Rollo turned Christian with a suitable meekness and seems to have taken his conversion seriously. The act of homage is supposed to have caused him greater difficulty, but an advantageous treaty has its own forceful logic and he managed it. By this philosophical acceptance he turned himself from a landless marauder (which had been his condition, however high his birth) into a Frankish aristocrat, and his men from pirates to landlords, farmers and freeholders, secure in their properties for ever. For them, the Viking days were over; the days of the Normans had begun.

Although elements of the old Scandinavian legal system were grafted on the new settlements, the one institution above all others which had safeguarded individual freedom, the *thing*, never made a Norman appearance. As a result, both law and the holding of land were guaranteed from above, rather than from below. Rulers, instead of relying on the freely-given support of those they ruled, made them beholden for princely law-making, protection and largesse. Thus the roots of an oppressive feudal system, later to stifle an older Saxon equality across the Channel, were laid down at the very beginnings of Norman history.

Whatever its burgeoning social institutions, however, the new settlement did not find that matters went uniformly well for it. When in 923 the Duke of Burgundy led a dynastic revolt against Charles the Simple, Rollo took the field against him, a loyal noble in his sovereign's train. This, though admirable, proved a mistake – conflict ended with the wrong king enthroned. As a consequence, Raoul, the erstwhile Duke, ranged Norman lands as earlier Vikings had once ranged his. It was above the lamentations of Northmen and their wives that flames now rose from ravaged rooftops, it was in their isolated farmsteads that marauders raped and murdered and the blood of the assaulted gushed across the straw of their own barns. Such treatment insisted on retribution – the Viking blood was still too turbulent in Norman veins for them to have learned a terror-stricken acceptance. Soon they were returning these bloody compliments on the far side of the River Oise. It is perhaps a wonder that the whole experiment, over which many Franks must always have had doubts, did not collapse then and there. Somehow, however, a peace was arranged, a new treaty signed – Rollo even found as a result that the area of his suzerainty had been increased.

Rollo, however, was lord only of his own Vikings; elsewhere, others raided, most notably in the Loire Valley. These now demanded from the new king land of their own comparable with Normandy itself, a request Raoul wisely turned down. With the inevitable logic of such confrontations, his refusal set the Vikings off on a slashing drive across Neustria. This was now in the hands of another of the Capetians, Hugh the Great, Duke of the Franks, and he and Raoul gathered an army and went after them. Felecan, as the Viking leader was called by the Franks, withdrew as far as Nantes; in 927, after a five-week campaign by Hugh, the Northmen were confirmed in their possession of that town, in return for their word that they would not distress their neighbours.

It took three years for their Viking passions to rise to the point where action was demanded; it would have been better had they disciplined themselves, for this time Raoul attacked them with a relentless determination and for a second time forced them to flee into their stronghold on the Loire. Their defeat, however, had put those with reason to hate them in good heart. On the feast of St Michael, in 931, the Danes were overcome as they had for nearly two centuries so often overcome others – by surprise. The Bretons, as fierce and independent as Vikings, put them comprehensively to the sword and almost broke the Danish power at one bloody stroke. There were some reprisals, a new campaign had to be fought five years later and it was not until 937 that Nantes was finally recaptured. But that was the end. What Vikings survived fled for the coast, the sea, other and safer lands. For the Franks, the long terror of northern axes was finally over.

Normandy remained as proof that those who spread terror sometimes reap a richer harvest than those who spread seeds. Its dukes had settled into dynasty, William Longsword succeeding when his father, Rollo, died in 927. He was a faithful supporter of Raoul and the Capetians, lands being added to those he already ruled as a reward for this fidelity. When he died in 942, a man who had been more Frank than Viking, a lifelong Christian, it might have been thought that Normandy had finally lived down its alien and violent beginnings. In the time of his young son Richard, however, there was a threat from within, from a revitalized Thor-cult, a paganism which turned the Christian Normans into a faction within their own community; and from without, when the restored Carolingians, in the person of Louis d'Outremer, tried to drive the sons of the settled Northmen from their lands. Christ and Capet triumphed, however, in the battle for the minds and allegiance of the Normans. As the Capetian House settled again on the throne of France, it drew Normandy into closer alliance with the rest of the country. Soon, its customs and its language began to lose their distinctive quality; Normans became to all intents and purposes Franks.

Less than a hundred years before, Ermentarius of Noirmoutier had written of 'the endless flood of Vikings', bemoaning the disasters of those times: 'Everywhere Christ's people are the victims of massacre, fire and plunder. The Vikings overrun all that lies before them and none can withstand them.' He listed the places that they had ravaged – Rouen is among them, 'laid waste, looted and burned', and Evreux and Bayeux. 'Ships past counting voyage up the Seine, and throughout the entire region evil grows strong.' Now the Vikings had themselves become 'Christ's people', Rouen was their legitimate stronghold, the 'entire region' – once their battleground, the granary of their extortions, a place to rob and leave – had become a monument to their true aspirations. They would adventure from it, to the far edges of Europe and beyond, but in two generations Vikings, Normans now and changed, had come to rest.

3 THE STRUGGLE FOR ENGLAND

A Viking tombstone from St Paul's Churchyard, London. This tenth- or eleventh-century stone is decorated in the Ringerike style which incorporates both English and Viking elements.

Peace in Wessex, and Alfred on the throne. An interlude – England beset, and Wessex at bay. Complex, intelligent, imaginative, courageous, literate because self-taught, richly robed in the papal Court of Leo IV at the age of four, fourteen years later a warrior commanding against Danes, Alfred, the only king called 'Great' in English history, stands as gigantic along the perspective of history as he did to his contemporaries. We can get quite close to him because the Bishop of Sherborne, Asser, who knew him, thought him well worth the adulatory effort of a biography. Although distracted by an illness – 'never an hour passes but he either suffers from it or is nearly desperate from fear of it' – Alfred, in Asser's words, 'did not permit the helm of government, once he had taken it over, to quiver or turn, though sailing amid the diverse raging whirlpools of this present life'.

Certainly there were whirlpools enough. East Anglia, Mercia, Northumbria – all had fallen to the Danes. In Dublin, across the water, a Viking ruler sat in established power. It was probably a force of his people which, landing in Dorset in 876, signalled the beginnings of a new Viking assault on Wessex. The invasion proved to be one half of a pincer movement. Based on Cambridge there was another army of Northmen, half that which had overrun Mercia in 874. Now, under its commander, Guthrum, perhaps no longer satisfied with the flat acres of East Anglia which it controlled, this force marched to join the newcomers on the coast. Wareham, a coastal town, was taken; Alfred, not prepared for the exigencies of a siege, paid the Vikings to leave his kindgom. They took his money, left Wareham – but, moving swiftly and by night, sent Guthrum's men riding westward to Exeter, while the sea-borne force set off to link up with them on the River Exe. In this way, the whole of England's south-west would be open to their ravaging forays.

Nature intervened, however, to forestall the violence of men. Off Swanage, a storm struck the Viking fleet. Over a hundred of their ships foundered among the waves, rocks and cross-currents of those difficult waters. Alfred, by now installed outside Exeter, became instantly and painlessly a victor; cut off from his support, Guthrum had to surrender. Again he promised to leave the kingdom; perhaps he even promised to return to the fens he had come from, but if so, he broke his word once more, for it was in Gloucester that he settled, poised above Alfred's northern frontier. The interlude of peace had degenerated into a sullen and fragile truce.

In those days, war conventionally ended in late autumn, to be resumed in early spring. It had its season and its period of rest. But now the *Anglo-Saxon Chronicle*

ABOVE This penny, struck to commemorate Alfred's occupation of London in 886, bears the monogram LONDINIA on its reverse side.
BELOW The Franks' Casket: the relief work in whalebone on its lid and sides illustrates scenes from classical, pagan and Christian stories. Made in Northumbria in the early eighth century, it is an outstanding example of Anglo-Saxon craftsmanship.

gives us its stupefied tidings: 'In this year the host went secretly after Twelfth Night to Chippenham and rode over Wessex and occupied it, and drove a great part of the inhabitants oversea, and of the rest the greater part they reduced to submission, except Alfred the king; and he with a small company moved under difficulties through woods and into inaccessible places in marshes.' To this winter attack, Wessex had no answer but surprise, defeat and submission. The West Saxons were scattered, many of them in flight across the Channel; many others had made formal submission to the Danes; only a steadfast or fortunate few re-mained at Alfred's side, free men, though harried and in danger.

If there was a time when Alfred burned the loaves he should have watched (thus immortalizing the cowherd's scolding wife who baked them), it was now, as he fled, the ghost of royalty in a land apparently unkinged. For it was clear that Wessex had fallen to new masters and that henceforth it would lie with the rest of England within the *Danelaw*. It was clear, that is, to almost everyone – only Alfred and a few others were exempted from this sensible clarity. Slowly, he gathered men to him; the Danes had always based themselves on fortified camps and now he built one, learning as good kings must from the successes of his enemies. Thus, entrenched on Athelney, an island deep in the marshes of Somerset, west of Sel-wood, he began his counter-attacks on the Danish strength – 'He continued fight-ing against the host,' as the *Chronicle* puts it. He seems never to have wavered, or so the histories suggest; there was never a pause during which one might presume his despair. There was only the necessary flight, the cunning encampment, the brisk efforts at attrition. The West Saxons had, in effect, taken to guerrilla war.

The next development was more overt, because now Alfred felt himself strong enough to begin an offensive: 'Then in the seventh week after Easter', the *Chronicle* tells us, 'he rode to *Ecgbryhtesstan*, to the east of Selwood, and came to meet him there all the men of Somerset and Wiltshire and that part of Hampshire which was on this side of the sea [which means perhaps those who had not fled from the country], and they received him warmly.' And well they might, standing beside Ecgbert's stone, hailing this single symbol of their continuing identity, of what despite all odds was still their unity. Yet how had Alfred summoned them, across devastated country ruled by marauders anxious to control those who had for so long stood out against them? It argues a greater resilience in the kingdom than the superficial history allows. Less than six months before, it had seemed as though Wessex was lost, yet here stood its fugitive king at the head of an army he had been able to summon across distances of up to a hundred miles.

He had chosen his moment with care. To the west, an attack on the northern coasts of Devon had been steadfastly repulsed, thus ensuring the Wessex flank. The Devonians, under their leader, Odda, may even have killed the great Ubbi, one of that triumvirate of reckless sons whom the legendary Ragnar Lodbrok is said to have sired. Encouraged by such neighbourly success, Alfred took only two days to catch up with Guthrum's army, which had thought itself to be marching out of Chippenham to put the Saxons decisively down. Such complacency was misplaced and might even have been their undoing; the Alfred whom they encountered was not now a man surprised in mid-winter and routed before his army could gather. This time, as the *Chronicle* lets us know, Alfred 'fought against the entire host, and put it to flight, and pursued it to the fortification, and laid siege there a fortnight . . .'. Such swift movement confounded the Vikings, who had had no opportunity nor even seen the need to prepare for a siege. When those two weeks had passed, they surrendered. Hostages and promises of a peaceful future were demanded and given; more, Alfred insisted on Guthrum's becoming a Christian, the kind of forced conversion usual at a time when the ceremonial formalities of a religion were assumed to bestow on those who undertook them their own spiritual rewards. Politically, however, as well as theologically, the move was an intelligent one, for Christian neighbours would be less alien than pagan ones, and the Christian English in the vast areas the Danes controlled might be better treated once their masters had become their co-religionists.

Such useful results would follow, of course, only if Guthrum viewed his baptism as gravely as Alfred did, and to ensure he did so, Alfred not only stood as his godfather but took his duties in that role very seriously. He treated his dangerous godchild with respect and even, one might have thought, affection, having him under his own roof for twelve days and giving him many presents. He even allowed the Danish army to winter that year in Wessex, which given the experiences of the previous winter seems to have been almost foolhardy in its trustfulness. Guthrum (or Athelstan, as he now was, this having been his baptismal name) responded honourably, however, and the following spring moved away. In this manner, Alfred beat off the Danish threat to Wessex and managed to keep his kingdom intact, a guarded enclave of Saxon freedom in a land otherwise pressed into homage or terror by the Danes.

Guthrum, meanwhile, whether Christian or not, remained a Viking (conversion never did a great deal to dampen the northern violence) and, turned back from Wessex, obviously considered Mercia's western territories easier prey. His move from Alfred's domains, therefore, took him no further than Cirencester, just to the north of them, whence he could glower across the fat pasture-lands and wooded hills of Hwicce, roughly the area of today's Gloucestershire and Worcestershire. Gloucester had an ealdorman or duke, Worcester a bishop, and these two were the strong men of the region. On the throne of Mercia sat the man in theory their ruler – Ceolwulf, the satrap placed there by Halfdan the Viking. Because they knew that they would find no protection from this king, the duke and the bishop made the decision to turn to Alfred as an ally and protector. This politically aware move had two consequences – it split the kingdom of Mercia once and for all, and it caused Guthrum to turn away from central England.

His adventures over for a while, Guthrum marched eastward, back into East Anglia. Here he divided the land among his faithful, established four earldoms, each *jarl* policing his area with his own army, and settled to administering the land, like other Vikings elsewhere in England, according to the law of the Danes.

In this way the *Danelaw*, that great eastern tract of Viking territory, was stretched further southward, resting there on the estuary of the Thames, as in the north it rested on the banks of the Tees. Uneasily, perhaps, but at some sort of peace, the divided country now lay for a clutch of years. The Danes consolidated, establishing their home-from-home by rooting themselves ever more deeply into the landscape, spreading their language, law, customs and preferences in a swift cultural seeding. The English, meanwhile, bided their time; they saw an archbishop once more installed at York and felt they had something to hope for, even if no more than a Christian stability. Alfred, wary, built up his new navy, bringing in Frisian sailors, men with experience of the sea, to strengthen the crews.

In 885, he had cause to use his ships, for Rochester found itself under attack from a new horde of Northmen. This was the start of a swift, tactical game of chess, with as always the fate of England as its prize. Guthrum, seeing a new opportunity, broke his word and sent his men swarming over his south-western borders. Alfred routed Rochester's besiegers, then used his fleet to capture sixteen Viking ships at the mouth of the Stour. Guthrum, always a Viking, counter-moved, and on water: he scattered Alfred's ships with his own skilful fleet, a larger one than the English, and looked for a moment to have the game won. But Alfred thrust forward, marched up the south bank of the Thames, swept into London and took it. Dominating the estuary and the lands to the north of it, he had clearly put Guthrum into check. Accepting this, the Dane ceded the game and signed a new treaty, giving up to Alfred Hendrica and Chilternsaete, the area immediately north of London – roughly the modern Hertfordshire and Buckinghamshire. Alfred also remained in London, a town he now fortified and made safe against attack; he put his own son-in-law, Æthelred, the Ealdorman of Mercia, in charge of its defences.

This complicated game of death and skill, ending in Alfred's complete triumph, continued and hastened the process which had been begun by the Ealdorman of Gloucester and the Bishop of Worcester. Almost all the English, outside Wessex as well as within, now looked to him as their natural and proven leader. In 892 he was given the opportunity of matching himself to this status, for this was the year when, defeated by the East Franks near Louvain, a Viking force of some 250 ships came careering across the Channel to land at Lymne, at one stroke putting the whole of Kent at risk. Immediately afterwards the great Hastein, who had once perhaps plundered the coasts of Italy, sent packing from Picardy by that vigorous King Odo, came sailing up the Thames with eighty ships of his own, intent on making England pay his Frankish debts. He too established himself in Kent, on its northern shore. England was once more beset.

It was clear to Alfred that the arrival of such a force would set the palms of England's resident Danes itching for the axe-handle. As long as he could maintain a balance of power in England by his own vigilance and the organization of his forces, peace might continue, but the tilting of that balance by a large horde of ravening newcomers was likely to lead to a gigantic and perhaps overwhelming

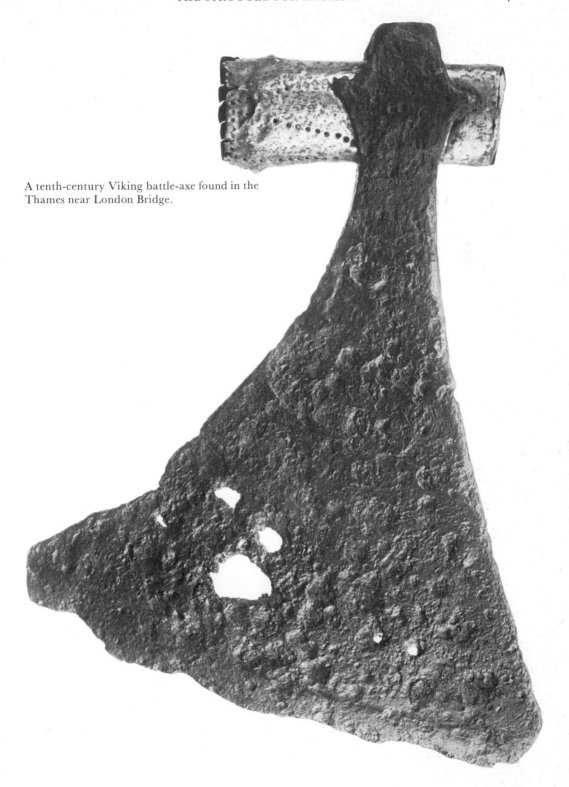

A tenth-century Viking battle-axe found in the
Thames near London Bridge.

King Alfred shown in an initial from a
twelfth-century Latin copy of the treaty
signed between himself and Guthrum in 886.
By it, Alfred gained control of extensive lands
north of London.

Viking break-out and the final collapse of the free areas of the country. Æthelred, of course, ruled in Mercia in place of the Danes' bought man, Ceolwulf, and Æthelred, married into Alfred's family, would see that the English Midlands stood with Wessex.

Alfred had also reorganized the *fyrd*, that militia of peasants which Saxon kings had always been able to call out in times of need. This responsiveness to crisis was both its strength and its weakness, for while it might fall upon a foe with the zest and enthusiasm of the newly recruited, a sustained watchfulness or a long campaign invariably saw its numbers dwindle – peasants, after all, find their *raison d'être* in tilling the land, not fighting over it. Alfred divided this army, so that one half was constantly on the alert, while the other peacefully tended its agricultural affairs. He had built, or rebuilt, fortresses throughout his kingdom, to give himself a network of defensive redoubts, many of them fortified towns maintained by their citizens; based on these, he could protect his people, rally them and, when the moment came, mount swift counter-attacks. All this, however, could be trampled under if the new Vikings and the large number of their already established countrymen were to join together in concerted attack. To avoid this, Alfred began his defence with swift diplomacy.

Because of his position of supremacy among the English, he was able to negotiate with leaders of the whole length of the Danelaw. He was given strong promises of neutrality from both the Northumbrian and the East Anglian Danes, to reinforce which he took hostages from the latter. In this way, he secured himself at least nominally. He must have known, and so must they, that they would stand with their Viking brothers and indeed throughout the campaigns that followed Hastein and the rest could always look to eastern England for asylum, sometimes for a supporting fleet, occasionally even for military help. It may nevertheless be that, had it not been for these oaths (given now by Christian men, if that made any difference), there would have been a major force sweeping down upon southern England from the north-east; even as it was, the battle was greatly prolonged by the succour the newcomers could find from their established compatriots, and by the fact that there were such large tracts of the country to which Alfred could not follow them when they fled. And this does not take into consideration the many occasions on which the Danelaw overlooked its sworn word and intervened directly in the fighting.

In Kent there was, for a while, a setting up of camps, a sending out of scouting parties, skirmishes, then negotiations. Hastein, in north Kent, agreed to talk with Alfred; while they parleyed, the southern party broke from their bridgehead in Appledore and thrust north-west to Hampshire, then north into Berkshire, then eastward. At Farnham Edward, Alfred's son and most able lieutenant, caught up with them, faced them and drove them back. As was the usual Viking custom, they looked to an island for refuge and found one at Thorney on the River Colne.

Edward would have kept them cooped up here, but his men had been in the field for their allotted span and were anxious to return home, an anxiety their shortage of food did nothing to lift. Alfred, bringing his own forces up to take their place, was diverted by the arrival of a fleet raised in the Danelaw and beginning to harry the coast of Devon. For a while it looked as though the Viking force on Thorney, unwatched and unguarded, would break freely into central England; just in time, a reinforced Edward, his brother-in-law Æthelred by his side, returned to invest the island a second time. The Danes surrendered, retreated and were followed by the English. At Benfleet they joined with Hastein's group. That experienced raider was away, plundering the nearby countryside, and had he not been, things might have gone differently. Without him, however, the Danish camp fell swiftly to the Saxons.

One can imagine it, probably circular, an earthen wall hastily but efficiently thrown up around it, the ships close by or perhaps even within this perimeter; sad huts of wattle-and-daub construction drably close to the beaten ground, the women and children at first brightly about them, but later huddling under their musty roofs as the attackers surrounded, briefly besieged, then ferociously attacked; the defences giving way, that wall a trap at last, the army broken and its dependents taken. Hastein's wife and sons were among those captured in this victory, but there was sometimes a magnanimity between the great dictated by expediency as much as by generosity – the turning of a year could shift the burden of mercy from one side to the other – and Alfred later handed them safely back. The English took the fleet, sailing away all the ships they could find crews for, then burning the remainder; it may be that the loss of his ships hurt the old Viking chief as deeply as that of his family.

Hastein was not long, however, in making a new camp, this time at Shoebury, to the north of the Thames Estuary, rallying there all the survivors. Perhaps he sent out a general call for help; certainly his numbers were swiftly increased by levies raised within the Danelaw. At the head of this force, he marched westward, possibly attempting to link up with Vikings then ravaging south Wales. If so, he reached Wales somewhat to the north of where a useful *rendezvous* might have been arranged, at Buttington, high on the Severn Valley. Ealdorman Æthelred steadfastly came after him, finding men in Somerset and Wiltshire as he marched, bringing in as allies a detachment from north Wales. Hastein tried to avoid battle, but, in danger of being starved into surrender, struck disastrously at the English. Soon he was scuttling eastwards again, to retire into Shoebury and lick his wounds a second time.

Regrouped and once more reinforced from within the Danelaw, the Viking force struck westwards yet again, so swiftly that Æthelred's army on the borders of Wales could not move into place to prevent Chester being taken. At this period Chester was a ghost town, one of many to be found in England then, and the ghosts inhabiting it were Roman. All over the country, the buildings of their great empire, its rule withdrawn from Britain four centuries earlier, dropped and mouldered and collapsed. Like clothes too large for one shrunken in body, they overshadowed the state men kept in these later and diminished times. They stood,

intimidating in their grandeur, quarries from which men levered the stones they
needed for their own mean walls and carried them away on creaking carts, leaving
the weed-grown, threatening streets to the wind, the adders and the long twining
of legend. As the anonymous eighth-century poet wrote (the translation Michael
Alexander's) :

> Snapped rooftrees, towers fallen,
> the work of the Giants, the stonesmiths,
> mouldereth. . . .

Chester was such a place, but it had been a great military centre once and even
after so long a time, Hastein's forces, within its fortifications, could defy the
English outside the walls. With winter closing in, it was too late for an ordinary
siege; Æthelred, however, organized what a later beleaguered people would call
a 'scorched earth' policy. Everything which the Danes might have used as food-
stuffs was systematically carried away or burned where it stood. By the following
year, the Danes had been squeezed out of Chester and forced to go marauding
across central Wales. At last, it may be wearily, they set out again, north-eastwards
to Northumbria, then south through East Anglia, to settle finally on the island of
Mersea, off the Essex coast – a long, circuitous march made necessary by the Saxon
army searching for them. The Viking force which had earlier attempted to strike
at Devon, turned back there by Alfred, now joined them on Mersea, and one can
imagine these ambitious and land-hungry raiders seething in their bleak encampment, held in check as they had been by the constant organized vigilance of
Wessex.

At the year's end, they had collected themselves sufficiently to sail up the River
Lea and make camp. There, an impudent twenty miles north of London, they
settled down, throwing up fortifications and from behind them threatening
Middlesex and the northern parts of Essex. Early in the summer of 895 the English
attacked them, but, with an unusual lack of vigour, had waited too long and
allowed the Vikings to become solidly established. They were repulsed, leaving
the situation worse than it had been before. Harvest-time was approaching, the
moment when hungry raiders swooped to take the newly-gathered riches of the
land from those who had sweated over them since the first ploughing. Alfred,
aware that the protection of these crops was a matter as much of prestige as it was
of practicality, marched to their defence. As often before, he showed himself more
intelligent in his leadership than the muscular Vikings might have expected;
instead of pushing his men forward for another glorious but doomed assault on
those well-defended walls, he set them to cutting timbers and carrying earth in an
effort to block the river beside the Danish camp. Seeing that if Alfred succeeded,
they would be left not merely high, dry and shipless but locked for good into their
encampment, the Vikings sent their dependents back to friendly East Anglia and
themselves marched rapidly away to the west. It was again on the Severn, this time
at Bridgenorth, that they came to a halt, building there yet another camp. On the

River Lea they left behind the precious ships above which, it may be, stragglers, looking back along the line of march, could see rising the distant black smoke of their destruction as the Saxons set them delightedly alight. In a way, that black column, blown sideways by the late-summer breezes, marked the funeral burning of their brightest expectations.

For now the war was over. The Vikings had had the freedom of central England, crossing Mercia again and again, as the mood took them or necessity dictated. But nowhere had they been able to settle, nowhere had they for long been allowed to plunder, nowhere had they managed to get their way, or even some part of it, without suffering disproportionate casualties. There would never again, it seemed, be easy pickings to be found in England. Mercia would never again collapse as it had before, to give some sea-weary pirate the land he had always dreamed of. The householders of the Danelaw, balancing what they had against what they might lose, were more and more reluctant to risk everything on the swing of a war-axe. Bridgenorth was Hastein's last rallying-point; all through the year 896, his men hesitated, grumbled, then drifted away. Some marched away to Northumbria, some to their wives and children in East Anglia. Many were settled within the Danelaw; many others were not, or refused the chance. These clambered back over the low gunwales of their ships and pointed those still-menacing prows out into the English Channel. Along the Seine, perhaps, or the Scheldt, they would find the fortune which had eluded them in England – or the grim death they had themselves eluded.

With the still dangerous Danelaw to police, Alfred now decided to strengthen his fleet. He made what the Vikings probably would have recognized as an elementary mistake (the logic of which complacent Spaniards were to discover six centuries later); he imagined that big ships invariably had the beating of smaller ones. In full battle, this may well have been true, for tactics in those days did not involve much manœuvring. Ships of a fleet would link themselves together and, in a body, take on the linked ships of the enemy. There would then follow a hand-to-hand battle, a matter of shields and swords and hissing arrows, in which man-power counted for much. It was perhaps this that Alfred had in mind when he ordered the construction of his new sixty-seater ships, built, the chroniclers assure us, on neither the Frisian nor the Danish patterns, 'but as it seemed to himself that they could be most serviceable'. In this seeming he was to be disillusioned, for his sailors found their new ships unwieldy, nine of them soon after they had been launched being out-fought by six of the Vikings', ignominiously going aground in a manner which suggests that Alfred had not taken account of the very shallow draught of Scandinavian vessels. It may be that this perhaps predictable set-back – the sea was after all the Northmen's element – made Alfred particularly angry; certainly when two of the Viking ships, having made his own look ridiculous, later ran aground themselves, he took the trouble to have their crews brought to him in Winchester, there ordering that every one of them be hanged.

This display of royal pique set its own seal on a new peace which must have given him some pleasure during the three years left to him. In 899, however, aged only fifty, he died. He had shown that, with vigilance and organization, the English could maintain their independence, that Wessex and Mercia could be made unattractive to the swiftest raider. He had taken a kingdom which had for months existed only in his head as nothing more than an idea and an intention, he had built it according to that idea and carried out that intention, and so had constructed a bulwark against piracy and annexation. He had forced men who were grudging with respect even for their own leaders to respect him, and had made that respect itself an instrument of his policies. In addition to all that, of course, he had reinforced literacy, especially in the developing English language, provided a code of law, guaranteed and even founded various establishments of the Church at a time when ecclesiastical influence was the primary civilizing factor in the Western world, and had by his combination of skills and interests not only energized the Saxon English in a new way but unified them in their admiration for him to the point at which they might, perhaps for the first time, truly take themselves as a nation.

One man's lifetime is not, however, long enough to give stability to a kingdom. His very strength threatens the state with which he has become identified, for when he departs it must be weakened and is sometimes overturned. Alfred was more fortunate than Charlemagne – his domains were narrower, his successors greater. His son Edward, always known as Edward the Elder, was a man who had already proved himself in his father's wars. Now he was to show that he was well up to coping with his own. His first threat was dynastic and came from his cousin Æthelwold; Alfred, after all, had succeeded to the throne despite his elder brothers' sons, a situation always liable to cause difficulties later. He had left Æthelwold lands, but these did not compensate an ambitious man for the whole kingdom. In need of allies, Æthelwold did not have to look far, though to throw such a glance was treachery: the Danes were always close at hand, always in theory poised to attack, always ready to assist the disaffected.

Fleeing to Northumbria, Æthelwold allied himself to Guthrum's successor, Eirik. Supported by Viking forces, he raided Wessex in 902. Stung, Edward sent a retaliatory army into the Danelaw, ordering it to cause a just amount of havoc and then to withdraw. The second half of this plan proved harder to follow than the first, and close to Biggleswade, in Bedfordshire, the Saxon army was overtaken and forced to battle. Nothing good for anyone came out of this fighting; the English, beaten, had many men killed and were forced to ignominious retreat, the Danes lost Eirik their king. Only the death of the throne-hungry Æthelwold may have been considered advantageous – quite possibly by both sides. Certainly as a direct result of this harassing to and fro across the frontier a peace was made, reaffirming the earlier treaty between Alfred and Guthrum.

Several quiet years now went by, but in 910 the Vikings could not resist the temptation offered them by Edward's absence – like many later monarchs, he was on the south coast with his fleet – and struck again. They cut their way through

Mercia, but found the King of Wessex more vigilant than they had thought. He raised levies and sent them as reinforcements to Mercia's Ealdorman, still Æthelred; together, his men and Edward's cornered the Danes at the beginning of their homeward march and, at Tettenhall in Staffordshire, utterly destroyed them. With this Saxon victory, the story of conflict in England takes a new turn, for now it was no longer the men of Wessex and Mercia who watched for Viking raiders and hoped against hope for peace, it was the Vikings themselves who were to be beleaguered. It would have been better for them if they had taken what Alfred's first treaty had offered them, a hold on half the island, rather than followed their persistent dream of conquest. But for men brought up on stories of ancestors so assiduously heroic, it must have been hard to resist the conviction that they would be less than their fathers if they too did not exchange the easy plough for the sword.

Their position now was made uncomfortable largely by the widow of Æthelred the Mercian Ealdorman, newly dead. Named Æthelflæd, she is one of the many ladies in history who step, fully armed and formidable, out of the shadow of their dead husbands, to take on the tribulations of what had been thought a man's world and to overcome them. When Æthelred died, it was she who, with her brother Edward's strong support, took over the ruling of Mercia. In this, she soon showed that she was Alfred's offspring, for she acted with that energy tempered with caution which had always been his hallmark. As the English began to put pressure on the Danes, they consolidated each new advance by the building of fortified boroughs. In this careful progress, she showed herself assiduous, throwing buttressed defences around Tamworth and Stafford in 913, Eddisbury and Warwick the year after. There was a short pause while she dealt with the Welsh, haplessly belligerent as ever in their western mountains, then the inexorable, step-by-step advance continued. In 916, she turned Warburton and Runcorn into her eastern redoubts. In 917, she took Derby and held it; the year after, Leicester.

From the Danish point of view, her pressure was that of one half of a nutcracker. The other half was crushing them from the south. In 913, Edward fortified Hertford and Witham and, although during the next two years he had to fight off two Danish counter-attacks and a raid by 'foreign' Vikings in the Severn estuary, before the end of 915 he had taken Buckingham and set up its defences. The following year Maldon was taken and fortified, and Bedford, and with the surrender of its commander, Edward took back the whole of the Chilternsæte, disputed land often in the past a springboard for Viking thrusts westward.

The Danes were now in danger of being pushed out of England altogether. Æthelflæd's push to north and east would soon link with Edward's to the north; in Bedford, he was now on the edge of the Midlands. Desperately, therefore, they struck at the Chilternsæte and the Hendrica beyond in an attempt to halt the English advance. They had lost the initiative, however, and had not now, perhaps, the depths of resources and the resolution to regain it. Their attacks failed; Edward took Tempsford, driving through the Danish defence and in the process

The British Isles

killing the Northumbrian king, a second Guthrum. Leaderless, suddenly out-
paced by history, the Vikings broke. Colchester fell, a feeble counter-attack was
beaten off by Edward's forces at Maldon; then, abruptly, Northampton's *jarl*
surrendered and so set a new fashion for submission, followed now by all the
leaders of the East and Middle Anglian hosts. Edward pushed forward to
Stamford, to be accepted by the Danes there as rightful king; as magnanimously
there as elsewhere, he allowed them, after this submission, to retain both their
lands and their laws. Nottingham, too, became one of his fortified *burhs*, and
possibly Lincoln as well.

To the north of him, Æthelflæd meanwhile threatened York, which was, it is
said, preparing to submit to her. But on the very point of triumph, this indomitable
lady had at last to make her own submission, for in this year of 918 she died.
Edward almost immediately pronounced himself her successor, a proclamation
there was only Æthelflæd's young daughter Elfwyn to dispute. It was, in any case,
to the clear advantage of the English that this son of Alfred, as intelligent and
resolute as his father, should continue his effort to reduce the Danelaw, an effort
on the whole more likely to be successful if its control lay in his hands. Nor did the
English alone feel this, for the Welsh hurried to offer him alliance, Gwynedd and
Deheubarth sending emissaries and messages of support. Their hard-learned
mistrust of the Mercians may, of course, help to explain their eagerness.

Encouraged, therefore, Edward continued, building in the year after his sister's
death fortifications at Manchester and Thelwall, and at Bakewell in 920. Established on the heights of Derbyshire, he now threatened the whole of the north. As
always, the Danes realized when circumstances had finally turned against them
and they could choose only between flight and submission. In earlier times, they
might have chosen flight, piling into their longships, pulling away from this
now-armoured shore with long strokes, hoisting their woollen sails and letting the
wind thrust them towards softer landings. But things were different now – there
were steadings to hold, crops and flocks to tend, harvests to look to. There were
children ready to inherit, and traditions that went with their inheritance. These
were what seemed important to the Danes now, and it hardly mattered to them
whether the king who could safeguard this security was one of their own or a Saxon.

There was not, after all, very much difference between a Dane and a Saxon –
their institutions were similar, their places of origin not too far apart, their
languages compatible, their customs overlapping. And both peoples were aliens
in a country where nevertheless they had lived long enough to consider it their
own. Edward, too, was manifestly just, a man not given to feud or unnecessary
vengeance, a man prepared to be as benevolently king to his Danish as to his
Saxon subjects. Thus it was that, as the chroniclers exultantly recorded, even 'the
king of Scots and the whole Scottish nation accepted him as "father and lord"';
so also did Rægnald and the sons of Eadwulf and all the inhabitants of Northumbria, both English and Danish, Norwegians and others; together with the king
of the Strathclyde Welsh and all his subjects.'

OPPOSITE The flying eagle from the shield
recovered from the Sutton Hoo burial.

The only surprising name in this catalogue of homage – which made Edward as nearly king of all Britain as any man might have thought possible – is perhaps that of Rægnald. For this man, scion of a legendary line with Ragnar Lodbrok as his ancestor, had been brutally busy in Ireland, on the Isle of Man, earlier in Scotland, and had only recently made himself king of York. Northmen from Ireland had, early in the tenth century, struck eastward, gaining a foothold in north Wales, then in the Wirral, then moving further east. There they had threateningly lurked, and stirred, and now and then drawn Edward's watchful eye. Finally the weaknesses left in the north by the struggle between the Danes and the advancing Saxons had given Rægnald his opportunity. Because of his family line he had of course a traditional claim to the north-east; it was in 919 that he made this claim good and set himself upon the throne of York (a triumph for the Dublin and Norwegian faction many Northumbrian Danes will have regarded with disquietude). He had therefore enjoyed that throne for only a year when he offered his homage to Edward – a homage, however, of political value, for it buttressed his own position with that monarch's support.

It was thus with great power in his hands that Edward died, in 924, leaving this augmented kingdom to his son, Athelstan. Brought up in the household of the Ealdorman Æthelred and his formidable wife Æthelflæd, Athelstan was as acceptable to the Mercians as he was, grandson of Alfred, to the people of Wessex. He was therefore able to take a step further the slow amalgamation of the English. It was a strength of the Saxons that one man led them, while the Danes, though united by tradition, were more fragmented in their leadership. Such lack of unity meant that the political evolution of their opponents had not been matched by their own, so that they had no choice of conduct open to them between the extremes of violence and passivity. The sudden break-out, to plunder and ravage, they understood, as they did acceptance of defeat and obeisance to a new master. What they did not understand was consolidation, sober, unified defence, fortification in depth and the solid purpose to maintain it. The long tradition of Viking mobility was always threatening to overwhelm their new allegiance to the land; when the going was difficult, the temptation to travel to where it might be easier was constant and not always resisted. For those who felt like this, Aquitaine and Frisia provided exciting alternatives and even if it was land and settlement they craved, Rollo's Normandy, newly founded, seemed to offer better prospects than the squeezed Danelaw.

One consequence of the Danelaw's essential fragmentation was the dynastic rivalries which constantly broke out, a rumbling of disputes over who ruled which section of the people. In Northumbria, these problems were the most acute and far-reaching, for they involved wider issues. The kings in both York and Dublin had traced their ancestry to Ragnar Lodbrok; both therefore had claimed Northumbrian supremacy. Rægnald, who had made the throne his own, was of the Irish line, a Norwegian, alien in many respects to the people he now ruled and altering the focus of their allegiance from Denmark to Ireland. The difficulties this

OPPOSITE The helmet found in the Sutton Hoo treasure. Almost certainly made in Sweden, it is probably similar to those worn in battle by Guthrum and his nobles.

caused, therefore, had made Edward's acceptance of him important and after his death this acceptance was confirmed when his successor, Sigtrygg, and Edward's son, Athelstan, extended the treaty into a new generation. Not for very long, however. The English Crown, having accepted Anglo-Danes as subjects, was not happy to see them come under the domination of the Irish Norse.

Sigtrygg, a relative of Rægnald, had been ruler in Dublin; although given Athelstan's sister in the traditional treaty-cementing marriage of those days, even his death strengthened the Dublin hold on Northumbria. His throne was taken by Olaf Kvaran, his son by a previous marriage, a boy of an age to need a regent; Guthfrith, his uncle, therefore followed family tradition, arose from his throne in Dublin and crossed the sea to take power in York. This final linking of Dublin and York was too much for Athelstan: he marched in that same year, 926, and sent the pair of them packing, Olaf to Ireland, Guthfrith north to Scotland. This immediately brought him the formal respect of a number of other independent British kings, notably that of Constantine III, King of the Scots, who with Welsh rulers made a special peace with Athelstan.

That they felt a need to do so expresses their anxiety. Two generations earlier, Wessex had been a hard-pressed southern kingdom, and for a while not even that. Now it had grown to encompass Mercia, the western parts of East Anglia, Deira and Northumbria. Athelstan might think of himself as king of the English, and might include some Danes in that definition, but local loyalties died hard and even for many Northumbrians he was an alien. For the Scots and the northern Welsh of Strathclyde, however, struggling to maintain their independence, he was as much an enemy as were the Vikings; grown so bloated, he was indeed the greater enemy. By 933, therefore, Constantine had accepted the logic of his fears and made common cause with those many Northmen who now accepted a Norwegian as the rightful king of York.

Despite hard fighting, despite English victories bloodily contrived and viciously exploited, the northern alliance against Athelstan grew firmer. A new Olaf now laid claim to Northumbria, this one the son of Guthfrith, the would-be Regent, who had died in 934. Gathering a fleet in Ireland, Olaf landed on the shores of the Humber and the defeat he inflicted there on Athelstan's minions was a signal to take arms which aroused not only the Welsh of Strathclyde but also those of north Wales itself. It was the northern Celts, however, who now joined with the Norwegians and the Danes to try to put down once and for all Alfred's ambitious House, to keep Wessex in its place and the country safely divided. Athelstan was not a king to flinch from crisis; his half-brother Edmund by his side, a famous Icelandic poet and warrior, Egil Skallagrimsson, in his train, he marched north.

It was at a place called Brunanburh that these tense preparations were finally released in the torrential climax of battle. The Irish Northmen stood under Olaf, the Scots under Constantine – called by Richard of Malmesbury 'a man of treacherous boldness and vigorous old age' – and the Strathclyde Welsh under their leader, Eugenius. This Brunanburh may have been today's Birrenswark, north of the Solway Firth, an ancient, flat-topped hill in Annandale, and it is in this sober countryside that the mind's eye must now place the swift gleam and clash of metal, the brightness of shields, the hoarse cry of men at the limits of courage and exhaustion, the glitter of blood, incongruously smeared across fern-leaf and grass-blade to blacken slowly in thin sunshine.

When Athelstan's army arrived, it found Olaf and his allies already established in an old Roman camp to the north. The English therefore placed themselves on the south side of the hill. Now there came call and counter call, challenge and counter-challenge, all the formalized interchange of provocation, courtesy and self-advertisement which were the preliminaries to the great military confrontations of the day. There was, like a false dawn, a false battle, when Celts on one side and Icelanders on the other lost patience with heraldry and propaganda and, breaking restraints, hurled themselves upon one another. That moment's ferocity, however, died down again; it was the following morning that sunrise set in motion what would be a day-long violence. Shoulder-to-shoulder now, the English advanced, England to be their prize; against them, steadfastly, Northmen and Scots defended their birthright and the tradition of disunity which had made them secure. Olaf fought, a young man arrogant in his certainty of kingship, determined to place himself where his blood-line led. Arrow-song and the rise and fall of blades, the soft giving of flesh under metal, the harsh breath of the hurt, and the afraid, and the weary. Men fell, howling, or lay, their worlds lost for ever, their faces under helmets and rimmed nose-guards robbed of particularity by death. And slowly the struggle turned against the northern party. The Scots, the Northmen, gave way, turned aside, began in ones and twos, then in dozens, to flee.

The *Chronicle*, jubilant, tells us of victory: 'With their hammered blades, the sons of Edward clove the shield-wall and hacked the linden bucklers.' Olaf 'was forced to flee to the prow of his ship with a handful of men' – the remnant of an over-ambitious host, huddled in their ships, rowing, disconsolately sea-bound, down the Solway Firth. 'There, likewise, the aged Constantine, the grey-haired warrior, set off in flight, north to his native land.' Seven of Olaf's noblemen, five kings and old Constantine's son were among the killed in that once-challenging, now-broken, army. It is no wonder that the chroniclers saw Athelstan and his brother as returning home 'exulting in war. They left behind them, to joy in the carrion, the black and horn-beaked raven with his dusky plumage, and the dun-feathered eagle with his white-tipped tail, greedy hawk of battle, to take toll of the corpses, and the wolf, grey beast of the forest.'

Athelstan now stood supreme in Britain, one of the notable princes of Europe. His sisters married into rulerships of the Franks and the Germans – Otto the Great was his brother-in-law, whom Widukind, the Saxon chronicler, would call 'the hope and resource of the whole of Western Christendom'. Charles the Simple was his brother-in-law, as was the Capetian Hugh the Great. Louis d'Outremer, the son of Charles the Simple, spent his childhood at Athelstan's Court. More importantly, Athelstan now considered himself the king, or at least the overlord, of everyone in Britain, thus hastening the long process of welding even the newly-come Danes and Norwegians into the structure of the kingdom. He was, it may be, helped in this attitude by the good relations he developed – or is said to have developed – with Harald Fairhair, the Norwegian king. Harald's son, Hakon, came as a foster-child into Athelstan's care, and, Snorri Sturluson tells us (one does not know with what accuracy) that 'he loved Haakon above all his relations.'

After Brunanburh, Athelstan could properly declare himself – and did so, on coin and seal and proclamation – *Rex totius Britanniae*, but this resounding and justly self-donated title died with him. When Edmund became king in 940, the enforced serenity of the kingdom began at once to be threatened, not surprising when one remembers that the new king was not yet twenty. From now on, indeed, there was to be played a murderous game of musical chairs about the Northumbrian throne.

The first sign of trouble came even before Edmund's formal accession, when in 439 Guthfrith's son Olaf took the now traditional route of Dublin kings and crossed to York, where fellow-Norsemen quickly helped him to that highly mobile crown. Soon Olaf had revived an ancient energy and was raiding across the Humber. At Leicester, Edmund was ready to face him but, by some flaw in tactics, terrain or resolution, ceded victory before battle could begin – or perhaps suffered an unrecorded defeat. In any event, Edmund gave up to Olaf a vast area of the eastern and central Midlands, from Derby to Lincoln, from Nottingham to Leicester, thus handing large numbers of unwilling and Christian Danes over to pagan Norwegian rule. This raised Olaf's morale so much that he was soon raging, Viking-fashion, across Northumbria. The north, it seemed, was his – but death snatched him elsewhere, and the picture changed.

What he had won fell to Sigtrygg's son, another Olaf, beaten once by Athelstan and destined now to be defeated by Athelstan's brother. For within a year, Edmund had won back what he had given – 'For a long hard time had the Danes been forcibly subdued in bondage to the heathen, till King Edmund, Edward's son, protector of warriors, released them again by his valour,' says the *Chronicle*, demonstrating how Saxon attitudes to some Scandinavians at least had changed in the previous century. Olaf, bending to the new direction in history's breezes, followed the example of his predecessor, Rægnald, and submitted to the English king, compounding this temporal humility with the spiritual one of conversion. Not a fortunate man, he was instantly turned out by his pagan and militant followers, who summoned instead another Rægnald, this one the brother of the first and more successful Olaf, Guthfrith's son. Neither submission nor revolt, however, could save Northumbria from Edmund, who marched again, captured York, threw out both claimants and took the throne himself.

In 946, Edmund died, still only twenty-five; his brother, Edward the Elder's youngest son, Eadred, became king in his place. He was at once busy in Northumbria, showing the flag and demonstrating that Alfred's succession remained in strong hands. But off-stage a different crisis would pose him problems;

Harald Fairhair had died and his heir had come to the throne of Norway. The new king, Eirik, was called Bloodaxe, not without cause – he had spent the years before his accession killing off as many of his half-brothers and potential rivals as he could reach. (It was the body of his equally unpleasant consort, Gunnhild, which some experts think rose semi-preserved to the surface of a Danish bog nine centuries after his death.) Harald had been robust, generous and prolific – it has been estimated that he had some forty sons – and Eirik's vigorous extirpation of large numbers of these raised him enemies in every corner of the realm. Lacking the tact and political skill to ride the currents of these storms he had raised, he soon became vulnerable to rebellion – and a rival was at hand: Hakon, Athelstan's foster-son. His arrival in Norway marked the end of Eirik's reign. Ousted, however, he did what many Norsemen had done in the past, he looked south and west – and saw Northumbria.

Oddly, it was the Archbishop of York, a man named Wulfstan, probably Danish, who seems to have been behind the movement to make Eirik Northumbria's king. There was a rebellion, the aggressive Norwegian faction won and Eirik Bloodaxe was installed. Again an English king marched into Northumbria, burnt roofs and rotting corpses the decipherable signs of his anger. The destruction of his own ambushed rearguard only made his efforts more determinedly violent, and the Northumbrians, the message now understood, for their own safety turned on Eirik. The Norwegian prince thus gained and lost two thrones within three years – and had still to gain and lose the second a second time. Wulfstan still remained, a man discontented with English rule, a king-maker who now set on the throne the twice-deposed Olaf. Eadred, unwearying, marched once more (his army, perhaps, less eager than he), and taking Wulfstan, imprisoned him. Anguished, the Northmen of Northumbria rebelled against the unfortunate Olaf and threw him out yet again – only to ask Eirik Bloodaxe to come back. As Harald Fairhair's favourite son, inheritor of that powerful tradition, he clearly had much appeal for them. One senses that, desperate not to lose their separate identity as the Danes had largely lost theirs, it was to reaffirm themselves as Norwegians that they turned, almost in nostalgia, to this far from commendable figure. This time, however, they had over-reached themselves. It was in the grimmest of moods that Eadred now rounded on them, in his mind nothing but their complete subjugation. Eirik was allowed less than two years to enjoy his regal insecurity before Eadred's purposeful approach in 954 sent him once more out of the kingdom. There would be no king to follow him, for he was the last independent ruler to be enthroned in York. Eadred made Northumbria an earldom and set over it Oswulf of Bamborough as *jarl*. The game of musical chairs, with its contenders from Dublin, Norway and Wessex leaping frantically to the music of arms, was over at last.

The Danelaw had returned under English domination. It was a much-changed part of England since those far-off days, early in the previous century, when Vikings had first come stalking up the beaches and the cliff-paths of the English

OPPOSITE Archbishop Wulfstan: from an early manuscript. He was Bishop of London and of Worcester before becoming Archbishop of York. He is famous for his denunciations of his countrymen, blaming the successes of the Danes on the Saxons' sinful lives.
LEFT and BELOW A bronze seal-die which probably belonged to Æthelwald, Bishop of Dunwich. It was found near the monastery at Eye.

coasts. Its language, its place-names, its laws and customs, the complexion and character of its people, had been altered for ever. It had been pagan, but much of it was now as fervently Christian as the outraged monks of Lindisfarne might have hoped for. Its nobility remained Danish, however, *jarls* supported by their countrymen, quiescent but not tamed, watchful of their interests and loyal to the Saxon Crown only as long as such loyalty brought them the security they had learned to value.

Twenty-five years of peace, with kings in England concerned more with the expansion of Church than of State, with storming the ramparts of heaven rather than defending their own. In 978 a child came to that throne, Æthelred, and perhaps it was the weakness this seemed to indicate which provoked a new wave of Viking assaults. In 980, when Æthelred was twelve, raiders clutched at Chester and savaged the surrounding countryside; Southampton was seized, and the Viking axes, as indiscriminate as in the past, rose and sickeningly fell upon the unprotected heads of the citizenry; Thanet was mauled. By the next year, the coastal communities of Cornwall and Devon were made tense, then tragic, by Viking attacks; a year later, London was burning, Dorset beset; in 987, Vikings were rampaging on the Somerset coast and the year after on that of Devon once more. It was as though a fire, long thought extinguished, had burst out once more about the strapped-down body of some unwilling martyr.

In 991, its flame struck savagely – and surprisingly revealed its victim to be already near death and ready to crumble into ash. In this year ninety-three ships came sailing up the Thames, their most important leader Olaf Tryggvesson, warrior, adventurer, Baltic pirate, later to be king of Norway; once arrived in England, he 'ravaged wide around the land', as Snorri recounts in the *Olaf Sagas*. 'He sailed all the way north to Northumberland, where he plundered,' the poet goes on, but Olaf paused short of that war-ravaged province to strip Ipswich and attack Maldon. He paused long enough, indeed, to allow the East Saxons to rally under their leader, Bryhtnoth, and march to the defence of Maldon and so into history. For there was a battle at Maldon, and a poet commemorated it, and that commemoration has come down to us.

As was usual, the encounter began with an emissary, his message both boast and insult:

> Then stood on strand and called out sternly
> a Viking spokesman. . . .

as Michael Alexander's translation puts it. What he suggests is

> . . . thou send for thy safety
> rings, bracelets. Better for you
> that you stay straightaway our onslought with tribute
> than that we should share bitter strife.

Bryhtnoth, however, was tougher than those from whom the Vikings had learned how to profit from terror. He 'shook the slim ash-spear' and, 'stiff with anger', made an unyielding reply: 'Spears shall be all the tribute' the Vikings would receive, for 'English silver is not so softly won.'

The armies were separated, the Vikings on Northey, the English on the mainland, a tongue of the sea between them, a causeway eight feet wide crossing this. The following morning, therefore, when violence began, the Northmen tried to storm the causeway. But three men, Wulfstan their Horatius, Ælfhere and Maccus his companions, held the charge, refusing to 'take flight from the ford's neck'. The East Saxons might have won the battle there and then, but chivalry altered their tactics. The Vikings asked for a fairer fight, and Bryhtnoth, 'overswayed by his heart's arrogance', agreed, falling back to new positions and allowing his enemies to advance on a broader and more practical front. Changed circumstances brought changed fortunes; for a while the Saxons withstood the attack, but then, under the bloodied spearpoints and cleaving axes of the Northmen, they began to fall. A dart hit Bryhtnoth; wounded, he fought on, but

> Then they hewed him down, the heathen churls,
> and with him those warriors, Wulfmær and Aelfnoth,
> who had stood at his side: stretched on the field,
> the two followers fellowed in death.

Now some of the English fled – those the poem calls 'the lack-willed' – but others stood fast, supporting courage with the elaborate vaunts of the doomed. To avenge their leader they now rallied and counter-attacked, these 'household companions, careless of life'. In the poem the last to speak, as things begin to go wryly with the Saxons, is Byrhtwold, clearly a man grown happily old in his earl's service.

> 'Though I am white with winters I will not away,
> for I think to lodge me alongside my dear one,
> lay me down by my lord's right hand.'

And so he did, and his companions with him.

With this defeat, much of the work so nobly and energetically done by Alfred's progeny slipped sadly into history. Æthelred was not a man of Alfred's pattern. He had come to the throne a bewildered child, flung to this difficult prominence by the murder of his brother, Edward the Martyr. Was it this which made him timid, unable to cause or to withstand the enmity of anyone? His name means 'noble counsel'; his nickname smacks of courtier's malice – 'unræd' or 'uncounselled', 'no-counsel', perhaps even 'evil counsel'. The linguistic shortcomings of later generations have transmuted this, and it is as 'Æthelred the Unready' that he stands in people's memories. Both versions of the joke are just.

It was Æthelred's misfortune to be king of a rich country at a time when Scandinavia needed treasure. The northern countries had become used to a constant supply of silver, brought westward up the Volga from Asia. Even in the countries of its origin and widest use, however, silver had become scarce, while the little that was available could not move as it had in the past because wars had interrupted the trade-routes. The Northmen, therefore, as they had so often, looked south and west to right the balance of their economy. Æthelred's kingdom lay fatly in their sight; it only remained to discover whether they could elicit from it the treasure they craved. They were not long to remain in doubt.

Accepting the perhaps Christian advice of his Archbishop of Canterbury, Æthelred now did exactly what the Viking herald at Maldon had advised and bought off the spear-storm with tribute. He did more, agreeing to feed the Vikings while they remained in his kingdom. It was thus a well-fed and well-satisfied throng which boarded its ships later that year and, to a relief in English minds attenuated by bitterness and doubt, set sail for the north. They bore with them their tribute, the first instalment of Æthelred's *danegeld*: ten thousand pounds of silver. It was not lost even on Æthelred, however, that not all the Vikings had gone; in 992 he sent a fleet to engage theirs, and though it was first betrayed and then predictably beaten, it achieved its object of harrying the Vikings out of East Anglia. In traditional fashion, however, they then struck elsewhere and were soon rampaging as their grandfathers had done through Northumbria. To defend this unhappy province, an army was raised, stepped forth to give the invaders battle, saw them perhaps too plainly and, newly faint-hearted, dispersed without unsheathing sword.

In 994 a new man appeared among the Viking leadership, Svein I, King of Denmark, Svein *Tjúguskegg* or Forkbeard, an implacable, hard-headed, intelligent man who knew an opportunity when he saw it, understood how to exploit it and then undertook that exploitation ruthlessly. Possibly before but certainly with him much of the old disorder through which the uncomplicated Viking qualities of courage, cruelty and greed had been expressed came to an end: his fighting men were soldiers, paid and maintained, and the operations they mounted were professional. Archaeology displays for us his military camps and barracks, meticulously fortified, aggressively placed, each capable of housing upwards of a thousand men. A king commanding such encampments did not come to England on a whim or to pay off boasts made in some moment of drunken bravado.

He and Olaf Tryggvesson, who had either come back or never been away, now combined and with ninety-four ships sailed up the Thames estuary to attack London. Hastily levied and mustered, the Londoners came out against them. The Vikings tried to by-pass them with fire, hoping to burn London into a condition which would make defence redundant. As in some later conflicts, Londoners stood firm, gripped sword and thrusting spear and, unlike faint-hearts elsewhere, struck the Northmen with a violence which threw them back the way they had come. Always ready to give up the difficult if the easy beckoned, the Vikings now sailed round the south-eastern coast of England, landing almost as they pleased, taking what they wished, murdering those who threatened to bar their way, burning the buildings which had housed them and then returning, laden and triumphant, to their waiting ships. If their preparations for raiding had been refined, their methods had not.

It was when these ravening marauders took to horse and began criss-crossing the very heart of Wessex, plundering what they saw and beating off whatever feeble efforts the English army could make to prevent them, that Æthelred's nerve broke. The price his people paid for this, apart from what the Vikings had themselves directly levied, was now sixteen thousand silver pounds. It is true that Olaf, as part of the bargain, allowed himself to be baptized, with Æthelred as his godfather, and that in the summer of 995 he sailed away to Norway, never to return (the matters he had to attend to there included the winning of its throne), but Svein had learned a lesson which affected him profoundly. He seems to have seen England as the supplier in a relationship which reduced banditry to commerce – for the money he took from her paid his soldiers, and the soldiers whom it paid took the money. As long as Æthelred could squeeze wealth from his people, Svein had control of a *perpetuum mobile* of economics.

Two years later, therefore, Vikings were back, and the next year, and the year after that. 'And the Kentish force came against them, and they fought sharply. But, alas, they all too quickly gave way and fled. . . . And the Danes . . . then took horses and rode wheresoever they would. . . .' Thus the *Chronicle*, setting down a tale of inefficiency and weakness – 'in the end, neither the navy nor the land-force came to anything, save toil of the people and waste of money and encouragement of the enemy' – which suggests there was little optimism even when, Svein's attention temporarily elsewhere, England was given the opportunity to prepare its defences. Such doubts were proved most dreadfully correct, for in 1001 Svein returned; Hampshire men were beaten, as were, later, levies drawn from Somerset and Devon, and throughout the south-west only fire robbed the ravens of the fruits of Viking atrocities.

Securely encamped on the Isle of Wight, gazing with the smirk of conquerors across the Solent at a land they must have thought of as almost their own, the Vikings waited with, one imagines, confident expectation for Æthelred's response. It came – the price of blackmail had increased again, for the bribe which would buy peace this time was twenty-four thousand pounds. But what fevers, what doubts, what sudden resolutions and abrupt despairs must have afflicted Æthelred's uncertain mind? No sooner had his own extortioners plundered those parts of the country the Vikings had left alone, no sooner had he handed over this enormous sum in return for unreliable promises and a compromised honour, than he himself broke the very armistice he had just so dearly bought. Did he really learn of a Danish plot against his life? It seems unlikely – Æthelred was the best king of England the Danes could have. If there was a plot at all, it would more believably have been concocted by a disgusted and frustrated nobility, some faction tormented by the long collapse of the kingdom's greatness. But his action hardly needs a rationale; in its senseless vindictiveness, it seems no more than the discreditable reaction of a weak man to his weakness. For on 13 November, St Brice's Day, 1002, by his order every Dane in southern England – that is, peaceful settlers on the one hand and on the other such Danes as had willingly entered his service – was seized and brutally killed.

One can imagine how the frustrations of the English, both king and people, were vented that day on the defenceless representatives of an army they had not been able to withstand. Here at last there was a battle the English would win! It was only a trusting handful of these aliens whom they could actually reach and cut and bloodily batter to death; the Danelaw was not within that sort of English jurisdiction, and most of the Danes in England were therefore safe from harm. And for that handful of corpses, for that moment's valueless frenzy, the kingdom would have to suffer. Northmen were not ones to lay vengeance easily aside for silver, and one imagines that, even by the evening of that murderous day, the English, both king and people, had begun nervously to realize it.

In the short term, however, Svein was to combine business with pleasure – his business as always the extortion of bribes, his pleasure now the extortion itself. He may have had special reason to enjoy the ravages he caused in England during that summer of 1003, for among those who had died on St Brice's Day had been, it is said, his sister Gunnhild. Exeter and Wilton in the west, Salisbury in Wiltshire, in East Anglia Thetford and Norwich – all fell to his revengeful hand, all were emptied of their riches. His only setback threatened to come at the hands of an Anglicized Dane, Ulfkel Snilling, who defended his East Anglia with the kind of resolution the English leaders themselves seemed no longer able to summon up. Certainly it was English irresolution which lost this battle for them and their Anglo-Danish allies, and a Svein who might have been penned and perhaps killed that day near Thetford survived and triumphed. Famine soon proved another resolute foe; for a year, the Danes withdrew.

In 1005, Svein fell upon the shores of Kent as ravenously as ever; later, based on the Isle of Wight, he made a winter march contemptuously across the breadth of Wessex, challenged the boasts of the English army, met them on the Wiltshire Downs and stampeded them. Unharassed, he brought his booty back under the agonized but impotent gaze of the citizens of Winchester itself, that ancient capital sustained no longer by an ancient pride. Æthelred turned desperately, as in the past, from his army to his tax-collectors; in 1007 he paid Svein the unprecedented sum of thirty-six thousand pounds of silver. Enriched, therefore, and grown in honour of a sort, the Danish king sailed for his homeland.

In the quiet time which followed, Æthelred tried again to scramble a defence together. He followed Alfred's example and ordered the building of a navy. This fleet, intended as seaward bulwark against Svein's return, assembled proudly off Sandwich. Its pride was short-lived. There was quarrelling among the leaders, factions were formed, threats were flung to and fro. Ships intended to belabour Danes were turned against one another, English swords struck for English and not Viking blood. Eighty ships were burned in these internecine encounters. Twenty others left the fleet altogether. Storm put paid to more. The commanders, including the King, gave the whole enterprise up and returned to their strongholds. The *Chronicle* tells us, sadly: 'And then afterwards the people who were in the ships brought them to London, and they let the whole nation's toil thus lightly pass away.'

How thoroughly it had passed away was proved shortly afterwards, when by strategic irony it was at Sandwich itself that the new Viking assault on England began, on 1 August 1009. Svein did not lead it himself, but a cluster of military luminaries did – Thorkel the Tall, Hemming his brother, Eilaf, of the line from which today's kings of Denmark descend, and perhaps Olaf, then nicknamed 'the Stout' but later to be king of Norway and, later again, dubbed saint. Kent, having watched that vaunted fleet melt away, learned its lesson from its king and paid the Vikings three thousand pounds to leave. Once more established on the Isle of Wight, they caused ruin and lamentation throughout the central counties of southern England. Soon the destruction had spread: Oxford burned, Ipswich opened to their axes, and only London – again and again – stood firm. By this time they had wintered in England and were once more vigorously on the rampage. In May, they met and defeated an army in East Anglia – Snorri's 'great battle at Ringmere Heath in Ulfkel's land', tribute to the vigour of that stubborn Dane Ulfkel Snilling, again left stranded by English allies of eroded courage. Nothing after this stood in the Northmen's path, and that path, wild and flame-fringed, now ranged the south-east: Thetford and Cambridge turned to ash and emptiness at their touch, while English commanders marched timidly to and fro in a tragi-comedy of confusion. 'And when the enemy was in the east, then our levies were mustered in the west; and when they were in the south, then our levies were in the north . . . whatever course of action was decided upon it was not followed even for a single month.' Thus the chroniclers, mourning a lost greatness, a lost kingdom.

In 1011, brought to despair by the winter burning of Nottingham, Æthelred admitted once again that he had no defences against his invaders. This time, the Viking assessment of his worth and their power had once more increased – the price fixed for peace was forty-eight thousand pounds. The gathering of such an immense sum was a difficult and lengthy bureaucratic undertaking in a kingdom so badly scarred; to keep English minds on their work, the Vikings pushed into Kent again, invested Canterbury and entered it through treachery, taking Ælfeah, the archbishop, as their prisoner. The capture of this ecclesiastical celebrity, however, and the manner in which he was treated, caused a split in the Viking party. First a separate sum was demanded for Ælfeah, but he refused to let himself be ransomed. As a result, at Greenwich he was brought before the assembled Danes and Norwegians, men made boisterous by victory and drink, violence their tradition, cruelty their entertainment. They humiliated him, flinging at him cattle-bones, pelting him with the heads of beasts, before smashing his skull with an axe-blow. Thorkel the Tall, it is reported by Thietmar of Merseburg, tried to stop them, attempting at one point to ransom Ælfeah himself; it was perhaps because he could not do so that, later the same year, when the Vikings finally left, he and his forty-five ships remained in England to serve under Æthelred. Olaf the Stout is said to have entered the English king's service at the same time, which suggests that Æthelred, despairing with some justice of his own commanders, had now turned more comprehensively than in the past to the use of mercenaries. One wonders what inducement, however tempting, could have led hard-headed soldiers to ally themselves with so desperate and rudderless a cause. No money, no new and dearly bought fighting force, can turn a weak and vacillating prince into a leader, nor his faltering advisers into strategists. We have the sad murmur of the *Chronicle*, as that enriched northern fleet at last slipped sleekly away through the Channel waves – 'All these calamities fell upon us through evil counsel. . . .' Perhaps it was about now that another Wulfstan was preaching in York Cathedral: 'Alas! for the misery and worldly shame the English must now endure through God's anger. . . . Instead, all these insults which we daily endure, we pay for with adulation of those who injure us; continually we give them money for protection and in return they daily make us smart for it! They harry and they burn, they pillage, plunder and carry off to shipboard . . . !'

Worse, however, was on the way. Perhaps it was, as has been suggested, to chastise the defected Thorkel the Tall or to forestall that Norwegian warrior's ambitions; more probably, it was the logical consequence of the years of easy plundering, of seeing every demand, however outrageous, obsequiously met; whatever the reason, in 1013 Svein of Denmark, no longer content to milk

King Knut and his first wife Ælgifu. In this
medieval manuscript they are seen presenting
a gold cross to the New Minster at Winchester,
whose monks are depicted at the bottom.

England, however eager England was to be milked, crossed the sea to annex the
entire beast once and for all. As intelligent as ever, he landed at Gainsborough on
the Trent, knowing what his appeal would be for the Danes of eastern England,
men who might have looked to English kings for leadership had there been any,
who had in the past given loyalty to the English throne, but who had now grown
tired of seeing it transmuted into silver for endless Viking bribes.

Almost at once, Northumbria, always volatile, and the Danish part of dis-
membered Mercia, submitted to him. Having secured his base by diplomacy, he
extended it by war. Marching south, he ripped through the centre of Wessex,
accepting the homage of Oxford and Winchester, before turning east to attack
London. Here, as before, the Vikings came across a steadfast and robust defence,
the Londoners now strengthened not only by Æthelred's own bodyguard but also
by Thorkel's Danes and Olaf's Norwegian party. The garrison struck at their
attackers as they were fording the Thames, weakening Svein's subsequent assault
sufficiently to withstand it. As a result the Danish king, not a man to waste his
efforts, raised the siege and stalked westward through the land, graciously to
accept the unstinted and immediate submission of Devon. With England's only
effective army locked into London's fortifications, it must have been with some
satisfaction that Svein sailed back to his starting point at Gainsborough. In a
matter of weeks, Northumbria, Mercia, Wessex and the West Country had fallen
to him; only London, untenable now, held out. Æthelred, who had married
Duke Richard of Normandy's sister Emma some years before, sent her and her
sons across the Channel for safety, then took ship himself and in his usual indecisive
fashion lurked for a while in the Thames Estuary and off the south coast, before
following his family and seeking a Norman refuge. London, bowing, surrendered
and paid tribute, Thorkel withdrawing sulkily to Greenwich. Hostages were given
up, submissions formalized. A Viking, after two centuries of plundering, invasion,
battle, settlement and defeat, sat on the throne of England.

It was a short reign, for early in February 1014, only five weeks after his
triumph, Svein was dead. His unconsolidated kingdom almost at once began to
splinter. Svein's immediate following turned to his younger son, Knut, for leadership. The English, however, seeing their opportunity in the immaturity of this
eighteen-year-old, suffered the welling-up of an illogical nostalgia for Alfred's line
and called on Æthelred to return – they would welcome him back and follow him

loyally, they plaintively assured him; they would even forget the errors of the past, if only he would rule them better in the future. Assuming himself (against the evidence) capable of this, Æthelred answered the call and was, indeed, soon marching north-east against the Danes, demonstrating a purposefulness new to him. Knut, wisely deciding to fight another day, set sail for Denmark, pausing only to put ashore the cruelly mutilated hostages sacrificed by the English for Æthelred's return.

Perhaps now there was a moment of happiness for Æthelred, a sense that for him too the tide could turn. But new disasters were already being forged on the black anvils of his destiny. In Denmark, Knut's elder brother Harald was the king; perhaps it suited him to have his brother safely enthroned elsewhere. Certainly he put his energies to raising a new force with which Knut might win back England; England herself relapsed into the easy disorder of Æthelred's other years. Thorkel and Olaf were paid a total of twenty-one thousand pounds, whether to go or to stay is uncertain; in the event, both left, Thorkel to offer his services and fleet to Knut in Denmark – a case, it may be, of the ship deserting the sinking rat. Knut's brother-in-law, Eirik, *jarl* of Hladir, Regent of Norway, faithful, experienced and ambitious only for his young leader, was another and perhaps more important recruit to the cause of Svein's son. While these preparations, so ominous for Æthelred, were under way, England suffered calamitous dissensions.

Into history, briefly and unpleasantly, stepped Eadric, Ealdorman of West Mercia, a strange and bitter figure, one of Æthelred's most devious and un-reliable counsellors. There was a double murder for which he was responsible, it seems, a crime compounded by royal injustice: Æthelred grabbed the dead men's property, imprisoned a widow. His son, Edmund, seizing perhaps an opportunity to stand for the right and be seen to do so, not only rescued but married her and, a young man in his twenties, set out in open rebellion against his father. Eadric, prime mover in the murders, thus became Edmund's enemy on his own account as well as his royal master's; factions bitterly faced each other. It was upon this disunited land that young Knut, in the late summer of 1015, set his fresh army, carried to England in a fleet two hundred strong.

Once again Dorset, Wiltshire, Somerset and Warwickshire lamented the Viking fury. Reluctantly allied, Edmund and Eadric marched against them. For the Mercian nobleman, however, it was Edmund in the end who was the greater enemy and he deserted; with forty ships of the English fleet, he entered the service of Knut. Alone, Edmund could only retreat. Knut now held Wessex, Æthelred London, Edmund the north – there were three kings in combat over England. Knut advanced, Edmund, unaided by Æthelred and that part of the army held as garrison in London, retreated again. Mercia fell to the Danes. Furious at the malignancy of Eadric, Edmund attacked his Midlands possessions, marching now with Uhtred of Northumbria.

In this most dangerous game of chess, played with the vulnerable flesh and blood of twenty thousand anonymous men, Knut now made a knight's move,

OPPOSITE One of the picture stones from Lillbjaro in Gotland. Carved in the local limestone from the fifth century onwards, they usually illustrated scenes from legend. This one, from the eighth century, shows a Viking ship in a Valhalla scene.

side-stepping Edmund's private violence in Staffordshire and Cheshire to take Uhtred's York. Outflanked, the Northumbrian was forced to submit. It was, it has been suggested, on the unpleasant Eadric's advice that Uhtred was murdered; in any event, he died and Knut placed *Jarl* Eirik over Northumbria in his stead. It seems that Edmund now at last made common cause with his father, but death severed that alliance, Æthelred slipping away from life at this crucial moment with a timing as precisely calculated to produce confusion as any he had shown during his unhappy reign.

London recognized Edmund as the king of England, a declaration defiant in its refusal to acknowledge that the bulk of the country lay in Knut's hands. The Danes, as so often before, set themselves to take the stubborn city; Edmund, who had reached it a little before his father's death, managed to get away, raising an army now in the still-loyal West Country. London, in the meantime, was tightly besieged, steadfastly defended. The Danes, their ships blocked by London's stubborn bridge, built a great semi-circular canal around its fortified southern end and dragged their ships up-river. Then they entrenched themselves about the now totally encircled town, and from these established positions attacked it again and again. No catapulted rock or thunder-cloud of arrows, however, no piercing war-cry or wild, advancing horde could daunt the besieged. Experienced now, proud of their history of defiant courage, perhaps even a little contemptuous of the Danes' efforts to take a town which had resisted them so often in the past, the Londoners stood firm and hoped for miracles.

And, almost incredibly, help was on its way. Tentatively at first, Edmund was advancing from the west. Knut sent a force under Eadric to halt him, but it failed. More and more men rallied to the young king; soon all Wessex joyfully hailed him; advancing with increasing boldness, he was at last able to raise the siege of London. More, he crossed the Thames and at Brentford defeated the Danes, an outcome to battle which must have seemed for the English like something out of legend. Now there was much movement but few engagements. Edmund had lost many men in his advance and returned to Wessex to recruit and regroup. Knut, too, having tried one last time to take London, withdrew northward for a while. But when the armies met again at Otford, in Kent, Edmund was once more the victor. Suddenly, time had run backward; it was as though Alfred's England had newly arisen. A man who thought so, in any case, was the appalling Eadric, who again turned his coat, one of the most easily reversible garments in the whole of English history. With the wiseacre certainty of bitter hindsight, even the *Chronicle* is moved to ponder the folly of this move.

It is curious how easily the monarchs of those days trusted the manifestly untrustworthy. Edmund had marched with Eadric in the past and seen him flee and then betray; Knut had accepted his treachery and made him a commander; now Edmund accepted him again. He must have known that the conflict for the rulership of England had reached its crux. He had struggled back from a disaster nearly as overwhelming as that which had overtaken Alfred; like Alfred, he had reached a

OPPOSITE Ninth-century silver rings found at Sandby, Oland, Sweden, possibly brought back by traders from central Russia.

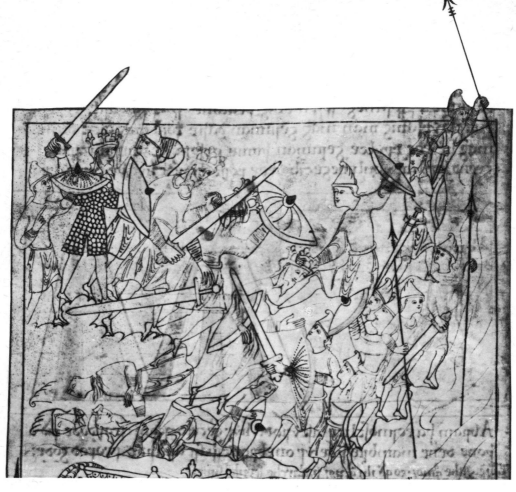

point where he could win the war he had so nearly lost. Eadric's men were the latter's passport to royal acceptance, of course – and yet, in the cruel politics of the eleventh century, it would not have been the first occasion that a king had accepted an army, but disposed of its leader. It may be there was no time; everything was in flux, Eadric plausible, battle imminent, the undisputed crown too close. With Eadric beside him, Edmund advanced into Essex. At Ashingdon, he met Knut's army.

Perhaps there was still a moment when all was poised, the two armies in balance, the weight of each locking the other, their conflicting cries harsh above the clash of metal or the dull collapse of flesh. Then, it may be, there was a wavering on one side, a jubilation on the other, a giving here, an advance there. In any case, Eadric saw cause to lengthen his register of treachery. One can imagine him at that moment, appalled by the consequences of his last, wrong choice. He turned and, with his men, fled from the battle. The *Chronicle* tells the whole story: 'He betrayed his king and lord and the whole English nation, and Knut won the victory, and

Anglo-Saxons fighting, from a contemporary manuscript.

with it all England.' Thus suddenly diminished, the English army collapsed; in a moment, Danish spears and swords and axes were busily among them. The losses were dreadful; it was here that Ulfkel, so often a lone stalwart against the invaders, was at last struck down. Edmund fled; for a few weeks, in Gloucestershire, it seemed as if for a second time he would attempt what Alfred had had to do only once; still with some part of the kingdom steadfastly his, he met Knut, and the two young men divided England between them, but everyone knew that this was a truce, that battle had only been postponed. (Among those who arranged this treaty, which gave Edmund Wessex and the West Country while Knut took the rest, was the one man with the best right of all to be in the middle – Ealdorman Eadric.) As all pondered on the future, the future, as so often, took its own course: aged only twenty-two, Edmund died. Already he had won back an honour his father had so often forfeited; his people had named him 'Ironside'. But Edmund Ironside was luckless in the end; buried early in December 1017, he left his world to Knut, the Dane.

So the struggle for England ended in a Viking victory. In 1018, sitting at Oxford, 'King Knut with the advice of his councillors completely established peace and friendship between the Danes and the English and put an end to all their former strife.' So, perhaps a little piously, the official statement of the time; yet it is true the war was over. Under Knut, Norway, Denmark and England were to be united in his single hand. Later, there would be dynastic struggle, with Knut's line dying out and Alfred's returning in the person of Edward the Confessor; there would be one last instalment of the northern break-out, when William of Normandy took England for himself. But the Viking wars had come to an end. One final payment of *danegeld* had to be made, an enormous bounty of 82,500 pounds, with which the Danish fleet for the last time turned from English shores, the oars steadily rising and falling, the bright sails lifting to the off-shore breeze, those voracious beaks and glaring avaricious eyes of the dragon-ships set in comfortable triumph on a homeward course.

And there was one last, satisfying royal chore to be performed, before England could for a while settle into the relative stupor of strong, benevolent rule. For his services, Eadric was given all Mercia to hold. It was his just long enough to give him comfort; then the betrayer was betrayed. His was, one may imagine, an execution at which few tears were shed.

The ruins of a Viking farm in the Shetland Islands. The first Norse settlements in the Shetlands and Orkneys, in the second half of the eighth century, appear to have been made peacefully, by men searching out pasturelands. Vikings came to conquer and colonize in the ninth century.

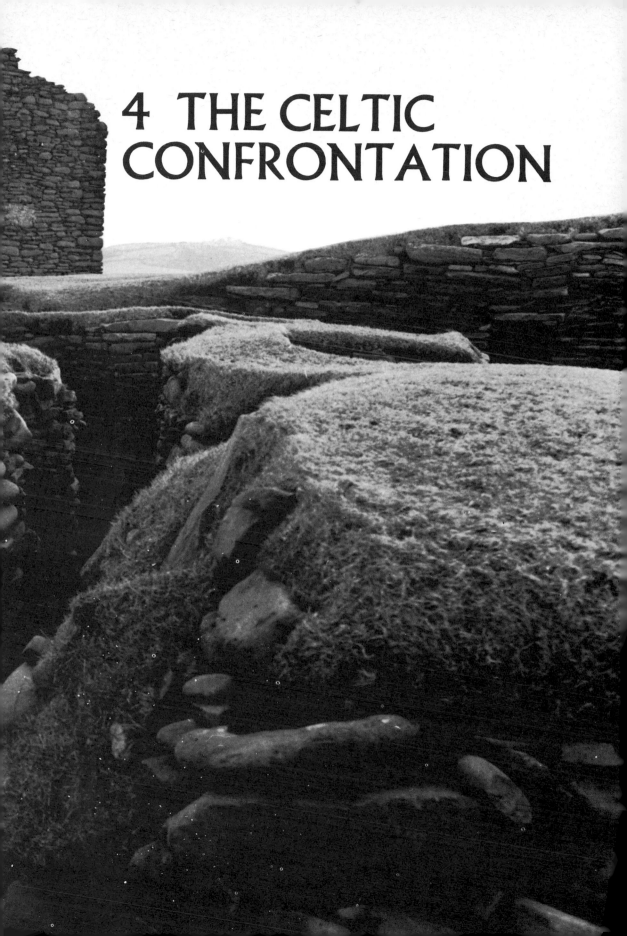

4 THE CELTIC
CONFRONTATION

Ireland: a country at the edges of the known world; even, for a long time, well over them. Empty for millennia, as the land groaned under the slow heaving of glaciers. Empty still as the ice receded and the hills slowly turned a welcoming green. In time, though, strangers arrived, from Spain, perhaps, and some from the north-west of Europe. They settled, scraping bone, chipping flint, learning the slow crafts of their era. The working of metal was a new skill, percolating to them over narrow seas – there was connection, therefore, some journeying to and fro between their island and its neighbour, or even, it may be, the mainland. But Bronze Age sophistication did not alter the composition of the people, nor the nature of their society.

It took iron to do that. Somewhere between the headwaters of the Rhine and the Danube, a vigorous and inventive people had stolen a march on their coaevals, stepping forth smartly into the Iron Age as though privy to the time-tables of history. With this edge in armaments, these, the Celts, thrust searchingly across Europe. In the fourth century BC, they reached the British Isles (elsewhere, they almost altered history, taking a sort of Celtgeld from defeated Romans in order to leave their city in peace). A branch of the people struck on into Ireland; these, called perhaps the Goidels, used their superior abilities to make themselves aristocrats, a fair-haired nobility lording it over darker subjects. Language, religion, social custom – all were changed.

As always, however, the conquerors sank into the loam and blood of the place they had conquered. Perhaps they were able to some degree to maintain their aristocratic aloofness, but separated from the world as they were on their rain-washed island, they grew closer to the people about them. By the eighth century AD, that closeness had been reinforced by the homogeneity of the Christian faith. Small kingdoms warred and High Kings rose and fell, but devotion everywhere gave testimony of how deeply the new religion had rooted in this fertile soil. Christ was worshipped in a hundred little wooden churches, the learned in their cramped cloisters were busy over manuscripts of gospels and psalters, metalworkers were casting the bells and crosses to summon the faithful or proclaim the faith, while stone masons hammered out the decorations on the houses of God and the tombs of the devout. And it was in the eighth century, as we have seen, that the Vikings had first burst in upon this devoted and serene seclusion.

For a while they held Dublin, proud Norwegians playing the same role which

The hilt of a ninth-century sword found in a cemetery at Kilmarsham, Islandbridge.

over a thousand years before the Celts had made their own. But dynastic war in Norway withered their roots and alone they were not strong enough to hold the Irish. Even when Cearbhall of Leinster, however, swept into Dublin early in the tenth century and bloodily cleared out these diminished strangers, their hold on Ireland was not entirely loosened. Many coastal settlements were almost purely Norwegian; in others, a mingling of the established with the newly arrived aristocracy added another genetic dimension to Irish heredity. In the wars and struggles for succession which characterized Ireland, as they did most other countries during those turbulent times, both the pure Vikings and those of mixed descent played an enthusiastic and sometimes profitable role.

Thus, when in 914 the Vikings from overseas once more turned their acquisitive attention to the wealth of this green island in the west, they found many allies already well entrenched there. With England closed to them by the energies of Edward the Elder and his indomitable sister Æthelflæd of Mercia, and the way to the fat lands of the Seine Valley blocked by the watchful Rollo and what would in time become the Normans, Ireland appeared irresistibly tempting again. Briefly, Rægnald of Ragnar Lodbrok's line skirmished and plundered, before setting off for the throne of York and a politic submission to the English king; another fleet began to lay waste country and coastline about Waterford; in 916 into the Liffey came sailing a vast and ambitious fleet, led by that Sigtrygg Gale who would also, a little later, make his mark on the hectic affairs of northern England. His aim was no less than the recapture of Dublin.

Under their High King, Niall Glundubh, the Irish marched fearlessly out. They had regained their kingdom once and were not prepared to hand it back in any rediscovered timidity. Defeated at Clonmel and driven back, Niall recoiled to give battle again. He allied himself with the men of Leinster, but the Vikings' military cunning was equal to that; attacking his allies at a moment when he could not come to their aid, they emerged with victory, swiftly fashioned and complete. Isolated once more, Niall retreated from the position he had taken up near Waterford, leaving that place and the surrounding countryside in the Viking clutch. Withdrawal, however, left his army intact; as the one effective native force in the country, it now became a magnet for alarmed and belatedly militant Irishmen. Early in 919, these gathered, the manhood of the many kingdoms, to bring to a climax the waiting and watching and months-long tension and find in battle the only solution for their pride. Sigtrygg, his retaken Dublin in the balance, rode out against them. On the north bank of the Liffey, near Islandbridge, the two armies met, the crash of their impact to echo round Ireland. Songs tell the story – Niall fell, and twelve lesser kings with him, a baker's dozen of royal ghosts to gibber about the camp fires of that day's victorious Northmen.

With such resistance, Ireland went to her new rape. Meath, Ulster, Armagh – across these ancient kingdoms the Vikings ranged; everywhere the peace of church or monastery was cracked open by the wickedly imperious axe. Great beams fell in a devil's confetti of sparks, flames robbed cell and cloister of even their austere furnishings; on cracking vellum, gold leaf blistered, then ran, the decorated word of God rendered illegible. For a while it seemed as if the whole of Ireland would bear this endless unreasoning wrath, but Dublin kings learned to play other tricks. Across the water, rich Northumbria beckoned them and that dangerous game of musical chairs about the throne of York in which Guthfrith, his son Olaf and that other Olaf, Sigtrygg's son, would leap and claw and stumble in the monomania of ambition.

In Ireland, therefore, violence died down. Once again, the Northmen were learning, it seemed, to live in their new condition as settlers. They traded, built houses, farmed steadings, married Irish girls. But not all the Irish were prepared to heave the expected sigh of relief and let bygones be bygones. Niall's son Muirchertach, for one, had inherited a tradition of pride and would not leave Viking Dublin unharassed. In 926 at Carlingford, the year after at Anagassan, his victories proved that the Gaill, the foreigners, were not, or no longer, invincible. In the years that followed, he fought many a vicious skirmish against marauding Vikings, by his efforts fencing off the rest of Ireland from the worst depredations of the Dublin-based. In 939, he took his battle further, sailing out to the Hebrides to attack the Viking strongholds there. His expedition had some success, but in the end his enemies waylaid him and it took a ransom paid to Dublin by his people to buy his release. Yet in 941, at the head of his great army, the 'Leather Cloaks', he marched into every kingdom of Ireland to demand hostages as a surety of good behaviour from those he was about to rule as High King – and he did not exempt the Vikings. Camping near Dublin, he made his demand of them also, and his prestige was such that they complied with it.

After his death in 943, the struggle was taken up by his successor, Congalach. In County Meath, this king won a comprehensive victory over Olaf Kvaran, Sigtrygg's son, and forced the Vikings to pay tribute, a reversal of the normal flow of extortion which must have satisfied the Irish. Olaf, however, was at this period still in the throes of his English ambitions, taking and losing that precarious throne at York as the tides of power flowed to and fro; it was not until 951 that, accepting Northumbria's having slipped from him for ever, he settled to his royal duties in Dublin.

Thirty years now went by which, if not tranquil, shone with some lustre in the history of the Viking settlement. There were, as always, Viking raids, Irish counter-attacks, confrontations, emissaries, ambuscades and treacheries, but the Northmen in Dublin looked strongly entrenched. Yet the continuous unrest about them, the opposition they always faced, the fact that they could never put their colony in the same condition, supported by the same recognition of its status, as the Danelaw in England, made Olaf's kingdom always vulnerable. These Vikings could never lay aside their history, as the English Danes had done, giving up for the sake of security the raiding tradition, winning wealth from the land and not from those who worked it; as a result, although at times and in places their relations with their Celtic neighbours were very good, the ancient enmity, greed on the one hand and mistrust on the other, always broke out again. In 980 the High King, now Mæl Seachlainn Mor, marched against the Vikings once more. Olaf sent out his army, commanded by his sons, and at Tara the two forces met. The Vikings were broken; fleeing thus, they surrendered Dublin. Despairing of earthly kingdoms, Olaf retreated to the Christian peace of the island of Iona and there, vassal to a different king, died in placid poverty.

Olaf's son had an Irish mother and an Irish name. In marrying a daughter of the High King, Muirchertach, Olaf perhaps had hoped to lay some diplomatic claim to the throne of all Ireland, if not on his own behalf then on that of his son. But this young man, Gluniarainn, now bent before his relative, Mæl Seachlainn Mor, with

Objects found in excavation sites in Dublin:
OPPOSITE, TOP A bone comb and parts of an
unfinished one, eleventh or twelfth century.
BOTTOM A carving of a Viking ship, loosely but
vigorously executed on a wooden plank. It
dates from the eleventh to the early twelfth
century. LEFT A figurine, probably a chess
piece, carved from the tip of an antler.
BELOW A section of a tenth-century post and
wattle wall.

an alacrity the meaning of his name might have made unlikely – for Gluniarainn means 'Iron Knee' – and so became the vassal and the ally of the Irish king. There may have been political shrewdness in this, for to the south, in Waterford, another Viking kingdom had grown up, separate from Dublin and a threat to its supremacy. Perhaps for this reason Gluniarainn marched out in 983, shoulder to shoulder with Mæl Seachlainn, against Ivar, the southern Viking leader, who had allied himself with the king of Leinster.

Six years later, however, he was himself embattled, shut into Dublin by the forces of the Irish king. For nearly three weeks the Vikings stood Mæl Seachlainn's close siege; then thirst drove them to surrender, and surrender forced from them the booty and taxes the High King demanded. Thus, when Gluniarainn died a little later, he left behind him a settlement impoverished and demoralized. It was therefore relatively easy for Ivar, the Waterford king, to establish himself in Dublin as well.

Such a concentration of Viking power must have seemed instantly threatening to the Irish. Certainly their High King now was too powerful to accept such an implicit challenge to his authority and, in 994, he hammered his way into Dublin once more. What he took this time included the symbolic heart of Viking rule there, for he forced the Vikings to give up what they had called 'The Sword of Charles', the very sign of their power, a blade said once to have glittered in the hand of Charlemagne himself. With it went Thor's Ring, equivalent to any great cathedral's most holy relic, the centre of ritual and that focus of divine power upon which a pagan Viking would swear his most binding oaths. Mæl Seachlainn did not, however, as perhaps he might have done, put an end once and for all to this alien dynasty within Ireland's shores. Instead, he allowed a new Sigtrygg, called 'Silk Beard', another of Olaf's sons, to take the throne of Dublin. His rule, however, was to be darkened by the eclipsing power of a ruler already mighty in the south, whose deeds the admiration of the poets would send echoing along the centuries.

Brian Boru – strong as the syllables which form his name, the legend of this king stalks through history, carrying it seems the whole legend of Ireland upon its shoulders. That vigour, that energy, that courage so fully rewarded, the battles which resound about it, the heroes, the heroines, the poets and their epics, the loves, lusts and deep drinking in its penumbra, the whole paraphernalia of myth, centring on it, on this one name, all are magnified and given an almost unbearable solidity by the certainty that its truth and the reality of the man who bore it guarantee the truth of that grimly glorious, embattled time. For after all, legend or not, Brian Boru was real, a son of a minor chieftain, Cenneide, lord of Dal gCais, a splinter-province in the kingdom of Munster.

Born in 941, Brian Boru never knew a time when the Vikings, in swift, straggling columns, did not sweep across land he thought of as his own. Like others, he might have accepted this, fatalistically seeing in it the punishing hand of God, a violent variant of the tax-gatherer. But he did not; with his brother and such men as they could muster, he took to the uplands, to the woods and dripping caves of what is now County Clare, moving from one darkness to the next and, out of this secrecy, appearing swiftly and briefly in the light of day to offer a moment of flickering brutality before disappearing again, bushes whipping into place behind his men, branches quivering for a while, the rain softly falling perhaps, while in the mud a horse and rider lay in the last pulsations of their blood.

His brother Mahoun made his peace at last, tired of danger, of sickness, of his band of companions dwindling, his friends one by one cut down. Bitterly Brian continued with those still faithful to him, delivering what check he could to the demanding raiders. Time and danger carved away the little he held; it is said that a time came when there were only fifteen men with him. But the resolution of the Dal gCais had yet another notch in it. Despite their sufferings, they resolved to put a new army in the field, this time to hack out for themselves a power-base from which they might more effectively withstand the Northmen. There was no king at Cashel – the throne of Munster stood ready for a claimant. There was a sounding out of neighbours, of allies. Mahoun would strike for Munster and against the Danes: who would stand with him in that endeavour? Connaught agreed, and so did chieftains from western Munster. Thus supported, Brian at his side again, Mahoun took Cashel and the crown.

Having secured their base, the sons of Cenneide waited for the moment when the Vikings would feel the need to meet their challenge. It took five years for that moment to arrive; then Ivar, the foreign king in Limerick, advanced in all his pride and fury to put these upstarts down. At Solloghead, a place not far from Tipperary, their armies at last plunged towards one another, the first arrows lifting through the air with the sun, the first men undone before the dew had dried, the blades high, stained already, then slashing downwards, men gasping, calling for justice or revenge, screaming their desperate farewells, the Irish at last at one with their history, the aliens betrayed by arrogance, by pride, but that slipping from them as towards noon they turned and ran.

Mahoun and Brian followed; one can imagine their jubilant songs as they marched across the hills southwards to Limerick. There stood a fortified encampment, earthen walls, timber-strengthened, enough to protect a garrison and ready to withstand a siege had any Danes the stomach for it. But at the first contact the fort gave way; no Viking had thought their march would end like this and they were not in the mood to resist. Ivar and a band of stunned survivors took ship, still the Northmen's last refuge; the oars dug deeply into the waves, perhaps thrust with the bitter anger of despair, while behind them their settlement tumbled, as they had made so many tumble, into ash and ruin. For the victorious king of Munster and his brother it must have seemed as though those dwindling ships, that dark, uncurling smoke, signalled the end of the Danish presence on their shores.

Ivar, however, was a man of vigorous ambition, of energetic pride. The following year, his camp had been re-established, supported by the enormous fleet he had gathered for his return. He constructed stockades and earthworks on the islands of the River Shannon to give himself a fortified base; to rebuild his diplomatic base, he sought out those Munster leaders who were not whole-heartedly delighted at the new eminence of the House of Cenneide. Seeing so powerful an alliance building against him, Mahoun reneged, as he had done once before. He gave up the crown of Munster. Yet the jealousy of those forced to watch his earlier climb was not appeased by this voluntary fall. Mahoun had to die, and in 976 he did so. It is not clear exactly how he died; it is clear that for his brother, Brian Boru, there was no doubt about whom to blame. The following year he went straight to the heart of this new and murderous conspiracy, attacking Ivar in his own Viking strongholds. Against his fraternal fury, the earthen walls of those island forts gave no protection. This time, Ivar did not flee; he fought, and having thus chosen or been forced into courage, died where he stood. Two of his sons died with him. A third son fled to the domains of one of the chieftains, Donnabhan, who had allied himself to the Vikings. Upon him Brian Boru fell with undiminished ferocity – the chieftain died, as did his fugitive guest, Ivar's son.

Revenge achieved, Brian set about a more politic violence. At the battle of Belach Lechta, near Ardpatrick, he settled the question of Munster's overlord. The king of Desmond, Mælmuadh, who claimed that role, came out against him, both Danes and Irish in his train. They had miscalculated in their allegiance, for over a thousand of them died that day. Munster bowed, with varying degrees of satisfaction, to Brian's power. For him, however, power was conditional unless it included domination of the Vikings. To the east, in Waterford, and the north-east, in Dublin, the untamed strength of the Northmen had its double focus. Between them and him lay Leinster and in order to contain that strength, if not reduce it, Leinster was a kingdom he had to control. It took him six years of diplomacy and skirmishing to achieve this, but by 984 the chiefs of that kingdom, too, recognized him as their overlord. The southern half of Ireland now lay passively in his hands.

This passivity lasted for fifteen years, a period Brian used to re-establish the culture and learning which had once been a feature of the land. By the end of the tenth century, therefore, life for many of the Irish had regained a serenity unknown since the beginning of the eighth. It was a flawed serenity, however. Perhaps this was due to the combative nature of the people; its direct cause was the rivalries which, still below the surface of everyday concerns, had all this time been developing. The country was, in fact, divided in three, and the reconciliation of these divisions lay only through the dark and abrasive aperture of battle. In the south stood Brian Boru, in the east the alien Viking lords and in the north the still-supreme Mæl Seachlainn Mor. Silently, these three forces tugged and strained against each other, conscious that for each of them overlordship of the whole island was a genuine possibility.

It was the action of a Leinster lord which now set these rivalries in violent motion. By allying himself with the Northmen, the Gaill, in Dublin, he proclaimed that he had thrown off Brian's suzerainty. Not a man to allow such a challenge to lie, Brian marched south-eastward with Dublin his goal. Guarding that approach to the city stand the Wicklow Mountains and in their western foothills, in Glen

A coin struck by Sigtrygg Silk Beard in Dublin. He was comprehensively defeated by the forces of Brian Boru at the battle of Clontarf.

Mama, the forces of Munster found the covering army of Leinster and the allied ranks of the Dublin Gaill waiting for them. With all his old energy, Brian Boru demanded the assault. Leinster men fought, then wavered and fled; the Vikings of Dublin, thus deserted and exposed, fell where they stood. They died almost to a man and, although Brian's army too was horribly mauled, no one now stood between it and Dublin. He was installed there by Christmas.

Sigtrygg Silk Beard, the king, fled for help northwards up the coast, but found the princes there not very eager to march against another Irish king, especially one of such ability, in the cause of the alien Gaill. Faced with a choice between something and nothing, Sigtrygg took the hard-headed Viking way, returned to Dublin and made his formal submission to Brian there. Marriages cemented, in accepted fashion, this coerced peace: Sigtrygg took Brian's sister as his wife, Brian himself married Gormflaith, sister of the king of Leinster, widow of Olaf Kvaran and divorced wife of Mæl Seachlainn. And Brian made another condition, one which after his recent disappointments in the north Sigtrygg was probably happy to accept – in future, the Vikings would fight in alliance not with the northern Irish kings, as hitherto, but with Brian's Munster levies.

This subtle and magnanimous policy on the part of Brian Boru, however, in its turn precipitated a new conflict – that between his southern kingdom and the northern one of Mæl Seachlainn, whose subjects and allies the Gaill of Dublin had been. Not a man to misunderstand circumstances, nor one to shrink from necessary remedies, Brian accepted the responsibility of the inevitable and moved first. By the year 1001, at the head of an army vast by the standards of Irish conflicts, the Vikings of Dublin now at his side, he was encamped outside Tara and demanding as his right homage from Mæl Seachlainn himself. Negotiation followed, marches, displays of force – more martial music than martial fervour. For Mæl Seachlainn was always an intelligent leader, a man in touch with power in all its elusive reality; it is likely that, even with the first transfer of Dublin's allegiance, he had

The 'Tara' brooch. This eighth-century Celtic
ornament was found in a wooden box with a
number of Viking objects at Bettystown,
County Meath.

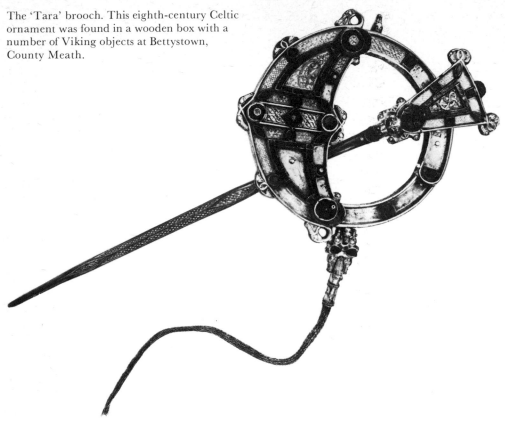

understood that the time for the southern king's supremacy had come. In any case,
by the following year he had made his submission without forcing Ireland to the
self-destructive folly of another war. In the two years that followed, with greater
or lesser reluctance, the kings of Connaught, of East Ulster and of Ailech had also
accepted Brian's overlordship.

From 1004 to 1012, a new calm descended on Ireland. There were border disputes, family feuds, dynastic quarrels, but they took place in the context of a wider
peace which, by and large, they did not threaten to disturb. The cultural renaissance Brian had brought to the south he now extended over the rest of the country.
But men of great estate are touchy, and a few years of security are enough to make
their followers forget the trials and terrors of more anxious times. So Mælmordha
of Leinster, making the most of an affront from Murchad, Brian Boru's son, called
an assembly of his lords and chiefs to pass the burden of this insult on to them. One
senses an irresistible excitement, a desperate, unprincipled glee – rebellion, the
freedom of the sword, fire again over Ireland: war at last! Eagerly these bellicose
nobles accepted as their own Mælmordha's sense of outrage. Within weeks, the
old alliance between Leinster and Dublin had been re-established. In the north,
urged by emissaries from Mælmordha, the kingdom of Ailech took up arms against
the High King. The whole island, almost in a moment, fell into turmoil, intrigue

and bloodshed. The rifts within the community as a whole did not stop short at the doors of Brian's modest hall, for his wife recovered an older allegiance and fled secretly to Dublin and the Court of her son, Sigtrygg Silk Beard, the ally of her brother of Leinster.

At first the burden of Brian's war was borne by his son. As Murchad swept vengefully through Leinster, Mælmordha retreated, to arrive pell-mell in the security of Dublin, demanding sanctuary. In the autumn of 1013, Brian Boru himself took command of his forces and drew the skeins of siege tightly about Dublin. The months wore on towards Christmas. Winter settled on the land; all was bleak. Behind their defences, Gaill and Leinstermen stood firm, albeit somewhat desperately. Brian's soldiers had each day to forage further for thinner fare. Before the new year, he had raised the siege.

But as the year turned, everyone in Dublin knew that this small victory was both partial and provisional. Sigtrygg himself – advised now, it is said, by the devious Gormflaith – sailed across the sea in a search for new allies. He had a good case, for Dublin was important to the trade and prosperity of the Viking world. Seeing it threatened, men sailed from the Hebrides in the north, from the kingdom of the Franks, from the still-raw and half-established colony of Normandy, even from Scandinavia itself. Sigurd the Stout, great *jarl* of the Orkneys, was brought from his fastness with a promise – that victory would give him the throne of Dublin, and the much-claimed hand of Gormflaith to lend legitimacy to that crown. Whether it was the lady or the kingdom her dowry which tempted Sigurd one does not know, but he agreed to sail. Seeing how powerful this bait was, Sigtrygg seems to have seen no reason not to dangle it before another fish – and so Brodir of Man was persuaded for the same prize to sail with twenty ships westward from his island to Dublin. Battle was a lottery, after all, and one of the two might die; if both survived, victory would put a new gloss on old promises.

For Brian Boru and those who stood with him, this gathering of rank after rank of alien spears must have carried with it dreadful possibilities. Hindsight suggests that Vikings would never have taken and held the whole of Ireland, but doubtless hindsight would have said the same of England had Svein Forkbeard been defeated. And this was the year of Svein's final victory over Æthelred; the Dane became king of England while Brian was still encamped outside the Dublin walls. To the High King and his faction, therefore, it may well have seemed that the continued freedom of the whole island was in the balance. Fortunately, Brian too had much to recommend him to potential allies. His rule had been just, moderate and peaceful. He was a good and intelligent man, with the prestige and the power to wring respect and a reluctant obedience from his vassal princes; often, his magnanimity also brought their friendship. Nor was his reputation confined to Ireland; Brodir of Man's brother, convinced that Brian was the best king Ireland could have, brought ten ships into his service, as well as much information about the army now forming in Dublin. Many of Ireland's most powerful men did not care to see the country's new cohesion thrown away for the sake of an anarchy which would profit no one but the overlords of Leinster and the Gaill. These too joined Brian.

So, throughout the early spring of 1014, the armies mustered: in Dublin, Sigtrygg and his brother Dubhgall, Sigurd the Stout, Brodir of Man, the Leinster detachments under Mælmordha, with behind all of them, exhorting, advising, intriguing, the much-married and once more (and doubly) spoken-for Gorm-flaith; to Brian Boru flocked the doughty and selfless Mæl Seachlainn, the southern O'Neill, the lords of Connaught and of Oriel, Ospak of Man, while with him stood both his son, Murchad, and his grandson, Tordelbach. The northern O'Neill remained neutral and Leinster balefully in Dublin, but the rest of Ireland marched with its High King, a national unity never seen before. Estimated at around twenty thousand strong, this army first swept through the Viking territories around Dublin. Towards the end of April, it arrived at Clontarf, on the Liffey.

Here, it posed a double threat, for on the south bank of the Liffey stood the Gaill's Dublin, while in the water off the Liffey's mouth lay the foreign Vikings' fleet. If one accepts the disposition of forces deduced by scholars, Brian drew his men up on the north bank, his right wing anchored on the Liffey, his left on the parallel River Tolka. The fleet was thus immediately before him, beached by or riding on the shallow inner waters of Dublin Bay. Sigurd and his allies had there-fore to come out to protect their ships. For Sigtrygg, on the other hand, it was the protection of Dublin that was of the greater importance, and in making sure that the bridge to the city was covered, his battle-lines became unduly stretched. In the centre, however, there was high ground (Mountjoy Square stands there today) and of this Mælmordha was able to take the fullest advantage. With his detach-ments on the ridge, Sigtrygg's brother Dubhgall holding the Dublin approaches on the left of the line, Sigurd the Stout and Brodir of Man guarding the way to the ships on the right and the sea behind all of them, the forces of Gaill, Viking and Leinstermen prepared themselves to battle for independence at the least and, at the most, the conquest of Ireland.

Dawn, then; 23 April 1014; rain-clouds, it may be, storming low from the west, the first slanting light thin, its growing radiance hardly to be noticed. Above the Irish ranks some seventy banners glowed, pennants flicking in the humid breeze. A stirring, a great, collective sigh, the clatter of metal, muted still; commanders stepping with confidence, real or assumed, out of their tented, sleepless nights. Yet two are missing, the highest commanders of all – Sigtrygg lurks in Dublin, while Brian Boru kneels on a spread skin in Tomar's Wood: it is Good Friday and he will not fight on such a holy day. He will pray, however, this old man, head bent, within earshot of death and destiny, his greatness that of Ireland, now submitting his authority to the authority of his God and awaiting the turns and tragedies of history.

Challenge, counter-challenge, a stepping forth of champions, one from the ranks of Brodir of Man, the other from those of Murchad. The fight between them, however, is indecisive; almost at once, it is overtaken by the wider combat.

Mælmordha and his Leinstermen come careering down the slope before them, the air wild with their battle cries. The force of their charge, the fierce thrusts of spear and sword there, drive back the Munster detachments. Brodir of Man follows his champion and the example of the centre. Soon Murchad's lines are bending, are struggling backwards, fighting still, but almost overwhelmed.

Two miles to the south, however, the story is otherwise. The men of Connaught have held the Dublin Gaill, they have advanced against them, Ospak of Man beside them, and the Vikings are beginning to turn; some are already streaming away over that precious bridge. Does Sigtrygg stand on a high place and see their flight? On the Irish left, Tordelbach, Brian's grandson, is driving forward, the stained blades of his men now forcing retreat upon Sigurd's Orkney Northmen. The whole line wavers; beyond the clouds, the sun climbs higher, hangs out of sight, a brilliant hawk, a patient vulture, its diffused rays lighting up with an impartial clarity the swift curve of the striking sword, the sudden blood, the anguished faces of the dying, the long inertia of the dead. Ireland is in the balance.

For the Vikings, it is their Leinster allies who now carry their best hopes. Mælmordha is still thrusting forward, still driving Munstermen in confusion before him. But is there, perhaps, something too swift in their retreat, in their readiness to give up the fight and run? If there is, the warriors of Leinster, certain of victory, do not sense it. They rush on, they scatter after pockets here and there of stubborn opponents, knots of men tangled with metal, sharp to the attacker, still keen and thirsty for victims – knots which hold, then curiously come undone, melt away; Munstermen running again, those of Leinster exultant after them. . . . Abruptly, to their left, a line of helmets, a cry, men springing out of the ground, an onrush of spears. Foxy Mæl Seachlainn, gone to earth, now comes leaping out into the light again to take his fellow-king of Leinster in the flank. His men come up-ward from their shallow trenches; among the Leinstermen, all is confusion. Their cries of triumph waver, they turn to each other, they call, seeking a rallying point. Too late; their heedless charge has scattered them. Cut off from one another, they give ground. Their retreating weight falls upon the flank of Sigurd's men, and Brodir's.

Now the first confusion, like a plague, spreads, redoubling, through the Viking forces. Murchad rallies; Brodir of Man, forsaking marriage plans and hopes of wider reign, runs like a terrified boar through woods in early leaf. His men, abandoned, die under Murchad's charge. Only Sigurd stands firm, stout in action as in name. He becomes in himself a rallying point. Under his still-potent banner, the Leinstermen reform. Brodir recovers himself, if not his men, and joins them. The Dublin Gaill come across to take part in this new stand. Grouped under their new leader, they thrust forward. Like a sea, the Irish army boils past on either side of them. Soon they are cutting their way through Brian's rearguard. Perhaps then they should have turned, made their way once more to their city and their ships; maybe they would have if they could.

Ahead of them, however, through the spaced trunks of trees, they see an unexpected tableau – a handful of warriors, a silent, waiting circle, behind them an old man on his knees, deeply in prayer. Is it a priest, Brodir wants to know. No – it is Brian Boru, High King of Ireland. With a cry, Brodir runs forward, smashes his way through the few defending shields, his sword rises, whirrs briefly in the spring air, crashes down upon the defenceless man. The blade bites, bone falls away, the royal blood seeps from the severed flesh. Turning, Brodir calls his boast to the world – he is the hero who felled Brian!

Did Sigurd know that Brian Boru was praying in Tomar Wood? Did he think that by killing him he would tear the heart from Irish courage? He was wrong if he did so. Murchad and Tordelbach had turned their men, were bringing them back. Dublin and the sea now lay the far side of them; whoever wanted to reach those havens would find the passage bloody. And so it proved, for Sigurd, knowing he had to try to board his ships, turned once again and made the attempt. He died, though Murchad, Brian's son, died with him. Brodir, cornered, fought for a while, then was taken and brutally killed. (In *Njarl's Saga* we are told that his belly was slit open and his intestines dragged out of him as he was led round and round an oak tree – he 'did not die before they were all pulled out of him'.) The Viking forces broke, split; in groups, in ones and twos, they raced through woods and across open hillsides, wide, curving runs to try to pass safely by the Irish flanks. But the two rivers hemmed them in; almost gaily, the Irish pursued, their frenzy that of men who had gathered their victory from the very arms of defeat.

At the sea's edge, by the Weir of Clontarf, groups of soldiers ran – pursued, pursuing; foam rose high about them as they plunged towards the ships, then abruptly reddened. In the shallows, corpses paled, waved feeble limbs as the water moved them, suffered the first soft nibbles of the fish. Ferociously, Tordelbach raced through the thin waves, his sword lifted above the spray of his own running. Then he was gone, cut down perhaps, finally drowned, the third generation of his royal House to die that day. At the Dublin bridge, too, there was carnage, despair, exultation; only twenty of the Dublin Vikings, it is said, managed to cross the Liffey to the fragile safety of their own city walls. Some seven thousand of their comrades and allies lay dead; so did some four thousand of their enemies. Something of the Irish destiny had been determined – such trials of a people's fate demand their price.

It may be that, in following the Irish poets and chroniclers, who themselves hovered over the riven corpses of Clontarf like the ravens they wrote about, we make too much of the battle's importance. Perhaps if Brian Boru had lived, a permanent peace might have been built on these bloody foundations; if his son and grandson had lived, a permanent dynasty might have established a unified Ireland. As it was, although the threat of Viking domination and Leinster auto-cracy had been repulsed, nothing really altered at all. Munster fell to bickering about the succession, and a kind of civil war; Mæl Seachlainn stood once more as High King; the Gaill remained in Dublin – these obstinate foreigners, humbled perhaps, and soon indeed taught a new and ferocious lesson by Mæl Seachlainn, but still with their own laws and rulers. The only emotion which united them all, and that briefly, was the genuine grief felt at Brian Boru's death, and the praise they brought in tribute for his prowess, magnanimity and might.

Wexford and Waterford, Cork in the south, Limerick on the Shannon to the east, Dublin above all – the Viking settlements grew, traded, prospered. For nearly forty years Dublin flourished; in 1052, however, in another of Ireland's endless wars, its king was ousted and the Irish Diarmait, of the Leinster line, ruled there in his stead. In one sense, this was the end of Viking autonomy. Northmen were to reign briefly in Dublin again, to struggle for it, to hold it and lose it, to lose their other strongholds too, finally to see a king of Leinster, Diarmait MacMurchad, turn to the Norman English across the Irish Sea for help.

Exiled in 1166, he returned in 1169 with eager mercenaries in his train. Dublin fell to him, and Waterford; Asgall Torquilsson, the deposed king of Dublin, and his ally, Svein Asleiferson, were foiled in their attempt to take the city back; then, in 1171, the last curtain fell on the Viking struggle for ascendency over Ireland, for in that year, with the Leinster king, Diarmait, dead, Richard Strongbow crossed the sea to take his kingdom. A new strain of Norsemen, altered by the centuries of separation, still discovering their own power and the extent of their ambitions, had arrived to oust the old. These, the Norman-English, did achieve that ascendency which had eluded their earlier Scandinavian cousins; the cruelty and callousness with which they used it led to the long disaster of Irish history, bedevilling all those who came after them for eight appalling, blood-spattered centuries.

Throughout these years of Irish struggle, the Scots, too, had suffered Viking raids, many of them from marauders based on Dublin and hungry for greater power. Rægnald flickered about that coast, soon afterwards falling upon English holdings along the Tyne. A Scottish army helped defeat him at Corbridge; it was after this that, seeing better chances to the south, he took York, held it a year and then submitted to the English Crown. That submission, mark of the success of Alfred's House, resulted in many strange alliances, one among them a new trust between Scots and the Dublin Vikings.

Olaf Kvaran, the young king of York, in flight from Athelstan and desperate for friends, found them in Scotland. His marriage to the daughter of the Scottish king, the grey-haired Constantine, was one of the visible signs of that alliance against Saxon England which brought Athelstan vengefully over the border, to punish temerity and put a curb on unnecessary independence. At Brunanburh, in 937, he achieved his purpose and, perhaps as a direct result, as the century wore on, the focus of power in Scotland moved north again, to the half-dependent, Norway-orientated Viking colonies in the Orkneys under their hard and often wily succession of *jarls*.

By the time of Sigurd the Stout, destined to die bravely if to little purpose at Clontarf, with Caithness on the mainland as part of their earldom, the Vikings of Orkney were raiders again, ranging as far as Ireland and holding, for a brief

A tenth-century Celtic cross at Clonmacnois,
County Offaly, Eire. In the background is a
look-out tower used by the Irish to detect the
approach of Viking raiders.

space, the Isle of Man. Sigurd understood something of the obligations of power,
too, returning to the small land-holders of the islands a portion of the rights bargained from them by the great Turf-Einar. By marrying a daughter of King
Malcolm II (great-grandfather of that other Malcolm whose simulacrum,
Shakespeare-invented, has stalked Macbeth these last four centuries), Sigurd
gave his power a wider base, and this his son, Thorfinn, named 'The Mighty',
inherited and extended.

Malcolm, at whose Court he passed his boyhood, made Thorfinn Earl of Caithness and Sutherland; further holdings were disputed by the sons of his father's first
marriage, but by 1030 only one of these remained to contest the inheritance. At
this point King Olaf of Norway intervened – that Olaf the Stout who had once
played his part in the destinies of England too. He was as anxious as other
Norwegian monarchs to demonstrate his overlordship over the Orkneys; he did
this now by dividing them, allowing one part to Thorfinn, the other to his half-
brother, Brusi. In 1036, however, Brusi's son Rægnald appeared with a claim
endorsed by the new king of Norway, Magnus, for two-thirds of the Orkneys.
Thorfinn, although not always slow to maintain his own rights, accepted this, and
seems for a while to have taken to his nephew, with whom he fought in enterprising alliance around the northern coasts of Scotland and Ireland.

Eventually, however, such proud and undisciplined warriors as these could not
contain their conviction that all and not part of this domain should be theirs alone.
With these tensions to unsettle their relationship, they quarrelled and fought, their
struggle, as so often between relatives and one-time allies, becoming bitterly
savage. Their ships met, prow to prow on those black northern waters, the men
tumbling across the linked decks, shields high, swords sweeping life away, the dead
falling sideways heavy as fruit, to drop from wooden safety into the insubstantial
waves below. Thorfinn was victorious, Rægnald fleeing to Norway and the
sanctuary of the Court. He was not there long; landing secretly, he made his way
with a small party to Thorfinn's house and, as the *jarl* slept, burned it over his head.
One hears down the centuries the raucous jubilation as the flames stretched towards the sky, inverted northern lights, drinking horns raised as the beams fell
inwards below their galaxies of sparks. Such celebration would have been premature – unseen, Thorfinn escaped, half-carrying his wife, and made his way to
Caithness. With such an enemy loose, one might have thought that Rægnald
would take precautions, yet that Christmas Thorfinn was able to turn fire against

The Calf Crucifix, from a ninth-century altar
frontal in the Isle of Man, illustrates the
merging of Viking and Hibernian traditions in
art. It owes much to the Viking Jelling stone.

the arsonist. Now it was he and his men who yelled in joyful ferocity as the flames
tumbled Rægnald's Orkney house, it was Rægnald who attempted to flee through
the maze of smoke and ruin. He was unluckier than Thorfinn, however, and was
seen, and hunted down, and killed.

Thorfinn the Mighty was a great ruler in the north of Britain, his lands wide, his
law strong. In a sense, it was the high-point of Viking ascendency in the area. The
massive forays of the Norwegian king, Magnus Barefoot, around the year 1100,
although they reaffirmed Norwegian power by their swaggering, bullying progress, were cut abruptly short by Magnus's death in an irrelevant battle in Ulster.
After this, although under Norwegian overlordship, the history of Viking Scotland
and the surrounding seas and islands is one of division, of adventurers making
uneasy gains, only to lose them to others luckier, crueller or more energetic than
they. Often, the blood-line of claimants was diluted (though from the diplomatic
point of view strengthened) by inter-marriage with Scottish chieftains and nobles.
Names swim up out of the turmoil: Godred Crovan, the Icelandic adventurer who
set himself on the throne of Man, then flexed his muscles and extended his power
into Ireland and Scotland; Olaf, his son, whose forty years of benevolent rule
brought peace to an area the calm of which his father's violence had shattered;
there was the sainted but ineffectual Magnus Erlendsson; and Rægnald Kali, who
seized the Orkney domains with savagery but ruled them with benevolence and
Christian zeal; and so on down those violent centuries, usurpers, upstarts, regents,
claimants, viceroys, pirates and bandits, all moiling and hallooing about the sea-
battered cliffs and the sloping meadows, the sudden bays and grey-green hills of
northern Scotland, their blood winding across the wind-cropped grass as they
died, their successors setting up in savage yet insubstantial state, often to die in
their turn, cruelty, torture and death the constant terms of defeat, a relative wealth
and a local power the rewards for victory.

For beyond the influence of their incestuous battles the Viking world had con-
tracted, or altered, or even disappeared, and their power, for all that the crown of
Norway guaranteed it, could be no more than local. They played out the repetitive
scenes of an ancient drama, its plot alternating between the noble and the repul-
sive, but its relevance constantly diminishing. At the end, it took on the appearance of some *revenant* reconstruction, a ghostly flickering through chambers of
history long abandoned by the living. The Viking style was still there, the ambition

and even the energy, but the scale was too small, the period too late; the world had outgrown them. Finally, treaties and marriages brought the Norwegian allegiance to an end; in 1472, the Orkneys came under the Scottish crown. Murder still stalked the Highlands and islands, massacre and usurpation still studded their story, but by formal declaration their part in the saga of the Northmen had come to an end.

Wales was the hedgehog. Prickly, the men of Gwynnedd in the north, of Glamorgan in the south, stood stoutly by spear and sword and made landing hard for the Viking. The great Rhodri Mawr, lord of all north Wales, fought a long battle against the invaders during the second half of the ninth century, sometimes winning (as when defeating and killing Orm, Danish leader of a fleet ravaging Anglesey and the mainland), sometimes losing (as when, in 877, he came as a temporary refugee to Ireland), but always presenting to the raiders the stern, implacable front of a prince determined to maintain his territory to the limits of his energy and time. After his death and the turn of the century, raiders came from Ireland, searching for new holdings, for lands from which they might harvest

A stone gaming board found at Buckquoy, a Pictish/Viking settlement in the Orkneys.

wealth, power and the status of nobles. But in that century, they and other Vikings were held up by another great king, Hywel dda of Cardigan who, by 942, had pulled into unity the many warring princes and factions of Wales, struck up an alliance with England and given the country a single code of law and the self-awareness to channel its unwavering desire for independence into a constant, wide-awake defence.

Alas, Hywel the Good died, as even great kings must, and the strength went out of his kingdom with him. Once more Wales fell into factions and opposing dynasties and, where before the country had been largely immune from Viking attack, it now became one of the normal stopping places for illustrious pirates in search of plunder. Eirik Bloodaxe came, a great leader who, as Snorri Sturluson tells us, because he had little land 'went on a cruise every summer, and plundered in Scotland, the Hebrides, Ireland, and Bretland, by which he gathered property'. And Bretland – Wales – felt the demanding weight of others on a similar quest: Turf-Einar, the Earl of Orkney, devious, proud and hungry, ('ugly', Snorri tells us, 'and blind of one eye, yet very sharp-sighted withal'), and Svein Forkbeard, who would die as king of England but spent some of his days in Wales as a prisoner, and Olaf Tryggvesson, who 'steered to Bretland, which he laid waste with fire and sword . . .'.

Wales now, not as adequately defended as in the past, was vulnerable to the raids of Vikings who had no longer to bring sizeable fleets across the difficult waters from Scandinavia, but who were securely based, in kingdoms of their own, in Dublin or the Isle of Man. Godfred Haraldsson, a Dane from Limerick who had succeeded his brother Magnus as the king of Man, made many forays into Wales, for a short while holding Anglesey, in 980 bringing destruction to the Lleyn Peninsula (where later generations would wander through a holiday peace), two years later landing with unabated ferocity on the Pembroke coast, returning in 987 to see what new plunder he might wring out of unhappy Anglesey. It is said that there he took some two thousand prisoners; perhaps it was this which persuaded the most powerful of the country's kings, Maredudd ap Owain, to play almost the part of a Welsh Æthelred – he ransomed the prisoners for one penny a head, a little later hiring mercenaries from the Dublin Irish to help him in his battles against the English. Neither payment nor alliance, however, brought immunity:

Anglesey was ravaged once more and in the year Maredudd died, St David's was attacked, its cathedral sacked, its bishop and most of the population to whom he ministered cut down as they ran for safety or knelt in stubborn prayer.

No one now knows what peaceful residue this protracted tenth-century assault left behind it. Elsewhere, coasts subjected to so consistent a series of small invasions developed, almost as though by contagion, Viking colonies, villages which concentrated on the land, on trade, on peaceful crafts, and the inhabitants of which learned the skills and easy friendships of good neighbours. Doubtless such settlements put roots down in Wales as in other countries; there are, indeed, place-names in south Wales which suggest that this was so. Perhaps the Welsh learned an Irish lesson and developed some tolerance for these busy newcomers. Certainly ties developed with the Gaill of Dublin. Gruffydd ap Cynan, King of Gwynedd, had a Viking mother, Ragnhild, grand-daughter of Sigtrygg Silk Beard; he was brought up in Viking Dublin, persuaded Northmen to fight in the many armies he needed to raise during his reign and always used the long-established settlements of the Northmen in Ireland as places of refuge when, as it frequently did, his throne became too volatile and dangerous to hold. So the war-routes across the Irish Sea became sea-roads for traders, for friends, even for relatives sailing to wedding or wake. The coasts of Wales settled into near-safety. King Magnus Barefoot, in his great voyages from Norway, did sweep into unhappy Anglesey again in 1098 and insisted that he had become its overlord, but he sailed away and it is unlikely that many people took his claim very seriously once he had gone. Perhaps there were raiders after him, isolated pirates determined not to allow the ferocious traditions of Viking freedom to disappear for ever, mad, frenetic warriors who came hurling briefly out of the turmoil to the north, Svein Asleiferson of Orkney and his friend Holdbodi in pursuit of some Welsh chieftain perched in fortified safety on tall Lundy Island, but on the whole Wales had no more to fear from Northmen. As with the Irish, it was the grim, insatiable Norman-English whom they had to face now, that purposeful grinding down of their liberty which, eight centuries later and whether for good reasons or bad, they are still resisting.

A section of the twelfth-century tapestry from
Skog Church, Hälsingland, Sweden, illustrating
Viking history. This section, dramatizing the
struggle between Christianity and paganism,
shows three priests ringing bells to frighten
away evil spirits.

5 VALHALLA
–AND AFTER

The old gods died hard. Believed immortal, they had been long-lived, established in a universe accepted by everyone, its cosmology especially created to give them their place. Their natures had arisen out of the natures of those who had created them, mirroring the admired and masculine characteristics of their worshippers – harsh, hard-drinking, boastful, angry, boisterous, heavy-humoured and lustful. Their virtues were the virtues of their devotees – courage, fortitude, resilience, perhaps cunning – and the stories told about them led men who had heard them since childhood to try to emulate the gargantuan feats they described.

Yggdrasil, the world-tree, the holy and all-encompassing ash, constantly attacked by the gnawing dragon Dread Biter, by a malevolent rotting of the trunk, by the four browsing stags which consumed its leaves, constantly protected by the three guardian Norns: this was the framework of the universe. On that tree Odin hung to learn his cosmic wisdom, his transcendental sacrifice, echo, perhaps, of the crucifixion (although redemption of mankind was by no means its purpose), the pattern for the ritual hangings carried out in his sacred groves. Its image was potency, the phallus, the lingam, a constant reinforcement and reminder of the Vikings' emphasized virility, the almost entirely male values of their world.

Asgard stood at the centre of this universe, the great, cloud-topping mountain where the gods had their homes to roister or sulk in, and where Valhalla keeps an open door for the ascension of deserving heroes. Those who lived in Asgard present to us now the usual confusing clutter of names, of ancient gods, great once, but overtaken by changes in human sensibility, of overlapping attributes, of sectarian preferences, the whole given a mysterious inner logic by that Indo-Aryan ground-swell whose steady but almost imperceptible movement surfaces only in an occasional name, an occasional characteristic. Thus we have All-father, a variant perhaps of the Vedic Sky-god, Dyaus, altered by the Greeks to Zeus; for the Romans, a version of his name, Dyaus-pitar, or Sky-father, became the familiar Jupiter. In Scandinavian mythology, his attributes – but not his name – became those of Odin. Thus the divine was transmuted.

Odin was the chief of the Æsir, the principal fellowship of the northern gods; to them were added, in an unexpectedly conciliatory manner, gods of, as it were, a different tribe, a divine race called the Vanir. Frey and Freyja were of these outsiders, two great figures easily accepted as having a status little less than that of Odin himself, or that of Thor. Odin had gained his pre-eminence at the expense of

Tiwaz, or Tyr, a god relegated – no one knows when or in what manner – into a strangely feeble god of war. Odin descends not from the Vedic Dyaus but from his divine companion, Vāyu, the wind-god. Certainly some of Vāyu's ruthless cunning and even some of his unprincipled licentiousness (he once struck a hundred princesses hump-backed for preserving their royal honour in the face of his advances) were retained by Odin, although over the centuries he developed a transcendental, brooding dimension which was hardly to be found in the early Indian gods. He was also the god who led the souls of the deserving dead to their elysian destination, and for this reason the Romans equated him with Mercury. Nordic theories of heaven, of course, like their ambitions on earth, reflected their preoccupations; the highest level of heaven, as a consequence, became that warrior's meeting-hall, Valhalla.

For many of the eligible warriors, however, it was not Odin whom they revered above all but rather Thor, the heavily muscled and endlessly energetic thunder god. It was he who had been most closely created in their own image; it was he who owned the objects they most coveted – Mjöllnir, the great hammer which was both Thor's weapon and his symbol and which, flung, would return each time to his waiting hand; the iron gauntlets which made it possible for him to heft so demanding a weapon; and the great belt which, girded about him, increased his already gigantic strength by a half. Despite his adventures, Thor was what the Vikings liked to imagine they were – more knight-errant than bandit. It was the Giants he attacked (not unprotected coastal settlements or demoralized riverside towns), and not for the sake of plunder, but to keep Asgard – and humankind's Midgard, too – safe from their threatening violence. Certainly they could identify with his appetites, his shock of red hair bright in the firelight, the drinking horn rammed into his vast beard, his head thrown back in simple satisfaction, just as they laughed, optimistically, at the way he could sometimes be tricked by his enemies in a manner they, of course, always guarded against.

The Vanir gods may have originated in Asia and thus been brought northwest by migrations and cultural contacts, although it seems at least as likely that they were established in Scandinavia even before the Æsir. Njörd is their chief, in one aspect the god of the sea, but in another possibly a version, transmuted across the genders, of an earlier earth-goddess named as 'Nerthus' by Tacitus in his account of Baltic tribes, the masculine ending here perhaps significant. Njörd's children are Frey and Freyja, brother and sister both beautiful, he rivalling the adored Baldur, she pre-eminent. Frey is a fertility god, his name developed from that root-word *prij* from which the name Priapus, too, derives. Certainly orgy and sacred prostitution seem to have been associated with his worship. His likeness in countless figurines, each endowed with a penis respectfully disproportionate, littered the Viking world. He is also, though less clearly than Baldur, the beautiful young doomed one, the Tammuz and Adonis whose myths later became intertwined with those of Christianity, as did that of Frey himself. In the very early English poem *The Dream of the Rood*, for example, the line describing Christ as

A bronze image of Frey from Rällinge, Södermanland.

'Lord of mankind' stands in the original as *Frean mancynnes* (although this may have been a poetic archaism, for much earlier 'frea' had meant 'lord' with no divine overtones) and the phrase 'Christ Almighty' appears as *Frea Aelmightig*.

Freyja (her legend intertwined with that of Frygg) was among the more amenable of Asgard's deities and was frequently appealed to by mortals in need of help. She shared with her husband, Odin, the task of gathering in souls, however, and as a result was sometimes associated with those battle-hungry maidens the Valkyries. She has, perhaps because of her responsibility for the dead, a strong connection with witchcraft and necromancy, her serene reputation complicated a little by this. Her beauty, too, often made her a source of heroic and divine contention (when Thor's hammer was stolen by a royal giant, it was Freyja he wanted as ransom; when the great mason built Asgard's wall, it was Freyja he wanted as payment). She, like her brother Frey, is in the end a fertility deity, a goddess of

OPPOSITE Viking sword with a hilt of silver decorated in the south English style, found at Dybeck, Skane, Sweden.

nature and the earth. She travels about the cosmos in a small cart drawn by two cats, a strange and almost sinister mode of transport oddly out of place among the robust inhabitants of Asgard.

Baldur was the second son of Odin, 'so blond and fair of face that a great light shines from him', as Snorri tells us, and about him there is a sense of purity and complex mystery which sets him apart even from the handsome Frey. In Baldur, above all, lie enshrined the half-transfigured lineaments of the Adonis myth (*Adonei*, 'my lord' in semitic languages; *baldr*, Old Norse for 'lord', *bealdor* in Old English). Baldur the beautiful was killed through the machinations of the tricky Loki. Struck down by mistletoe, the only part of creation not pledged to do Baldur no harm, the shaft flung by his own blind brother Hödr to whom Loki had handed it, the young god died in purity, leaving consternation among the gods. A messenger was sent to the Underworld, while Baldur's body, watched by his divine companions and accompanied by his wife and his horse, was burned on its ship-borne pyre. Hel, Underworld's queen, agreed to release Baldur if it could be proved that every living creature in the world really mourned him. Thus the whole universe wept to display the sincerity of its sorrow – with the single exception of the twisted Loki: 'Let Hel hold what she has,' he snapped, his hate, as always, crackling down the centuries. Thus Baldur remained among shadows, released only into that new and purified world arising after the last agony of the old gods, Ragnarök.

The blood, the early death, the lamentation, the final resurrection – all must have helped to make more easily assimilable the later stories (though Baldur is a god who in any case came late to eminence) of the death and elevation of Jesus. There are hints of this, too, in *The Dream of the Rood*: 'Wept all creation,/ keened the king's fall' might refer even more easily to Baldur than to Christ; so too might the later line, 'All wounded I was with shafts.' As with Tammuz, Adonis and Mithras, Baldur provided a mould from which Christian missionaries were later to press credible and quite accurate representations of the Jesus whose worship they proposed.

'The father of lies' is what Snorri calls Loki, the phrase perhaps familiar to a Christian writer. Certainly the spiteful, faithless and embittered mischief-maker of Asgard was a mixture of Lucifer and not so much Mephistopheles perhaps as Machiavelli. Indeed, the name Loki may well be related to the Latin *lux* which is the root of 'Lucifer', though his light was the glare of the forest fire, that violent, destructive flame, baleful as well as beautiful, dangerous always, but hypnotic to some. (His father bears the name Fárbauti, 'Dangerous Smiter', his mother is Laufey, 'Leafy Island', a *skáld*'s phrase for 'tree' – thus, lightning smites tree, fire results.) After Loki had refused to weep for Baldur and so sentenced him to existence among shades, the gods caught him and bound him with the entrails of his own son, torn to pieces by his brother, who had been conjured by furious deities into the shape and nature of a wolf. Shackled to three rocks, Loki lay (and perhaps still lies) positioned below a venomous snake, its mouth opened so that a constant stream of vitriolic poison fell upon his upturned face. His faithful wife Sigyn, how-

OPPOSITE A Viking head carved on the Oseberg wagon. Even today we recoil from the single-minded ferocity of this Norwegian warrior.

Two silver and bronze-gilt amulets possibly
meant to represent the Valkyries, *c.* 850.

ever, placed herself beside him and caught the venom in an outstretched basin;
whenever she has to empty it, the pain of the endless flow brings Loki to convul-
sions – which we experience as earthquakes.

Thus there was well-established in the Nordic mind a pantheon including an
overseeing father, a divine sacrifice, a concerned and beautiful lady and a
scheming contriver of evil, figures which might with some ease be modified into
the iconography of the Christian Church. The notion of heaven and hell was also
familiar, Asgard and Hel being widely accepted as the true destinations of the
Viking dead. For northern pagans, however, heaven had a different aspect than
it had for Christian devotees; there was nothing of the meek and gentle about the
concept of Valhalla, that 'hall of the slain' which rewarded with eternal battle and
endless carousing the fiercely brave, the deservedly victorious and the indomitable
defeated. Indeed, Valhalla, although one among that cluster of magnificent
buildings which housed the gods of Asgard, was by no means easy to enter, for its
entrance was protected by a tumbling, brawling river and by Valgrind, the barred
and grudging gate which opened only to the especial few. Each of its 540 doors,
however, could accommodate eight hundred warriors marching shoulder-to-
shoulder, spears were its roof-rafters and the slates they supported were shields.
The fortunate who were allowed entry were chosen by the Valkyrie, the blood-
enraptured maidens whose wild rush across the sky signalled as surely as the flight
of vultures a distant carnage, battle and the bloodied heaps of the dead. Arrived
in Valhalla and greeted by the assembly of his muscular peers, the chosen hero
would face an eternity of doing what he most preferred – Snorri tells us that 'as
soon as they are dressed, they don their armour' and march off to their daily battle,
an exhilarating violence robbed of its ultimate danger now that they have passed
through Valhalla's gate, both distracting them and giving them the appetite
necessary to face the feasting and drinking in which the rest of their time will be
spent. At the time of Ragnarök, however, their swords will once more be called
upon in all reality and the threat to which the gods succumb will also lay them
low a second time.

Ragnarök, the world's end, the doom of the gods – a strange conviction for a
religion to proclaim, taking from its gods the very fount of their otherness, that
which makes them distinct from men: immortality. A terrible winter, three years
long, a collapse of morality, greed everywhere and a breaking of all faith, all

bonds; this in Midgard, where men must live. In Asgard, the death of Baldur has signalled the coming end; Loki, enemy now of all those who so ferociously punished him, will soon find allies in the Giants, those lurking presences at the edges of the world whose growls, stratagems and forays have always threatened the equanimity of the gods. Sun and Moon are devoured, each by the great wolves Hati and Sköl, then the wolf Fenrir, whose jaws stretch across the firmament, one of the dread brood fathered by Loki on a giant ogress, breaks loose, while its sibling Jörmungand, the World Serpent, rises out of the boiling sea, its venom a deadly fountain. The Fire Giants advance over the buckling bridge, Bifröst, that great rainbow collapsing and falling now under their weight. At last Loki himself bursts his dreadful bonds and comes ravening from his imprisoning rocks in search of his last revenge.

The gods rush to arms and so do the Einhergar, the chosen heroes of Valhalla. Against them are ranged the Frost Giants, their race immemorially old, sworn enemies of Asgard; the Fire Giants under their fearsome leader, Surt; the sons of Hel following the exultant orders of Loki. The trumpet of Asgard's watchman, Heimdral, calls its legions to their last battle; throughout the earth there is the trembling of a universal dread – it is the trembling of Yggdrasil as in terror it contemplates the end of the order it has sustained for so many aeons. Odin drives forward, the glittering point of his spear Gungnir threatening Fenrir, the great wolf. As he thrusts home, those vast jaws open and the wolf's maw engulfs the god. So Odin dies, although instantly revenged by his son, Vidar, who tears the beast's fanged mask asunder and so kills it. Frey dies too (the sword in his hand not his best, for that he had given to his servant, Skirnir, to run a lover's message for him); it is Surt who destroys the beautiful Asnir god. Thor confronts the World Serpent; one glimpses him with whirling hammer deep in the venomous mist which surrounds the monster, the dull clatter of his struggling rising above the battle's wider clash. And the World Serpent, confounded, falls away and dies, a last victim of the thunder-god's might. In weary triumph, Thor turns away; he walks nine paces before, even his strength not proof against that virulent poison, he collapses, dying. It is the Giants now who triumph, their theme destruction; from Surt himself flames lash out to engulf the earth and lash the heavens into cinder.

The end, then; but not without resurrection. There would be the surviving sons and daughters of the mighty, Baldur to return to sunlight – not the warmth of the first sun, now wolf-engulfed, but that of a second, the first sun's daughter – and with him the shade, permitted life again, of his inadvertent killer, Hödr his brother. Two sons of Odin – one of them that Vidar who had so swiftly avenged his father's death – and two of Thor's would be there to take up the burdens of divinity, Thor's sons bearing as tremendous legacy Mjöllnir, the mighty hammer. So too there would be one pair of human survivors, an Adam and Eve to repopulate the new and greener earth. Times would be sweet then, and life a marvel, humanity busy in its remade pastures, their gods easy in the heavens. There were even hints that a new All-father would come to govern this more placid universe, a god expected yet not to be named, in whom some commentators have seen a covert and interpolated reference to Jesus. Others, however, seeking for bearings in the many Indo-European myths which tell a similar story, consider that originally it was Odin himself who returned (or more probably the older chief of the gods, Tyr) after an absence appalling enough, but only temporary.

In all this, too, there was much material for the missionaries to work on. The kind of vision offered by the Book of Revelations, the idea of apocalypse and re-birth, of a universe remade for a juster and saner, a God-fearing and law-abiding mankind, were not concepts alien to the Northmen's thinking but had already been developed through the strong emphasis laid on Ragnarök by their own religion. On the other hand, if the persons of the gods and the structure of some myths allowed Christian propagandists to infiltrate their own doctrines into minds already prepared to receive them, if such gods and myths permitted an overlay of Christian story and so made the new religion more easily acceptable, there were many aspects of the older, pagan ways which the Vikings had to jettison upon conversion, or else either combine with the later doctrines or practice surreptitiously.

It must not be thought that paganism was any more homogeneous than is Christianity – there is evidence, especially from Iceland, that even atheism was not uncommon – and it is clear from the place-names which survive that, in one area or another, this or that god has at one time been predominant. In Denmark, for example, the syllable Tyr is peculiarly frequent, occurring there and hardly anywhere else; Thor, too, is often to be met with, but the use of his name is common throughout the Viking world. Odin, common in southern Sweden as well as in Denmark, is hardly found at all in Norway, where the cult of Frey and his sister Freyja seems to have been widespread. In Norway, too, the name Ull, Thor's stepson, expert archer and skilful on skis, is frequently used. Such names may indicate that in those designated places there stood centres of worship dedicated to that particular god; they may show, on the other hand, no more than the optimistic devotion of a farmer or householder expressing his personal allegiance and hoping for the god's consequent concern.

Worship itself seems usually to have centred on some feature of the landscape, occasionally something natural, a great rock, a hillock, often a place such as a grove or a cairn where nature had perhaps been given some assistance. Sometimes such assistance flowered into the construction of a full-blown building, although these do not seem to have been in any sense splendid, forerunners of Christianity's cathedrals (a tradition which, perhaps, explains the hold their own particularly spare version of Protestantism has on today's Scandinavians). Often, shrines remained unroofed, or the gatherings of the devoted were held in buildings which at other times had other purposes; these were probably farms to which neighbours might travel for prayer, dedication, sacrifice and feast.

It was, in fact, the sacrifice which at such meetings was the basic act of worship. What was offered heavenwards included the whole range of objects within mankind's control and gift, for the gods were greedy, capricious and powerful. Later, animals thus sacrificially slaughtered were eaten at great feasts from which those taking part derived a conviction that they were being given a new strength by their gods – food accepted by Æsir and Vanir had been passed by divine generosity back to them. Perhaps more importantly, these gatherings reinforced a community's sense of itself and of its corporate reality, binding it together in its relationship with Thor, Frey, Odin and the rest, and sustaining it by the latters' acceptance of its vociferous devotion. Isolation, long winter, land sometimes thin and not over-fertile, perhaps even a sense of being overwhelmed by the size and endless implicit demand of bony landscapes, threateningly high-ridged or broodingly flat; the powerful sea beyond, patient, heavy as much with threat as with promise; the enigmatic sky over all, shrieking as winds drove north-easterly across it, awhirl with blizzards – with such conditions to prime them, meetings like this, devotional in intent, must often have ended drunken and orgiastic. Dimly through the smoke and the centuries one can see the burly figures of these worshippers, faces oddly aflicker in the unsteady glare from the central fire, beards already matted, grease glistening on cheek and hair, drinking horns now jammed again through those ferocious bristles as, leaning back, they drink, the horns rising towards the ceiling like inverted trumpets, the thick ale spilling down their chests, about them the cries and laughter, the careful insults and wild prognostications of their neighbours. It is no wonder that it was at feasts like this that boasts were made which later exploits had to honour, for their form was a vow, its witness the god whose presence permeated such a place at times of sacrifice. Thus awe of the gods became one element in that apparently endless, almost unearthly energy which fuelled the convulsive Viking assault upon the world.

Not all worship, however, ended in the magnanimity of festival or the conviviality of a shared drunkenness. A constant feature of northern paganism was human sacrifice; we have the account, possibly a little biassed by his own convictions, of the Christian chronicler Adam of Bremen, who, although admittedly writing from hearsay, makes vivid for us the scene in Uppsala's sacred grove. He describes the place, with its three gold-decked statues, that of Thor, whom he calls 'the mightiest', in the middle, Odin and Frey on either side. Offering was made to Thor if plague or famine threatened, to Odin at times of war, to Frey, naturally, at weddings. Every nine years, he tells us, there was a festival held there from which 'no one is exempted.' He describes in some detail the sacrifices: 'of all living things that are male, they offer nine heads, with the blood of which it is customary to placate gods of this sort. The bodies they hang in the sacred grove adjoining the temple.' In this grove every tree 'is believed divine because of the death or putrefaction of the sacrifices. Dogs and horses hang there with men, and a Christian told me he had seen seventy-two bodies suspended there side by side. Furthermore, the songs usually chanted in this kind of sacrificial ritual are many in number and unseemly – it is, therefore, better to keep silent about them.' There are notes to Adam's manuscripts, added at about the same time; one of these says that such festivals continued for nine days, that every day a man is sacrificed, along with other creatures, the total of men and beasts slaughtered by the end making up that number, seventy-two, of which Adam's witness spoke. (Nine nines, however, do not make seventy-two.) The vernal equinox, it adds, is the time when this grisly festival is celebrated.

Another and perhaps less reliable chronicler is Thietmar of Merseburg, writing in the eleventh century of rituals which used to take place in Lejre, in Denmark. This is a place which was perhaps famous then as a centre of pagan devotion, but which is known to us as the town near which Beowulf – legend undying, hero looming at us through his integument of epic lines – first landed on the way to his dark struggle with the fearsome Grendel. Thietmar says that here, also in every ninth year, people would gather during the month of January in order to celebrate Yule 'by, among other things, sacrificing ninety-nine humans and as many horses to their gods, as well as dogs and cocks, and also hawks'.

For ordinary people, at their own religious centres, there were usually three festivals a year – one in midwinter, one at the beginning of summer, one at harvest time, all chosen, as such celebrations were throughout the world, to help along with divine favour the normal fertility of nature (although among Vikings the early-summer gathering had a special significance, for at these they prayed for victory, for the gods' helpful intercession in the raids and campaigns on which they were about to set out). Those who officiated as priests at such ceremonies were already the leaders of their communities, chieftains, *jarls* and kings. In this way,

Detail from the tapestry from Skog Church. The figures probably represent (left to right), one-eyed Odin, with a tree beside him, and carrying an axe; Thor, with his hammer; and Frey, holding fruit or an ear of corn.

A Bronze Age rock carving from Bohuslän, showing a sacred spring wedding.

religious and secular power were united in particular individuals, and only social standing among men permitted a public approach to the gods. Thus the sacred feast and the carousing of a chieftain in his hall were not necessarily separate events, nor would a great man of this kind have either a religious or a secular aspect; his pre-eminence included both spheres, was apparent in both and was in each a function of its existence in the other.

Since these same men were, by virtue of their positions, powerful as both legislators and judges, the making and administration of laws were given an extra weight and significance by the constant involvement of the gods. A community united in its ritual feasting was not less nor in a different way united when assembling for discussion or trial (in Norway, the name *Vébönd* or 'sanctuary ropes' was used to describe the ropes marking off the place of that committee which discussed points of law). The different aspects of life spilled over from one to another in a way which our effort to separate church and state may make it difficult to understand – though in court our witnesses still swear on the Bible in a way no Viking would find unfamiliar.

Worship was not, however, as much a public as a private and household affair. It was not even a matter of revering the great gods, for much of it centred on devotion for one's ancestors, an aspect of paganism strong enough to survive for centuries the conversion to Christianity. It was for this reason that the Underworld and those who inhabited it seem in the Viking mind to have had a dark immediacy sometimes more peremptory than all the bright antics of Asgard's fellowship. Death and preparation of the dead for the new life they had now begun, funeral, burial and remembrance all played a very large part in Scandinavian worship. Nor was this concern entirely benevolent or disinterested – Vikings dreaded the 'dead walkers', a variety of uncontrolled and uncontrollable northern zombies much given to making a malevolent display of their enormous post-mortem strength. Graves were filled with useful objects – everyday utensils and agricultural implements as well as weapons – suggesting that surviving stories of Valhalla are rather impoverished compared with the rich expectations of a full life-in-death which the Vikings actually held.

The ultimate destination of the dead was in any case a matter for divine choice, several of the gods being thought of as calling in their own when the time came, these chosen ones to live in halls other than Odin's Valhalla. And there was, of course, the abode of Hel, reached through a vast cave, a mouth of darkness looming in a place of rock and chasm, the way back then barred by the appalling hound Garm. A gold-roofed bridge provides the only means to cross the River Gjöl (its name means 'howling' or, perhaps less dramatically, 'echoing'); beyond begins the domain proper of Hel, the Underworld's great queen, her name derived from that of her own terrible realm. Its topography is threatening – 'Hills of Darkness', 'Gate of Corpses' – and its inhabitants often monstrous. Fenrir the great wolf waits there, fettered until his brief victory at Ragnarök; it is here that bound Loki struggles in his pain; all about are writhing snakes and dragons vicious and envenomed; Hel's own enormous palace, named 'Sleetcold' according to Snorri, stands there, while everywhere there rise the dead souls' wails, their cries of misery, grief and despair.

There were thus a number of possible futures for the dead, from being bound in their bodies and becoming agencies of doom among the terrified living to sinking into the ice and mists of Niflheim, which some said was the lowest of the worlds; from stepping into the happy boisterousness of Valhalla to joining Freyja in her sometimes orgiastic revels in Folkvang, her own hall. It is clear, therefore, that there was a widely-held conviction in the Viking world that there was a continuity of personal existence in which death was only an episode among others, albeit one of the more important. Birth and battle, death and afterlife – these were all of equal value in the picture the Northman had of himself and his times. However, a person's entry into so new and unknown a condition as was likely to meet him beyond the grave made necessary a ceremony of some complexity. Since it is clear from grave goods that the Vikings expected a continuity not only of personality but also of status, the most complicated funerals were likely to be those of the wealthiest and most powerful men, and here there is much evidence that this was so, not only from the graves themselves, but also from eye-witness account.

Ibn Fadlan was secretary of an embassy from the Caliph of Baghdad to the Bulgars sent to the Middle Volga in 921 and he has described a funeral which, that of a leader among the Rus, is taken to exemplify such ceremonies throughout the world of the Northmen. He tells us that a poor man is laid in a small boat and then burned, but someone wealthy has his wealth divided, a third going to his family, a third to provide drink (which he called *nabidh*) at the funeral, a third to clothe the dead man himself. The drinking and the celebrating, we are told, continued for ten days, there was music and sexual intercourse and so potent was the *nabidh* and

Glass gaming counters found in Viking graves
at Birka in Sweden. They were probably
brought back by raiders from Egypt. BOTTOM
A ship burial site at Blomsholm, in Bohuslän,
Sweden, showing stones grouped round the
prow of the ship. RIGHT A Viking sword,
ceremonially bent as part of the burial ritual.

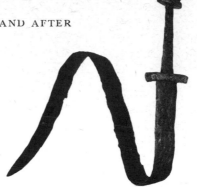

so deeply did the mourners drink of it that sometimes one of them, too, would die.

The man who had died had been buried, perhaps to help in preserving the body
for its cremation. Meanwhile, 'the people of his family ask his young women and
men slaves, "Who among you will die with him?"' A girl responded, her answer
final and irrevocable; it usually was girls, Ibn Fadlan points out, who volunteered
in this way. She was now put in the care of two young women 'who watched over
her and accompanied her everywhere'; clothes for the deceased were prepared,
during which time 'the slave drinks every day and sings, and gives herself over to
pleasure.' The dead man's ship was hauled from the river and made ready,
propped upright on the bank. 'Then they brought a couch and put it on the ship
and covered it with Byzantine brocaded tapestries and with cushions of Byzantine
brocade.' An old woman, 'whom they call the Angel of Death', prepared the bier –
'She is in charge of embalming the dead man and preparing him, and it is she who
kills the girl. The one I saw was strongly built and grim.' The corpse was then
dressed, food was placed about it, and weapons; a dog was killed, and two horses,
two cows, a hen and a cockerel, and these too were placed with the dead man.
Then the doomed slave-girl went into the ten several tents or pavilions of the dead
chieftain's kinsmen, 'and the master of each tent had sexual intercourse with her
and said, "Tell your lord I have done this out of love for him."'

On the day of the funeral, a Friday, the girl was brought to the ship and there
was lifted into the air three times, saying the first time, 'Behold, I see my father and
mother,' the second time, 'I see all my dead relatives seated' and the third time,
'I see my master seated in Paradise, and Paradise is beautiful and green; men and
young boys are with him. He called to me – let me go to him!' When the girl was
finally brought into that last ship-board pavilion where her master lay, six men
went in with her, to have sexual intercourse with her, while outside the rest of the
assembled men beat upon their shields, a heavy, ominous noise one can imagine,
its purpose to cover the girl's last shrieks so that 'the other girls should not be
frightened and thus seek to escape death with their masters'. After the six men had
ended their ritual copulation with the girl, now apparently fuddled by the quanti-
ties of *nabidh* she had been given, 'they laid her by the side of her dead master; two
held her feet and two her hands and the old woman known as the Angel of Death
came in again and put a rope about her neck and gave the crossed ends to two men
to pull. Then she came with a broad-bladed dagger and thrust it repeatedly

between the girl's ribs, while the two men strangled her with the rope until she was dead.'

After this the closest relative of the dead man, naked, approached the ship, carrying a burning brand; he walked with his back to the bier, 'one hand holding the kindled stick and the other covering his anus' and so set fire to the ship, the others then pressing forward, each one with a burning brand of his own. Watching this, someone said to Ibn Fadlan (through his interpreter) that he thought the Arabs were fools, '. . . "because you take those you love and honour most and put them in the earth where insects and worms devour them. We burn them in the blinking of an eyelid, so that they enter Paradise that very moment." ' Within an hour, ship, dead chief, girl slave and grave goods, all had been consumed by the fire. Then the Rus built 'something like a small, round hill, in the middle of which they set up a great post of birch-wood.' On this they wrote the name of the man and the name of their king 'and so went on their way'.

Elements in this description fit what has been found throughout the area of Viking ascendency – the killing of a companion for the dead certainly occurred in Norway, Sweden, Iceland and the Isle of Man; animal bones are common in rediscovered graves, as are weapons and other utensils, and the building of mounds or cairns to mark the sepulchres of the respected was also very frequent. There was, however, another side to this concern for the dead and their fate, a feeling for and a fear of the way they interacted with the living. This, allied to the widespread awe of the gods and their powers, led to the growth of what is always the obverse of a well-established high religion – superstition, sorcery, witchcraft and possession.

One of the most important of these practices, looked at askance by orthodox pagans, was called *seid*. In this a person with shamanistic powers would clamber on a platform and there go into trance, aided in doing so by the rhythmic chanting of his companions. It was believed that in this state the spirit of the shaman became free of its body and was able either directly to affect other people, if necessary even entering them, or else to divine the future by learning of it from other spirits. There were sometimes difficulties when such sorcerers attempted to regain consciousness and a special song would be sung to help them in their struggles. Prevalent, too, were talismans, figurines of gods and goddesses imbued with something of the power of those they represented. Sometimes such amulets were no more than symbols, a circumstance which made the Christian motif more readily acceptable – in fact, a mould has been found in north Jutland from which could be cast both the new cross and the more ancient T-shape of Thor's hammer. It appears that such staples of world-wide witchcraft as the use of images, or the hair-clippings and nail-parings of someone hated, in order to work them some mysterious harm, were widely known and often condemned even before the arrival of Christian missionaries. Divination by various methods other than trance was also commonly practised, local sprites and spirits were often believed in, dreams were thought of great significance and throughout the Viking world runic charms of all kinds worked or failed to work their ambiguous little miracles.

LEFT Thor's hammer; a representation from Kabbara, Scania. BOTTOM A tenth-century silver Thor's hammer from Fossi. The tenth-century crucifix from a grave at Birka (BELOW) executed in filigree and granulation, illustrates how similar Thor's hammer and the Christian cross were.

What one sees, therefore, is a vigorous and far-flung religious life, concerned at one end of the spectrum with such mysteries as Odin's search for knowledge (for his use only; not for him any thoughts of humanity's salvation) and the gods' long awareness of their coming doom, and at the other shot through with the impurities of fear, superstition and magic. Actions of all kinds were seen to have their place in a universe ultimately ordered by the essential, all-pervasive structure of Yggdrasil and the wayward but awe-inspiring machinations of the gods. Death was explained, and in a way which allowed the dead a reality and an authority which reinforced the original conviction of survival. Throughout the Viking area, feasts and festivals, the chanting of kings and noblemen officiating as priests, the collective drinking and ritualistic copulation of the regular gatherings, all helped to build, maintain and increase the sense of community which otherwise feuds and wars might have destroyed. In many ways, the whole Viking endeavour was no more than the active aspect of the Viking beliefs, a version of their own legends, an extension of the ancient sagas, an attempt to force the undivined future into a shape of their own choosing. Considering this, therefore, one is forced to ask why these vigorous, self-sufficient and often self-satisfied northern communities ever succumbed to Christianity at all. This used to be a simpler question to answer than it is today, for to Christian historians the superiority of their own beliefs seemed self-evident. Today, with Christianity itself on the wane, one sees the conversion of the Vikings in a quite different way: what on earth possessed them to jettison a religion which had served them so well for a new preaching totally at odds with almost every aspect of their lives?

It must be understood that the acceptance of a new god into the pantheon presented no great difficulty to the pagan mind – his efficacy was all. A god who seemed useful might have a part to play; it did no harm, in any case, to propitiate him as much as possible. Apart from that, as Northmen travelled across Europe and frequently did not return, but settled where they found land and opportunity, some of the tight homogeneity of Viking society began to unravel. Vikings of the new settlements often developed close ties with their Christian neighbours, sometimes intermarried with them and certainly took from them aspects, however superficial, of their culture. In their ideological isolation, such settlements of erstwhile raiders, however large the territory they occupied, were not well placed to resist the blandishments of the Christianity which surrounded them. Those who travelled between such settlements and the Scandinavian homelands carried the new theological message with them, a message also brought and preached with a heady and effective fervour by a series of great missionaries. Politics, too, played their part, for, as we have seen, conversion to Christianity was often the price Northmen had to pay for the lands they were allowed to annex or the power Christian monarchs were prepared to grant them.

There may also have been reasons for the change less clearly discernible. It may have been, for example, that as the institution of kingship developed and brought with it the hierarchies of at least semi-feudalism, the neo-Platonic hierarchies of the Christian universe became a more acceptable model than that of the old religion, in which, despite the existence of All-Father, Odin, each god had power in his own right, all gods faced the constant struggle with the resentful Giants, the world was ringed and undermined by terrible beasts of evil intent, while the future held the forbidding darkness, the bloodshot gloom, of Ragnarök. The emphasis placed on this laid over the ancient beliefs a heaviness, a blackness, to which Christianity seemed to provide an antidote: love was preached, light, redemption – it was Baldur risen, spring come again and Ragnarök denied. It is almost as though the weight given to that last battle and terrible approaching defeat was too great for people to bear, as though by insisting on its importance those who most desired the perpetuation of the traditional beliefs played the greatest part in paving the way for the success of the new ones.

There may just possibly have been one more element at work in this process of conversion; far to the east, Islam was on the ascendant, Christianity hard-pressed, Asia rampant, Europe threatened. Might it be that some sense of continental solidarity led during those years to the gathering-in of all Europe's forces under the single symbol of the cross? Perhaps that is far-fetched; what is clear is that, from the ninth century onwards, Christianity, now gradually, now swiftly, eroded or overcame the pagan certainties of the Viking world. That such a change was for a long time and in many places more formal than deeply felt or understood is not surprising when one considers how fundamental were the differences between the old creed of warrior or fertility gods and the new one of forgiveness, humility and peace. Nevertheless, such a change occurred, and whether its acceptance was formal or not, it altered for ever the lives of these sinewy raiders, traders, farmers and pioneers of the North.

Often conversion in the early days was no more than a political move, of the same sincerity as the marriages so frequently arranged for diplomatic convenience, to be forgotten and dissolved as necessity changed. In 826 Harald Klak, already thrown out of Denmark by his fatigued and reluctant subjects, made baptism the bribe which brought the Carolingian Louis the Pious to his aid. He and four hundred of his followers were inducted into the Church at a ceremony at the imperial palace at Ingelheim and returned to Denmark in temporary triumph, bringing with them one of the key figures in Scandinavian conversion, Anskar, a monk who became a bishop and, posthumously, a saint. His first mission to Viking lands, however, had little time to put down roots; in 829, the Danes proved themselves as reluctant as before to live with Harald as their leader and threw him out a second time. This must all have been a great disappointment to Louis, who had already sent off Ebo, Archbishop of Reims and papal legate, to fish for converts beyond the Franks' northern frontiers.

After a missionary journey to Sweden, Anskar, in his early thirties, was made Archbishop of Hamburg, sharing with Ebo the papal legacy to the peoples of the north (this designation including Finns and Slavs as well as Scandinavians). It was while he was there that, as has been described, he was forced to flee, sacred relics

The baptism of Harald Bluetooth by Bishop
Poppo, from the twelfth-century altar of
Tamdrup Church, East Jutland.

OPPOSITE Viking jewellery (c. tenth century) used to ornament a woman's dress,
found at Birka: two oval brooches, beads of cornelian, rock crystal and glass, and,
in the centre, a trefoil brooch.

bundled up and in his desperate care, before the politically ferocious horde of Horik the Dane. This was in 845; in 849, now styled Archbishop of Hamburg and Bremen by the mission-conscious Louis, still ambitious for Christianity, he was on his way to Denmark again to find Horik as politically magnanimous as a little earlier he had been aggressive. Permission was granted for the building of a church at the trading centre of Hedeby, where the constant flow of merchants, some of whom were Christian, gave it a congregation and a purpose. When a second Horik came to the throne in 853, however, having hacked his way to power in a not unusual manner over the murdered bodies of cousins and brothers, he closed the church. Anskar hurried back to Denmark to repair the tenuous Christian connection and not only got the church opened again but was even permitted to hang and ring a bell above it. In Ribe, in west Jutland, a second church was opened; thus the new faith established its early footholds among the Danes.

Despite the activity of the missionaries, despite such easy introductions to the new religion as the *primsigning*, a word derived from the Latin *Prima signatio* and meaning little more than the handing out to curious heathens of the cross-amulet as a first sign of their interest, Christianity in Denmark made only indifferent headway until, here as elsewhere, the energetic intervention of a convert king would make it abruptly the standard and acknowledged faith. There was a century of wars and piracies, a kingdom of Swedish overlords, the rise and fall of many improbable heroes, before the renewed mission of one of Anskar's successors in the see of Hamburg and Bremen, Unni, found Gorm the Old in cantankerous charge of Denmark. A pagan in the traditional mould, Gorm is remembered in the sagas not really as one who carved out a kingdom (that was a commonplace of northern heroism), but as the father of Harald *Blátonn* or Bluetooth and of his sister, the slightly sinister Gunnhild, wife of Eirik Bloodaxe, the fancied identification of whose body, as it rose mummified from Danish bogs, so excited nineteenth-century archaeologists.

Harald Bluetooth seems to have become converted as a matter of policy, for his neighbour was a Frankish monarch as anxious as Louis had been a century earlier to see Denmark Christian. Otto the Great, whose championship of the faith also had its political side, seems to have sent a bishop named Poppo as a missionary to Harald's Court. A confusion of Ottos in the minds of chroniclers places now, in the 960s, battles which were to take place later, ascribing Harald's conversion to the consequences of defeat by the forces of the Holy Roman Empire – 'thereafter', Snorri recounts, 'King Harald allowed himself to be baptized, and also the whole Danish army.' Adam of Bremen has a similar tale to tell, while the Saxon Widukind describes a crucial theological debate in which Harald challenged Poppo to prove his faith by ordeal, the imperturbable missionary then demonstrating the superiority of Jesus by removing his hand undamaged from a white-hot iron glove.

Whatever the details, Harold's acceptance of Poppo's preaching appeased the pious Otto, who turned to other imperial matters, such as the spreading of his rule

OPPOSITE Tenth-century gilt-bronze weather vane from Soderala, Hälsingland. Before its years on a church tower, it flew on the prow of a long ship.

through northern Italy, leaving Harald free to pursue his own similar ambitions in Norway and Sweden. That his conversion was seen by both Harald and Otto, however, as an act of homage by the lesser to the greater monarch was confirmed when, in 973, the Dane was among those kings who bowed before the imperial throne at Quedlingburg.

When the first Otto, however, was succeeded by the second, Harald was soon busily nibbling at the edges of his domains. It was at this time, therefore, that an Otto was forced to take effective retaliatory action and it was in the wake of these successes and under the pressure they produced that Harald at last saw to it that the whole of Denmark should become a Christian state. In the end this may have helped to lose him his throne, for his son, Svein Forkbeard (later to be, briefly, king of England), found no difficulty in gathering allies against his father and some of these may well have been long-affronted pagans. The work of conversion, however, once under way, was not to be turned back. Svein himself seems to have understood quite clearly that Christianity was, as it were, the ideological wave of the future, that paganism meant isolation; his son, Knut, was a practising Christian, active and devout, a bridge between the long-established Church of his English domains and the still-developing Christianity of Denmark. The new faith had come to stay, its subtle trinity worshipped everywhere in place of the old, multi-headed pantheon of Asgard.

Norway, the history of which intertwines with that of Denmark, also needed the intervention of strong men and politics more than that of the missionaries to become totally Christian. There were one or two earlier and abortive attempts at this − Hakon the Good, Athelstan's foster-son and Christian in the English fashion when he arrived to take over Eirik Bloodaxe's forfeited throne, would almost certainly have liked to see Norway change to the new faith. Instead, it was he who changed, understanding that those about him were not ready for conversion and that to rule them he and they needed to share a single faith. His subsequent reign does much to prove that magnanimity, generosity and a concern for justice were not the virtues exclusively of Christian monarchs − although it may be argued that his early training and beliefs contributed to his style as ruler.

The sons of Eirik Bloodaxe and the ambitious Gunnhild eventually ousted Hakon; the eldest of the five brothers, Harald Greycloak, became king. He was Christian and seems to have been zealous in his faith − too much so, perhaps, for his own good, for it is likely that his despoliation of the pagan holy places led to the fervent and profound anger of those who were devout in their ancient beliefs. This may have been among the reasons for his being trapped and killed in unexpected battle in north-east Jutland − 'He himself advanced the foremost of his troop, hewing down on each side,' Snorri assures us, but his bravery had no reward and Norway was partitioned, some coming under the direct rule of Harald Bluetooth, the rest being held under the Danish king's suzerainty by the *jarl* of Hladir. This man, Hakon, effective ruler of western Norway, worked as hard to restore paganism as Harald Greycloak and his brothers had to destroy it. It must have seemed ironic to hard-pressed missionaries that the bleak winters and light harvests which had followed the attempt to make Norway Christian now gave way to rich summers and heavy, profitable harvests – Thor the Thunder-god, patron of farmers, was not to go under without a fight.

In the ninth century, Harald Fairhair had been a notable ruler in Norway, perhaps the first to consolidate royal power there, although building on foundations laid by that redoubtable warrior Halfdan the Black; now, some 130 years later, a new king of his line was to thrust his way to power in that same craggy country. His arrival would have an effect on the spread of Christianity there. Olaf Tryggvesson, apparently surviving massacre and the formidable enmity of Gunnhild and her brood, surviving constant flight and even slavery in Esthonia, had eventually passed his late childhood and early manhood under the secure protection of a relative in Novgorod. At the age of eighteen he had gone *á viking* – as Snorri puts it, 'Olaf then made ready, went on board, and set out to sea in the Baltic.' He won booty, renown and a wife. Later, as we have seen, he fought with the Danish Svein Forkbeard in England, lending his sword for a while to that ambitious man's attempt to overthrow the uncertain Æthelred; he raided widely throughout the British Isles, carried himself everywhere with the bearing of a hero, a born leader – and somewhere during this period was converted to the Christian faith.

According to Snorri, not one to avoid a good story in the interests of mere fact, this conversion took place in the Scilly Isles, where a hermit, reputed to be able to foretell the future, warned Olaf that he would be wounded, although this was intertwined with better news – he would become 'a renowned king' and do great things, many of them for Christianity; and upon recovering from his wounds, he would begin by having himself baptized. When Olaf was duly wounded in a skirmish, precisely as the old man had predicted, Olaf naturally wanted to know how he had gained his powers. 'The hermit replied that the Christians' God himself let him know all he desired'; impressed, Olaf had himself baptized forthwith. The *Anglo-Saxon Chronicle*, on the other hand, tells of Olaf's being conducted 'with great ceremony to the king at Andover, and the king stood sponsor for him at his confirmation, and gave him royal gifts', in response to which Olaf gave his word 'that he would never come to England as an enemy again' – a promise given considerable weight by a Danegeld payment of sixteen thousand silver pounds and in the event faithfully kept.

In Norway, Hakon, that *jarl* of Hladir who had been *de facto* ruler there since Harald Bluetooth had partitioned the country, had fallen upon old age and unpopularity, despite a just and not dishonourable governorship. Thus, when there landed at the southern entry to the Hardangerfjord a young leader, renowned and heroic, Harald Fairhair's great-grandson, already triumphant overseas and now rich, come with his ships and his men to claim the throne of Norway, Hakon was left without resources. Everywhere men flocked to Olaf Tryggvesson; Hakon, it is said, had his throat cut by his own body-servant, Kark, while he lay in semi-hiding under the roof of his mistress. At Trondheim the *thing* accepted Olaf; to the south, those lands which had been under the Danish Crown and Harald Bluetooth now seem also to have opted for Olaf and their Norwegian identity. Exultant, determined to strike for the faith he had so recently embraced, it must have seemed to Olaf that his life had become a cornucopia from which wonder after fertile wonder might be extracted.

It should perhaps have been so – Olaf, young, girded in strength and bright with fame, his youth, his upbringing, his campaigns and marriages the raw material of legend, seems to have been the Viking dream made flesh, the epitome of that vigorous self-image which had made a thousand heroes clamber into their longships in the quest for wealth, land, title and fulfilment. Alas, within five years that brightness, dimming, was to flicker a last and useless time and then go out for ever. It is not really clear what brought him down; it is likely to have been, as it had with Harald Greycloak, the mesmerized zeal with which he approached the business of converting his heathen subjects. This was not calculated to bring him the loyalty of those who had doubted him, or to keep that of those who had welcomed him. 'Early in spring,' Snorri tells us of the year 997, 'King Olaf set out from Viken with a great force westwards to Agder, and proclaimed that every man should be baptized. And so the people received Christianity, for nobody dared oppose the King's will wherever he went.'

Such tactics neither made true converts nor safeguarded the kingdom; they failed therefore at both the religious and the secular level. Olaf's resultant isolation was no position for a ruler in those days, when only a secure power-base protected kings from greedy neighbours and ambitious rivals. And there were both to plague the Norwegian king – in Sweden, a new king had consolidated that country, Olaf Sköttkonung, a Swede who had extended his overlordship to include the neighbouring and hitherto independent, if subservient, Gauts; in Denmark, Svein Forkbeard cast about for ways to widen his domains and, it cannot be doubted, burned with resentment over the loss of those Norwegian provinces which, so recently under the Danish Crown, had opted for Olaf Tryggvesson at their first opportunity; finally, there was Eirik, the dispossessed *jarl* of Hladir, Hakon's son and a man whose intelligent advice to both Svein and Knut would give him in the end great status in the new Viking kingdom of England.

This confederation it was which brought Olaf down at last, waylaying him at sea somewhere near Hälsinborg as he was sailing home from what may have been an attempt to recruit an ally in his wife's former husband, Boleslav the Pole, King of Wendland. Perhaps he was betrayed, led into a trap, abandoned; what seems certain is that he was outnumbered, surprised, immediately valiant, eventually defeated. The story is that he leaped overboard, evading those determined to catch him, his tall figure falling, cloaked, mailed, gleaming, into the dark water, the world about him a shout of triumph, a wail of defeat, his last sight perhaps that of stretched spears, raised swords, axes, grey metal gleaming as dull as northern skies, then the sea he had so often mastered closing about him, his body already

The Jelling Stone. Jelling, in Jutland, was the site of the Danish royal cemetery. Harald Bluetooth set up this stone in memory of his parents, probably between 983 and 985, and it bears the earliest known Scandinavian representation of the Crucifixion.

sinking, gliding through those layers of shifting cold, out of the sight of men and into legend. For inevitably the legend arose – he had swum to safety, casting off his coat of mail as he went, had been picked up and taken to the safety of Wendland, had been seen, years later, as a pilgrim in the Holy Land, as a monk in Syria, an anchorite in Greece. The historically certain thing is that he disappeared that day, and Norway was altered in consequence.

Svein Forkbeard took a part, Olaf of Sweden was recognized as overlord of another, *Jarl* Eirik ruled the rest; thus Norway, once more partitioned. Christianity, meanwhile, formally widespread, but with its roots neither deep nor established, continued its struggle there. Paganism had lost its official supremacy and it is proof that Olaf Tryggvesson had been at least partly in sympathy with the true movements of his times that it recovered neither its former position nor its traditional vigour. His forced and formal conversions had had the effect of giving his country at least a Christian veneer. It is important to remember that for many people all religion was entirely a formal matter, a question of ceremony, incantation and ritual. Faith was not distinct from magic, words of prayer and names of gods were powerful in themselves, mystery was automatic when the right process was learned and repeated, the universe was a machine motivated in ways permitting the participation of the learned, the wise and the ordained. Thus the new rituals and ceremonies, once they were believed to permit access to transcendental forces, could be accepted, adopted and sedulously followed – without altering for a moment the essential cast of mind of the devotee. Seen in this way, Olaf Tryggvesson's effort, finally self-destructive though it proved, responded to his people's needs and may even be considered successful. Certainly those who wrote about him at the time, or during the next two hundred years (with the exception of Adam of Bremen who, deploring his adherence to English teachings in preference to the pure Roman dogma dispensed at his own cathedral, condemned him as a sorcerer and fortune-teller), seem agreed that the true arrival of the Church, not only in Norway but elsewhere in the Scandinavian world, can be said to have occurred during Olaf's reign.

It needed a second Olaf, however, to consolidate his work, one who had also been busy in England and one who was also to come to an unpleasant end. This was Olaf Haraldsson, known as the Stout, who took advantage of Denmark's English involvement to seize for himself the throne of Norway. His claim too was bolstered by his belonging to the House of Harald Fairhair and in 1016 most of Norway accepted it. Olaf, who had been baptized in Normandy some three years earlier, seems to have taken the missionary side of his work with some seriousness. Later, this was to seem pious and dedicated on his part, but these missionary kings knew their politics: the common and comfortable rule was that as the king went, so went the people, and if they did not the implications of their refusal were wider than the merely theological. Thus a ruler's energetic advocacy of the Christian faith was often dictated not only by a desire to prove his own allegiance to Jesus but also by a desire to prove his subjects' allegiance to him.

In terms of what its people believed, Norway was a patchwork kingdom. As Snorri points out, 'In the upper ends of the valleys, and in the habitations among the fjelds, the greater part of the people were heathen; for when the common man is left to himself, the faith he has been taught in his childhood is that which has the strongest hold over his inclination. But the King threatened the most violent proceedings against great and small who, after the King's message, would not adopt Christianity.' This attitude of belligerent proselytizing was in some ways at variance with another of Olaf's preoccupations, one which was the foundation of his proper claim to be a good and enlightened king – his respect for the rule of law. In this he showed the incorruptibility of the most ideal judge allied to the zeal of an eager legislator; he worked from the precedents laid down by Hakon the Good, but added, deleted or amended as his own intelligence dictated.

By introducing legal standards which stretched without variation throughout the country, he began the necessary undermining of the great and mighty, whose legal arguments had been conducted largely with the sword-arm, while at the same time strengthening another strand in the tapestry of nationalism which time and circumstance had been busily weaving over the years. He reinforced this by using as his representatives not so much the great *jarls*, rulers of whole localities with the state and status of minor kings, but rather what might be termed the squirearchy, the farmers of good birth and solid standing who made up the bulk of the land-owning class. It is an unhappy fact that the enemies he made himself among the princes would not in the end be counter-balanced by the friends he made among the farmers.

His most important labours, however, were for the Christian faith, their most tangible results the establishment of a state Church. This, too, was a matter of law, at least on the one hand; on the other, there remained the Mafia methods of the earlier Olaf Tryggvesson, a matter of sudden descents, imprisonment, torture, the crippling or even blinding of those unswerving in their devotion to Thor and Odin, and the vigorous despoliation of those gods' holy places. However, Church law, introduced like the secular code through the *things*, soon permeated the country, supported by a programme of church building which placed some outpost of the faith within reach of almost all the population. Because of the successes of Knut, the traditional Danish rival, in England, it was to the archiepiscopal see in Bremen that Olaf turned for help and advice, sending his chosen adviser in religious matters, Grimkel, and many others to be consecrated in that cathedral on the German shore.

It was, in the end, his rivalry with Knut and the Danes that brought him down. He made alliance with Sweden; in company with Onund, Olaf of Sweden's son, he decided to attack Denmark. Knut, however, his English kingdom consolidated, saw that he could no longer rely on rivalry between Norway and Sweden for the safety of his Scandinavian frontiers, turned on Olaf with his usual vigour – and at once discovered that he had friends. Thorir Hound, Erling Skjalgsson, Einar Thambarskelfir – such were the names in Knut's roster of his suborned. Olaf of

Norway, his dreams of invasion dwindling to the reality of aimless skirmish, then to thoughts of retreat, found himself finally beset when Knut, with a great fleet, arrived off his coasts in 1028. Sweden had at least for the moment prudently disengaged herself from her neighbour's predicament; the affronted aristocrats and, it may be, the coerced ex-heathens flocked to Knut; everywhere the Dane was accepted and in some places welcomed with great warmth; Olaf fled, and once more a *jarl* of Hladir, Hakon Eiriksson, was set over Norway as a Danish regent.

In Viking times more than any others, perhaps, it was individual mortality which altered history. *Jarl* Hakon died, drowned as befitted a Northman, in faraway Pentland Firth; there were claimants to his regency, Knut's son Svein arrived to consolidate in his own person his father's rulership – and from the Court of Yaroslav in distant Russia, travelling in haste to make what he could of his enemies' confusion, there came the deposed Olaf, intent on regaining what he considered his own. He had 240 men with him, some 480 were loaned him by the Swedish king, a number of others rallied to him, adventurers, the riff-raff of a turbulent world, half mercenaries, half bandits, those disaffected now with the rule of the Danish Knut, old friends, ambitious gamblers – a motley army of well under four thousand spears, those who wielded them largely heathen, though ironically gathered under the banner of a king committed to the triumph of Christianity. Against these stood what was said to be the largest army ever

A Viking baptismal stone at the church of
Norum in West Sweden. It shows the legendary
hero Gunnar in a snake pit, one of the many
trials he faced.

gathered in Norway, apparently outnumbering Olaf's force by something like
four-to-one. Undaunted, Olaf brought within his shield-wall the *skálds* who, he
said, would thus be able to witness at first hand the remarkable triumph about
which they would later have to sing; what these poets thought of their situation,
elevated from the re-telling to the making of history, they mostly did not survive to
record (although, to be fair, the fighting poet was no strange figure in Viking tradition). High summer, then, the year 1030, the place Stiklarstadir in the Tröndelag,
and the fighting went as it had to, given the forces involved. Olaf's army broke too
swiftly even for the traditional heroics – Snorri, a man reverential to Olaf, says
only that 'the battle began before half-past one, and before three the King fell.'
There was, perhaps, an eclipse that day – though either it or the battle may have
been nudged along the calendar by chroniclers who felt their conjunction made for
more acceptable drama – and if there was, it will have been appropriate, for the
death of Olaf was no more than a temporary darkness over his fame, a beginning
more than an end.

Almost at once, it seems, people began to speak of the miracles worked by Olaf
slain; on that same evening of battle the blood of his hidden body gave back the
sight to a passing blind man, and from then on his benevolent spirit seems never to
have settled to its heavenly rest. There is no surprise in learning that a year later
his uncorrupted body was lifted from its grave, to be reburied in the church at
Nidaros he had himself founded to the honour of St Clement twenty years earlier,
nor in realizing how soon after his death his protégé Grimkel proclaimed him too a
full-blown saint. It is more surprising to discover how vigorous this sanctity
proved, how widespread its reputation became, how much it did to give Norway
that national identity Olaf's law-making had already helped to establish and how
firmly it continues to this day to underlie Norwegian Christianity. As the country's
patron saint, Olaf has had a rule serene, unrivalled and likely to continue at least
as long as Christianity itself.

In Sweden, as in Denmark, it is Anskar who stands at the beginnings of the
Christian tradition, arriving there from Denmark in 829 after a journey during
which pirates almost managed to take his life and that of Witmar, his companion.
It was on foot, therefore, without baggage, without even his books and psalters,
that he arrived at that great trading centre, Birka. The king, Björn, aware like all
the Scandinavians of the power of Anskar's Carolingian patron, received him with

A scene from the Sigurd Saga carved on a rock
in Sweden. The dragon Fafnir, which frames
the carving, is slain by the legendary hero,
Sigurd, both for its knowledge and the gold
it guarded.

politeness, permitted him to preach and observed with equanimity the conversion
of Hergeir, Birka's town prefect. With this local leader's help, a church was built
which probably, like the one at Hedeby, catered for the Christians among the
itinerant traders who crowded the streets and marts of the town, as well as standing
central to a slightly circumspect if sincere missionary effort.

It was Olaf Sköttkonung, however, who made the first countrywide attempt at
converting the Swedes (his name, which has been translated as 'Tax-king', suggests however that it was not for his piety that his people singled him out).
Baptized himself in 1008, he made a violent foray against the great shrine of
paganism in Uppsala; his lack of success was made plain by the description of it
Adam of Bremen was later to write. The aristocratic guardians of tradition were
too strong to be robbed of their faith by any such frontal attack. It was, instead, the
King who recoiled, setting himself up in Västergötland where, spiritually bas-
tioned by the operation of devout missionaries come from England to spread their
version of the Word, he could leave both the conservatively devout and the
devoutly conservative to their heathen devices. Within a century, however, even
that ancient centre of prayer and sacrifice, its allegiance to the Æsir centuries old,
had changed the direction of its faith (if not its function or its status) and accepted
the complex unity of the Christian trinity in place of the anarchy of gods and
heroes previously worshipped there. And within the next hundred years, Sweden
too would have its sainted monarch to rival Olaf of Norway and the later Knut of
Denmark – Eirik Jedvardsson, canonized for his bloody work in beating with the
keen edge of sword and axe the gentle worship of Jesus into the heads of recalcitrant Finns.

Far to the east, the great Vladimir of Kiev at the end of the tenth century
dragged his people into the incense-clouded, gold-shot Christianity of Byzantium;
in the west, missionary bishops built their turf-roofed churches in Iceland, in
Greenland, even perhaps in faraway Vinland, their prayers there rising into a
heaven not prepared to hear them for another four centuries; thus throughout the
Viking world the old gods were abandoned, and with them the isolation and something of the special unity of Northmen. Losing that, they gained an ethical structure which laid down clear rewards for acceptable conduct, clear punishments for
sin. It was as if a declaration had been made that the virtue of courage was no longer
enough; humanity, even in the turbulent north, needed more emphatic guidance.

Conduct may not have altered much, but the way people thought about conduct did. Crime could be less self-evidently explained away by calling upon self-interest; law was given a transcendental and therefore extremely powerful basis. Such institutions as slavery were undermined by a new uneasiness about the importance of every individual endowed with a soul and so potentially in touch with God. To work for rather than against others was seen as worth while, clearing as it did the difficult path to Heaven, and if not everybody undertook good works almost everybody could see where the goodness lay in such works as were undertaken. The coming of Christianity did not end the Viking age – far from it – but it altered the consciousness of these Scandinavian marauders, giving them new incentives on the one hand, taking from them old ones on the other. It was certainly an indication that the emphasis had swung from raiding to settlement, from loose and temporary confederations of equals to the settled hierarchies of kingdoms, from recourse to the sword to recourse to the law, from the conviction that one could carve out for oneself on the battlefield a place in the eternity of Valhalla to the hope that one might apply through one's manifest virtues for a place in the eternity of Heaven. Violence did not abate, ambition was not placed on leash, adventure did not end because mitred bishops sang their Masses in Hedeby and Uppsala. But the world was no longer a treasure casket which any muscular young man with a sword, trusted companions and an oar in a longship had the right to rifle – the days of primal wildness were gone for ever.

Rock carvings of ships like those used by the
Vikings, found at Tune, Østfold.

6 THE BYZANTINE ADVENTURE

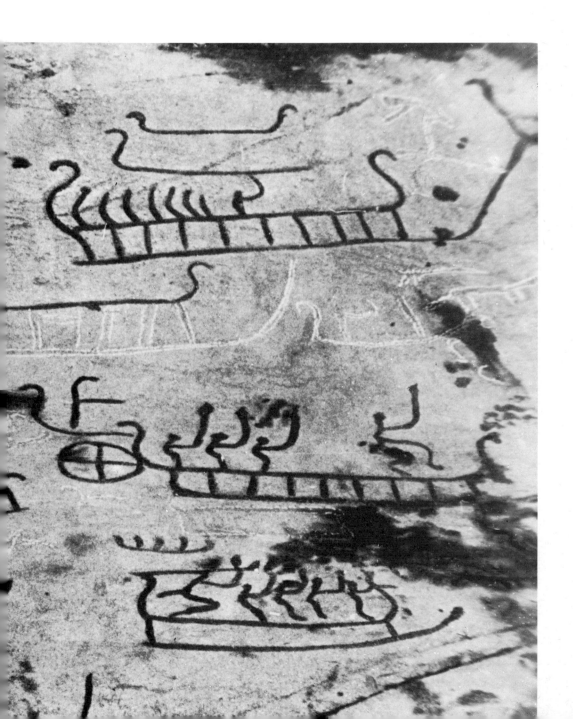

It was in 911 or early the following year that 'We of the Rus: Karli, Ingeld, Farlof, Vermud, Rulov, Gody, Ruald, Karn, Frelav, Aktevu, Truan, Lidul, Fost, Stemid', representatives of 'Oleg, great prince of the Rus', signed the treaty 'for the maintaining and proclamation of the long-standing friendship between Greeks and Rus' which recognized the reality of Rus power along the Dnieper trading route. It implied a diplomatic acceptance of equality between Byzantium and Russian Kiev which was later to beguile these transplanted Northmen with ideas of impossible conquest, but it was an act of recognition nevertheless of the status and importance of the great Oleg and his people.

It must not be thought, however, that the eastern Vikings had entered a new phase of luxurious city living. An Arab traveller, the geographer Ibn Rustah, describes Rus of about this period living in unhealthy, marshy conditions on an island in a lake. They had no land of their own to cultivate, he says, but brought all their food in from surrounding Slavonic communities. It was a territory rich in furs, an area, too, which supplied many of the slaves who still did the heavy work of Europe. The Vikings pursued both, travelling widely to trade, as Ibn Rustah says, and keeping their money in special belts. He comments on their exquisite clothes, on the gold armbands worn by the men, on their many towns. He comments on their loyalty to each other – 'They do not split up, but stand as one man against their enemies until they have conquered them' – and on their legal system – 'If one has a complaint against another, he takes him up before the prince'; single combat decided those conflicts which the prince's wisdom failed to solve. Fathers, he says, left their sons no legacy but a weapon, telling them, 'You own nothing but what you can get for yourself with this sword.' He talks of their religion, which here as elsewhere involved sacrifice by hanging, the creatures offered including men and women. He describes the insecurity of their lives, a man not being able to slip away into some nearby wilderness even to defecate without taking an armed guard with him. Such was Viking existence during the early decades of the tenth century in so renowned a centre as Novgorod, considered the most likely scene of these descriptions.

Mysterious Oleg died. He had been a great figure, prince and founder of the state, leader, focus for legend and myth, obscured for us by the impossibilities and contradictions of the chronicles, his irrefutable monument the existence of Kiev itself. An Igor succeeded him, son of the equally mysterious Rurik who had led

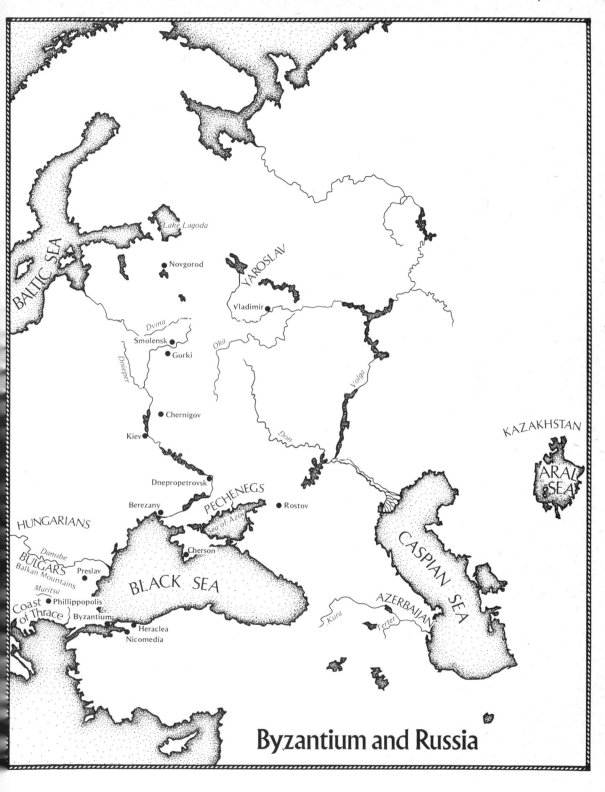

Byzantium and Russia

the Rus eastwards in the previous generation. (There was a Rorik, brother of that Harald Klak who had tried to take the Danish throne with the aid of Carolingian Louis and the Christian faith; he had held land in Jutland some seventy years earlier – can he, given the span of years, really have been Russia's pioneering Rurik and this Igor's father?) Some twenty years after his accession to the throne, some ancient Viking itch – dormant or until then kept appeased by constant conflict with the predatory Pechenegs – or perhaps some insult, some dispute, brought Igor to the determination to attack Byzantium.

Again the moment was well-chosen – the Byzantine army was fighting in Armenia, the navy was sailing the Aegean, frustrating Muslim flotillas. A Rus fleet crossed the Black Sea, its size said by Greek chroniclers to have been vast, their figures of ten thousand ships and more a tribute to terror rather than accuracy; Liudprand of Cremona puts the number at a thousand and so probably brings the attack into truer proportion. The Emperor, Romanus I Lecapenus, put his defences into the hands of his ministers, Theophanes and John Curcuas, the latter already a legend for his exploits against the expanding might of Arabian Islam. Into fifteen old hulks they placed the equipment necessary for the use of that Byzantine secret weapon, the famous 'Greek fire' coveted by so many ambitious princes (its secret probably crude petroleum, expressed under pressure and ignited).

Under Theophanes these battered-looking but threatening old ships sailed out and, near the east coast of the Bosporus, came across Igor's massed fleet. One may imagine the amazement, perhaps even the laughter, which greeted this patchwork flotilla as Vikings, hardened by battle and sea-voyage, turned the prows of their ships hungrily towards what they must have assumed a negligible enemy. But war-cry shrilled to scream, confidence thinned to amazement, then to terror, attack disintegrated, as the world turned black and purple with flame, the slow Byzantine ships vomiting out their smoking death as below them the swift galleys of the Russians swung away into confusion, all their precise seamanship now shrivelled in this awe-inspiring heat. Sleek hulls, tall masts, furled sails, all burst into flickering flower; men blazed, flesh glistening, or flung themselves into the clear but deadly water, to sink there under the weight of armour or of pain. The desperate survivors scrambled for the open sea.

All this, however, was only a foretaste of what Igor's forces would have to suffer. Driven back, they rallied and, recalling Viking traditions, began to raid the southern coasts of the Black Sea, ravaging ports and settlements on the shores of Bithynia and Paphlagonia. They were not the only ones, however, who could rally their forces at need; from Byzantium there now emerged a vengeful force under Theophanes. Having scoured Bithynia, from Nicomedia to Heraclea, the Vikings were ready to withdraw, their earlier set-back soothed by the universal balm of booty. Were they singing, perhaps, when abruptly the great Byzantine fleet appeared on their horizons? They must have thought themselves clear, safely on their homeward journey, their adventure certain after all to show a profit, when

Objects brought back from the Middle East by
Vikings: LEFT A bronze Arabian brazier found
at Hamrånge, Gästrikland. ABOVE Tenth-
century bronze flask, Persian in form, found at
Aska, Östergötland.

once more, out-numbered now as well as out-manœuvered, their escape cut off,
they had to face that dreadful fire. Like some appalling and cosmic fury, the flung
flames pursued them; trapped, they shrivelled, insect-black, in a brightness not of
their choosing. Later, baldly, their chroniclers were to write, 'The Greeks have
something which is like lightning from heaven and, discharging it, they set us on
fire.'

Igor escaped; few others managed as much. Determined on revenge, he gathered
new armies, recruiting from as far away as Sweden, bringing in Slavonic levies and
accepting as allies the Pechenegs with whom he had fought for so long. With a new
and enormous fleet, supported now by cavalry, he set out again, optimistic, perhaps brash, in 944. 'Behold, the Russians are coming in countless ships, and their
ships have covered the sea'; thus the dispatch of the governor of Cherson, a salt-
producing town on the Crimean coast, warning the Byzantine emperor of Igor's
impending arrival. The Russians' optimism may have been matched by Byzantine pessimism; certainly Romanus now decided that diplomacy should continue
war by other means.

Igor, placated by gifts, turned back to Kiev, while his Pecheneg allies, eager to

plunder someone and not particular about whom it should be, swung north-
eastwards with everyone's blessing to ravage the lands of the Bulgars. Plenipo-
tentiaries from Byzantium now hammered out with Igor's representative a new
treaty, one notably less respectful of Russian demands than the earlier one had
been. Both the numbers of merchants who could enter the city at a time and the
amount of silk they might take out with them when they left were limited, and they
would henceforth have to pay duty on what they carried away. Every autumn they
had to leave their special quarters in the outskirts of Constantinople, but would be
supplied free for their return journey to Kiev with a month's provisions. In return
for these mild trading concessions, Igor agreed to protect Cherson and its fisheries
from the depredations not only of the Bulgars but also of his own people. In 945,
fifty Rus notables signed this treaty, the names now not as simply Nordic as they
had been three decades earlier, but many of them probably of Slavonic origin; the
Scandinavian character of the Rus was slowly being eroded. That the state they
had founded was of significance, however, was proved by the fact that Byzantium
took the care to draw up this treaty at all – the trade route along the Dnieper was
still of great importance to the Greeks and whoever controlled it they took
seriously.

A description of the Kiev of this time, and of the people who inhabited it, comes
to us from the hand of what must be one of the most eminent chroniclers of the
period – Constantine VII Porphyrogenitus, Emperor of Byzantium. He was partly
the writer and wholly the editor of a compilation known to us as the *De Adminis-
trando Imperio*, a survey of the empire's history and geography, of the empire's
neighbours and how best to manage relations with them, and including in Chapter
42 a description of the world northward from the imperial borders. Intended as a
text-book for the Emperor's son, it has become one of those fortuitously rich mines
into which historians disappear to emerge years later, pale from lack of sunlight,
their chosen nugget triumphantly in hand.

Kiev stood on the west bank of the Dnieper, high enough to avoid danger from
the spring floods which widen the river from under half a mile to over six. During
the winter, the Rus who were based there travelled through the far-flung lands of
their vassal neighbours, collecting from these Slavonic tribes the stipulated tribute,
a protection racket producing profits of money, furs and slaves. With the spring
and the consequent thaw, they would return to Kiev, where there gathered now
the trading fleets of the north, boats come down-river from Novgorod, from
Smolensk, from Chernigov and Visgorod. In June, with the waters of the river
receding, the collected fleet would move down to Vitichev to be taxed, setting off a
day or so later to face in convoy the hazards of the rapids and the assaults and
ambushes of Pecheneg pirates. Significantly, the Emperor when describing the
cataracts (near modern Dnepropetrovsk) gives us their names both in the
Scandinavian form and in their Slavonic equivalents, suggesting a bi-polarity of
language usual between overlords and subjects. At St Gregor's Island, where an
enormous oak tree may have had religious significance (the island was St Gregor's

for the Byzantines – for the Rus it was certainly another's), a sacrifice was offered before the fleet moved on to Berezany, an island where a man named Grani once cut runes into a stone to commemorate a comrade, unluckily dead, this Karl's memorial becoming for us the most easterly on which Nordic runes have ever been discovered. And from Berezany, Constantinople beckoned, great market of two continents, a golden beacon calling to it fleet and caravan from every accessible corner of the world.

Arabian authors also described the Rus, as we have seen, Ibn Fadlan saying he had never beheld men of the size of these river-travellers, nor with such ruddy complexions, each one wearing a cloak and bearing sword, axe and knife as an armoury constantly to hand. Glass beads, he says, were greatly prized by the women and would be bought for high prices, thus foreshadowing the experiences of other travellers in a later world's distant places. That these people had not forgotten their Viking traditions is clear from the reports, rumours and fantasies of piracy and rapine which clutter their reputation.

According to the traveller Mas'udi, some five hundred Rus ships sailed across the Sea of Azov at some time around the year 914, and on up the River Don. They then spent a week dragging their ships across to where the Volga flows down to the Caspian Sea. Following this river, they sailed on southward from its mouth to attack the Persian coast, westward to savage a defenceless Azerbaijan. They made the Baku area their storm centre and from there, relentless as a tornado, whirled through a defenceless country plundering, murdering and, we are told, taking as prisoners children whom they could later sell as slaves. The Caspian, however, though large, is finite, no more than a great lake; when the people on its shores decided to face their tormenters together, the Vikings' future closed in. Muslims and Christians united into an army, its spearhead those fearsome and dangerous Jewish converts, the Khazars; after a three-day battle near the mouth of the Volga the Rus fleet was smashed. Those who survived were now too small a band to guarantee their own safety and before they could reach the familiar waters of the Black Sea, they too had been overtaken by enemies new and old. None, it is said, lived to return to their homeland.

More successful, perhaps, was a raiding party some thirty years later which sailed two hundred miles up the River Kura, then up its tributary, the Terter, to smash its way at last into the town of Berda, capital of Arran, over the bodies of five thousand troops sent out to stop them. Murder, there as elsewhere, was the Viking fashion; in streets littered with corpses, the rampaging Rus ransacked the white houses, the few survivors listening terrified in shadow and hiding-place to their laughter, their shouted boasts, the crash of axe and sword-blade as the caskets of the frugal were opened, or the skulls of the recalcitrant. Then sickness came, to hand these conquerors as implacable a death as they had offered others; outside the town, the provincial governor rode at the head of thirty thousand men. There were skirmishes, battles begun and broken off, none decisive in themselves but between them enough to give the weakened Rus their warning. They left, dragging

rich plunder with them; the local inhabitants, however, did not go without reward, for on their return they dug up those Rus warriors whom dysentery had
killed and robbed them of the fine weapons which, there perhaps more than elsewhere, their companions had felt they would need.

In Kiev itself, Igor died. His son succeeded him, a boy named Svyatoslav – the
name an indication of how the steady pressure of the majority Slavonic culture
was now beginning to erode Rus self-sufficiency. It was the prince's mother, however, the Princess Olga, who ruled Kiev as regent while the boy grew up. She died
a Christian, though she seems not to have been born one, and in this too an important change becomes apparent. Christianity, in a people so closely linked to
Byzantium, had long ago begun its penetration, but there is little evidence that
until this period it had made much headway. Now, in 957, Olga paid an official
visit to Constantinople and while there, it is said, was baptized.

It is in another of the interesting compilations made by Constantine VII
Porphyrogenitus, his *Book of Ceremonies*, that we learn most about this visit with
its great feasts, its sumptuous but official hospitality, its forbidding protocol. The
Russians were introduced, strictly in order of rank, Olga therefore the last, rising
through hierarchies of courtiers and officials like some stately balloon through

Coloured and ornamented beads of glass
alternating with silver and gold, typical of the
jewellery favoured by Viking women.

nodding successions of clouds. She progressed past vistas of grandeur and a
promenade of gardens, to arrive at last before a dais covered in purple silk where,
standing before two golden thrones, Constantine and Helen, his Empress, awaited
her. There was music, there were exchanges of elaborate courtesies; later, imperial
children appeared, there was some relaxation; Olga was invited by Constantine to
speak of whatever she wished. Formality returned with the prepared banquet, the
imperial couple now on their thrones, Olga beside them. 'When the other princesses had been introduced in order of rank by the master of ceremonies, and when
they had bowed to the ground, the Princess inclined her head slightly and sat down
at the place where she stood. . . .' In the hierarchy of the imperial Court, only
those in the six highest ranks were permitted the privilege of sharing the Emperor's
table. Later, Olga received as a present the sum of five hundred *miliarenses*, handed
to her on a golden plate, and the rest of her party received gifts in proportion,
down to the eighteen servant girls who were each given eight *miliarenses*. It was
apparently during this visit that Olga was christened, the ceremony guided by the
Patriarch of Byzantium, she herself taking as her baptismal name that of her
hostess, the Empress Helen.

It is not clear whether it was diplomatic convenience or missionary zeal which
dictated this sumptuous reception for the widow of an unruly prince, beaten back
from the gates of Constantinople less than twenty years before. In either event,
little of what was desired can have been unequivocally attained. Olga, returning,
found that she could not impose her newly accepted religion on her subjects – not
even with the aid of a German bishop, himself a sort of walking ecclesiastical snub
to Constantine and his proselytizing energies. Her envoys at the Court of Otto I
asked for him to be sent to Kiev in 959, a scant two years after her ceremonial entry
into the Eastern Church; when he arrived, another two years later, he was soon
forced to go home again by the hostility of a people who were in the throes of a
pagan revival rather than any hoped-for Christian conversion.

On the secular level, Constantine was soon protesting at Olga's failure to keep
her promises as the flow of slaves, furs, wax and mercenary troops he had expected
either dried up or, more probably, never began. Her reply seems to have been a
complaint that her fleet had been kept waiting off the Golden Horn before she and
her retinue were admitted into Constantinople, security measures she appears
somewhat belatedly to have taken as insults. The fact of the matter is that while

Svyatoslav Yaroslavovitch, Grand Duke of
Kiev, pictured with his family on the title page
of an eleventh-century collection of
manuscripts.

Olga could see that a Christian Kiev would be in contact with the major areas of
European civilization in a way its earlier paganism had prevented, she also wanted
her city, her country and her Church to preserve their independence. The best way
to ensure this may have seemed (as Tito's Yugoslavia, for instance, has demonstrated in the modern world) the manipulation of the tensions and rivalries
resulting from an ideological split between east and west – in tenth-century terms,
the conflict between the Christianity of Byzantium and that of Rome and the
Holy Roman Empire. Russia, dominating the continent's eastern trade routes,
had power enough for her to be able to use it as a bargaining counter. To the west,
the Baltic Slavs had opted for Rome; to the south and south-east, the Balkan Slavs
for Byzantium. Russia, between them, governed by its astute princess, maintained all contacts, kept open all possibilities.

The accession of Svyatoslav for a while pushed the balance down with an unpleasant bump against Byzantium, although not in a way which brought much
benefit to Rome. Despite his Slavonic name (or perhaps even, such are the vagaries
of psychology, because of it), Svyatoslav proved himself a most vigorous Viking.
He began by extending Russian hegemony to the Crimea, becoming overlord and
protector of the Goths there after his defeat of the Khazars on the northern shores
of the Sea of Azov. Far to the north-east, on the banks of that River Oka which
flows into the Volga at the modern city of Gorki, he subdued the Vyatiches; his
greatest campaigns, however, and those most clearly demonstrating an imperial
ambition, were against the Bulgars.

Byzantium had a new emperor, Nicephorus Phocas, a military leader soon
busily extending his empire's frontiers. The Bulgarians, long troublesome, in 965
sent envoys to collect from him a tribute to which they fancied they were entitled
by an earlier treaty; the Emperor sent them unpaid back to their king, Peter,
whom he described as 'a prince clad in leather skins'. Nicephorus, after making
threatening moves in the direction of Bulgaria, then sent gifts and money to
Svyatoslav, persuading a prince who needed little encouragement to fight his war
for him. In 967 a large army of Russians crossed the Danube, soon to have the
whole of northern Bulgaria in their hands.

The story then becomes a little confused, as Byzantine history tends to do. There
is a rumour that Nicephorus's envoy, Kalokyros, had ambitions to become emperor himself (a reason, perhaps, why he had been sent so far away) and as a result

Assorted coins, mostly Byzantine and Islamic, brought back by the Vikings from their travels in the eleventh century, and found on Viking burial sites.

persuaded the Russian Grand Prince to annex Bulgaria. It is likely that here, too, Svyatoslav needed little persuading. In any case, at Little Svetlav, near the Danube delta, he seems to have decided to set up the capital of his new and extended domain. It was a place, he is reported to have said, where 'all the good things converge: gold, precious silks, wine and fruit from Byzantium, silver and horses from Bohemia and Hungary, furs, wax, honey and slaves from Russia'.

Nicephorus, after all a Byzantine and as swift to see and parry threats as any other intriguer, realized the extent of Russian ambitions and at once made peace with the Bulgars. By a suspicious coincidence, almost immediately afterwards the irrepressible Pechenegs laid siege to Kiev itself, swarming up the Dnieper valley in what one has to suppose was an answer to Byzantium's wily – and well-paid – request. The winter of 968, therefore, saw Svyatoslav hurrying back to deal with this over-ambitious diversion; by the summer of the following year, he was once more in Bulgaria, this time determined to take and hold the country not for its own sake but as a base for an attack on Constantinople itself.

With auxiliary forces of Magyars and Pechenegs to increase their strength, the Russians smashed through all Bulgarian resistance, swept into Preslav, the capital, then overwhelmed the strategic and fortified city of Phillippopolis on the Maritsa, massacring the trapped inhabitants. By the end of that year, therefore, a victorious Prince Svyatoslav, standing at the head of an army of Russians, Slavs, Pechenegs and fierce, Turko-Mongol Magyars, secure in eastern Bulgaria, could look south-ward with an optimistic covetousness towards the walls and gold-encrusted towers of Constantinople. Again there stood a new emperor in that city, John Tzimisces; Svyatoslav dismissed his efforts to negotiate with contempt, demanding huge ransoms for the prisoners and territories now in his hands. If the Byzantines did not want to pay, he suggested that they should withdraw from Europe 'which does not rightly belong to them'. If they did not, 'there will be no peace between the Russians and the Romans.'

Byzantium, however, was still a great empire and was, moreover, moving into a resurgent phase. Its response was swift, vigorous and effective. An army was mobilized and sent to force the passes of the Balkan mountains; a fleet of three hundred ships at the same time sailed for the mouth of the Danube, its object to pen the Russians in. Unopposed, the Byzantine columns pressed through the rocky valleys and down into the plains near Preslav. The city fell; the Rus retreated. At

Silistria, on the Danube, Svyatoslav took up new and fortified positions. Relentlessly Tzimisces followed him northwards. The Russian army came out to meet
him, but foot-soldiers, even Vikings, were no match for heavy cavalry. They were
hurled back, to the trenches and stockades of the town.

Now followed three months of vicious stalemate. Armed with the heavy weapons
of siege warfare, the Byzantines poured their rocks and beam-like spears upon the
defenders. No sally, no desperate foray, could break their relentless watch. Inside,
sickness and starvation, the twin subversives of every siege, began their work of
slow assassination. Along the riverways, Byzantine ships patrolled, arsenals of
flame ready at any moment to incinerate those attempting to flee seawards.
Svyatoslav sued for peace – he would leave Bulgaria, never to return; the empire
and all its possessions in the Crimea would henceforth be safe from his ambition;
all he wanted was food for his men and a promise that Byzantium would use its
influence to prevent the ravening Pechenegs from attacking the Russians during
their return journey. Tzimisces agreed; the two leaders met on the banks of the
Danube to cement this catalogue of Russian humiliation. We have a record of
what the Russian prince looked like at this meeting, written by Leo Diaconus in
that year of 971. He was, he says, of medium height:

He had bushy brows, blue eyes and was snub-nosed; he shaved his beard but wore a long and bushy moustache. His head was shaven, except for a lock of hair on one side, a sign of the nobility of his clan. His neck was thick, his shoulders were broad and his whole stature was pretty fine. He seemed gloomy and savage. In one of his ears hung a golden ear-ring adorned with two pearls and a ruby set between them. His white garments were not distinguishable from those of his men, except for their cleanness.

The fates of the two men after this brief meeting were to be very different. Despite any intercession by Tzimisces, the Pechenegs waylaid the Russians and killed Svyatoslav; they took his skull, that shaven skull, lock-adorned, and they lined it with silver and made it into a drinking goblet. For John Tzimisces there was instead a triumphant re-entry into Constantinople, hymns of praise, a gem-encrusted sceptre, a progress in a golden chariot for the holy icon he had brought from Bulgaria, the Emperor following it on a white charger, behind him the captured Bulgarian King, taken during the campaign on the principle of killing two birds with one stone. It is significant of the importance of Kiev and the trading routes, however, that despite the total collapse of Russian ambitions, none of the traditional privileges enjoyed by its merchants was withdrawn.

In Kiev, with Svyatoslav dead, sons struggled towards power through a confusion of murder. The great principality had been nominally divided into three, giving each son a patrimony, but none was satisfied with anything less than the whole (in this children of their times as well as of their father). Yaropolk, governing Kiev, slew Oleg, ruler of the Derevylans. From Novgorod, the third son, Vladimir, fled to the Scandinavian heartlands. Eight years after his father's death, however, he returned at the head of a largely Swedish army, drove the over-extended Yaropolk out, slaughtered him in a fraternal way and took the entire Russian fief.

One of his first acts was to celebrate the pagan revival which had frustrated that German bishop by setting up on a hill near his city the wooden idols of a set of strangely unfamiliar gods. The most important deity, a thunder-god named Perun, glared at bedazzled beholders out of a golden head adorned with a silver moustache. Human sacrifices were made to these gods, and the chroniclers have recorded the abrupt lynching of a Christian father who had with paternal steadfastness prevented his son's being offered in this way. Such a virulence of paganism, however, seems in Kiev as elsewhere to have been rather a death-energy than a genuine resurgence; in 988 Vladimir accepted Christianity.

The *Russian Primary Chronicle* emphasizes the glory of Byzantine Christendom by somewhat fancifully describing Vladimir's conscientious search for a new religion: Islamic Bulgars arrive, but are dismissed because of Muslim teetotalism; Jewish Khazars do their cause no good by admitting that history has scattered their co-religionists in other people's countries; the Pope's emissaries prove equally, if less clearly, unsuccessful; the Greek legate, on the other hand, is made to deliver a vast and uninterrupted speech and when, later, the still uncertain Vladimir sends his own representatives abroad to investigate further, they report that, while among the Bulgars there is no joy, 'but only sorrow and a dreadful stench', and the

Roman service is without beauty, in Byzantium 'we knew not whether we were in heaven or on earth . . . we know only that there God dwells among men.'

It is more probable that for the politically wide-awake Vladimir, foreign missionaries were less important than domestic isolation in bringing him to his decision. Russia was now an established country, rich and powerful enough to demand equality of treatment from the outside world. Such equality, however, would never be granted by Christian princes to a pagan nation. Without foreign acceptance, Russia would stagnate alone. If religion was to be the cement tying it to a wider world, then for a European state Christianity was the one to choose. And if Christianity was chosen, it was politic to settle for the variety which had its nexus in that magnetically and at the same time threateningly nearby metropolis Constantinople.

The actual occasion of Vladimir's own conversion, however, seems to have been even more precisely politic than this; asked for his help by the Byzantine Emperor Basil II Bulgaroctonos, who was faced not unusually by rebellion, Vladimir sent six thousand men, making his price a marriage with the Emperor's sister Anna. Once the rebel leader, Bardas Phocas, was safely dead, however, the Emperor appears to have heeded Anna's pleas, she being, reasonably enough, unhappy at the idea of marrying a man whom chroniclers could accurately describe as *fornicator immensus et crudelis* and who was said to keep established in the various towns of his domain some eight hundred concubines and slave-girls. Vladimir, having kept his side of the bargain, became incensed at this imperial reluctance, marched on Cherson and captured it by the simple process of cutting its water-supply. Thus installed on the Crimean coast, the Russian posed an obvious threat to Constantinople, a fact which Vladimir underlined with bloodthirsty warnings. Basil II, occupied in the perennial Byzantine manner with a war against the Bulgars, capitulated and gave up both his sister and Cherson, neither the town nor the lady the first of their kind to be sacrificed to diplomatic expediency.

It was in Cherson, now part of Anna's dowry, that Vladimir complied with a Byzantine condition and had himself baptized by the local bishop (one suspects that perhaps the coming and going of missionaries and theologians described by the chroniclers may be no more than later invention designed to make palatable a conversion based on such blatantly secular considerations). Whatever the true facts of the Russian Prince's conversion, whether it was calmly decided on merit or diplomatically accepted, whether it culminated in baptism in Cherson, in Kiev or in Constantinople, whether it was the Emperor's will or Vladimir's own which was the prime mover in the business, it is clear that once he was a Christian, he took his religious obligations very seriously indeed. The glittering idol of the mysterious Perun was whipped through the streets of Kiev and flung into the Dnieper; an ecclesiastical building programme turned the new belief into a reality of wall and tower, of incense and rhythmic chant; priests from Constantinople and from Cherson preached before these brand-new altars; Christianity was proclaimed the one religion of the principality.

Various objects found on Russian sites:
LEFT A silver pendant in the shape of a bird
from Barsoff Gorodok, Siberia. BELOW An
eleventh-century pendant with chains and
horses' heads, found at Barsoff Gorodok.
RIGHT Tenth-century bronze oval brooch
found near Moscow. FAR RIGHT Eleventh-
century silver cup with an Arabic inscription,
found at Barsoff Gorodok.

It seems likely that the language of prayer and liturgy was Slavonic, a fact which recognized demotic realities. It did more – it became an instrument in the forging of the nation, in the creation of its literature and thus of its self-awareness and may be seen, as a consequence, as one cause of that historically inevitable effect, the severing of the new Russia from its Viking and non-Slavonic roots. As soon as Vladimir had brought about the widespread conversions he demanded, he organized the education of the children of the aristocracy. By this means, the Russian Church, although accepting its allegiance to the Patriarch of Byzantium, kept some measure of independence – an independence, however, always sketchy, and contrived in any case with the aid of the Byzantine clergy who had themselves a century earlier built up a tradition of Slavonic preaching in order to encourage the northward spread of their teaching. The later elevation of Vladimir into sanctity, ordained by the Eastern Church, certainly suggests that for them there was nothing subversive in the Russians' use of Slavonic in their worship.

Vladimir was succeeded, briefly, by his son Svyatopolk, known to history as 'the Accursed'. His crime was to murder his two younger brothers for purely dynastic reasons, an occurrence which was not so unusual as to arouse widespread abhorrence in itself, but which Christian legend has turned into a classical confrontation of the vicious and the meek. The two young men, Boris and Gleb, are shown as frankly terrified, pleading gently with their murderers instead of submitting in pride or retaliating in savagery ('Do not harvest from me my unripened life,' Gleb murmurs, unavailingly, 'do not reap the unripe ear of corn'). Such an acceptance of fear and death was swiftly seen as being of the very stuff of martyrdom, and the two soon joined their father in canonization. Only the church of Kiev demurred, its closeness to the scene of the crime doubtless making available to it the usual ambiguities; miracle and Byzantine pressure, however, soon brought it to confirm this dual sanctity. Svyatopolk the Accursed seems to have been more violent than sensible – having murdered two brothers, he ought perhaps to have gone on and disposed of the rest. As it was, when the survivors, Yaroslav of Novgorod and Prince Mstislav appeared before his gates at the head of a vengeful army, the ruler of Kiev found himself predictably friendless. So perish, one may hope, all those who are the cause of martyrdom in other men.

Yaroslav, who in concert with his brother Mstislav would now be ruler of Russia for over thirty years, brought his country to a pitch of prosperity unknown before, upon this wealth laying the foundations for much of its culture. At the same time he maintained and even strengthened the old Scandinavian connection in a way which suggests a strong pride in his own origins. He married the daughter of the Swedish king, Olaf Sköttkonung, and involved himself in the politics of the north by giving refuge to her sister's husband, the not as yet sainted Olaf of Norway. When, at Stiklestad, Olaf came to the end of dreams, his young half-brother, that Harald Hardradi whose Viking brightness English Harold would finally extinguish in 1066, returned to Russia to become one of Yaroslav's officers; later, he would marry his princely employer's daughter and carry her with him back to Norway and a throne.

At the same time, however, Yaroslav had no doubts that Kiev and the Russia which he ruled from there was a country in its own right, one he had the duty to make strong and magnificent. He celebrated victory over the Pechenegs in 1030 by some seven years later founding his own cathedral of St Sophia, Russia's first and a splendour of dome and tower, of mosaic and gold leaf to rival the great church in Constantinople itself. Paintings within the cathedral show the Prince and his family in reverent juxtaposition with the Trinity and its attendant hierarchies of saints and angels, thus establishing that Kiev's royal family were on visiting terms with God. Giving Russian Christianity both root and expression in this magnificent building, Yaroslav did the same for Russian literature and historical self-awareness by originating the *Russian Primary Chronicle*, that mixture of record, legend and rearranged fact from the confusing intricacies of which scholars must pick such truths as their discretion and its likelihood permit. Beginning with the Flood and the dispersal of mankind after God had shown once and for all at Babel who was to be master, the *Chronicle* establishes the Slavs as going back to the beginnings of history, one of the seventy-two nations which came into existence after Jehovah's counter-stroke against that over-ambitious tower.

At the same time, the Russian people were given a strong linguistic heart by the way in which commentators attempted to lend their alphabet an almost transcendental importance. Language spread the word of God; Slavonic was the language of the Russian Church; written Slavonic made God's word and the Church's preaching available to everyone. The letters in which the language became apparent were, therefore, as holy and as wonderful as the texts they communicated. As one author put it, a people who have no sacred books in their own language are like a naked body, a dead soul.

Given such a view of the language's importance, it is not surprising that almost at the same time as he was founding his cathedral, Yaroslav should have organized a sort of committee of the learned and given it the task of translating books from Greek into Slavonic. It is a measure of his grandeur and the task's significance that internal evidence from surviving texts suggests that these translators came from many different parts of the Slavonic world. Yaroslav also attempted to define the Russian laws, although the *Pravda Russkaya* or 'The Russian Law' in which Kiev's juridical legacy was at least partly enshrined is hardly a systematic codification of a legal system. What is apparent through it, however, is how little even so important a skein as the law in the culture of the country owed to Byzantium. Instead, it looks backward, to north Europe, and it is in the laws of England, of the Franks and of the Scandinavians that analogies are found.

Thus, although clearly in the Byzantine orbit, the Russian principality of Kiev-Novgorod maintained an independence and even, through its law and language, proclaimed that independence loudly. It is not surprising, therefore, to discover that proud Yaroslav had his difficulties with Russia's great trading partner on the far shores of the Black Sea. The fact that everyone accepted the Byzantine emperor's nominal jurisdiction over state and even Church did not mean an everyday acceptance of this condition, a practical obeisance, a structured and deferential humility. Thus when riot and street-brawl in Constantinople led to the death of a Russian nobleman at a moment when Yaroslav fancied he saw a weakness in Byzantine rule, he seized the opportunity to assert by violence that independent power in which he and all his people implicitly believed.

When Yaroslav's son Vladimir, Prince of Novgorod, appeared with a vast and partly Scandinavian force at the northern entrance to the Bosporus in 1043, he discovered the Byzantine forces, although in the disarray of surprise, under the control not of the weak Michael v, as he had expected, but of the stronger Constantine ix Monomachus. Every Russian merchant in Constantinople was instantly arrested; so were the hitherto trusted Scandinavian mercenaries of the Varangian Guard. Constantine himself led a makeshift fleet of heavy triremes and old hulks pressed into service up the narrow straits towards the Russian fleet. Since in the Byzantine manner Constantine had until then tried to negotiate with them, even offering compensation for the death they had come to avenge, Vladimir and his colleagues may have thought that little effort stood between them and victory. Even in that moment when, all terms contemptuously rejected, they stood tall on their after-decks and watched the wide crescent of defending ships come labouring northward up the narrows, they must have believed Byzantium almost on its knees.

Three triremes now swept to the forefront of Constantine's fleet. One can see their triple rows of oars stretch and flash, the sparkle of a brief foam, the disciplined surge forward. Towards them dance the slimmer, lower ships of the Russians, almost dainty by contrast. Now the larger ships, looming, ominous, block out the invaders' sky. And still the Russians call their defiance, the Swedish warriors clasp their spears, crouch with hungry swords, await the familiar battle. Then all is changed. As so often before in that place, flame alters the invaders' condition. In the black smoke which rises, all banners shrivel, all courage, all hope. Fire falls out of those clouds like a congealed lightning, settles on wood, on woollen cloaks, on flesh. As in a forest, it leaps from mast to mast and, as from a forest fire, the living must turn and flee before it.

Seven ships burned, moths to the terrible candle of Byzantium's 'Greek Fire'. Was there a storm then? It has been chronicled, a swirling of water, a battering of wind to complete fire's havoc. It hardly matters; the Russians fled, Constantine's fleet pursuing – all agree on that. Later, off the coast of Thrace, Vladimir's ships would fight a more successful engagement against a patrolling squadron, but that would do nothing but salve some remnant of their pride. They took to the land, seeking a hard path home. The Governor of Paristrion, a province between the lower Danube and the Balkan Mountains, brought out an army against them; weakened, disheartened, bewildered, the Russians were broken, then cut to pieces. Vladimir managed to return to Kiev, but with him came only a few of the host he had led southwards so confidently. Of the rest, those who had not died were prisoners; their right hands now decorated Constantinople's walls. Eight hundred captured in that final land-battle were taken to the Byzantine capital and there every one of them was blinded – significantly, this was a punishment meted out to traitors, to rebels: as Psellus, a statesman of the day, described it, for Byzantium this campaign had been 'the rebellion of the Russians'. It had failed, and there would never thereafter be a war between these unequal antagonists; Russia, having learned its place, would have to wait on history to amend it.

Yaroslav died. His great principality collapsed under the weight of dynastic bickering. Sons and grandsons scrambled for the pieces of his partitioned inheritance. The Scandinavian connection weakened; the new Slavonic consciousness dimmed, then overwhelmed, awareness of a proudly northern origin. Yaroslav's grandson (and Constantine's, fruit of the marriage which cemented the healing treaty of 1046), Vladimir Monomakh and his successor Mstislav I did something to revive Kiev's glory, but little to bring it back to any Scandinavian consciousness. For the Rus, the Viking days were over for good. Indeed, to some extent prosperous times were over for good, for they themselves now suffered from the swift violence of a new kind of land Viking, the Cumans or Polovtsy, nomad Turks who swarmed in from the east and, between 1061 and 1200, made more than fifty damaging attacks on the middle Dnieper valley and its trade route to Byzantium. That area's traditional raiders, the Pechenegs, were destroyed for ever; and upon Kiev itself, its route to the sea and Constantinople closed, a darkness descends, the gold and the magnificence retreat into history and legend, new centres such as Rostov enter into a bright importance, and the story of Russia winds forward into an era in which its Scandinavian roots would become an irrelevance and, later, an embarrassment.

Against the assertion of Pan-Slavonic propagandists, only the archaeological evidence and the bald statements of the runes stand as witness. But even in the middle of the eleventh century, Swedish Vikings were still travelling east to the land of the Saracen, the half-legendary Serkland, in search of wealth and of adventure; Ingvar Vidfarne led a band of companions the length of the Volga – a dwindling band, their adventure closing in on them like some vast fist, the wealth a receding dream, each man's singular death the only reality, and commemorated only in the careful tribute of the survivors. Twenty-four rune-stones were put up to them; the children of Gunlev raised one – 'He fell in the east with Ingvar. God help his soul.' Ingvar himself is remembered on a stone set up by his father Tola, not for him but for his brother Harald: 'In far-off lands they boldly sought gold. In the east they spread food for the eagle. They died in the south, in Serkland.' When he died, there somewhere near the shores of the Caspian, Ingvar was twenty-five, a hero, one from whose life a saga would be woven, as complete a Viking as any of his ancestors. Yet already, against the new structures of the Russian state, against the background of Scandinavia's established and Christian kingdoms, he seems an anachronism. Civilization would not for much longer find room to accommodate that anarchic wildness, that jubilant and blood-thirsty restlessness which had for so long been the Viking way.

Among the most binding and attractive traditions which characterized the Vikings was that of fellowship. The high value placed upon the bond between warriors surfaces in the stories, at least semi-legendary, of such communities as the one reputed to exist at Jomsborg on the Baltic, where men aged between eighteen and fifty, select, a brotherhood, lived by placing their courage and their tempered skills in battle at the disposal of those who needed and could pay for them. No woman was ever allowed inside their walls, the death of any one of them would be avenged by the others, none was permitted to raise his hand against a comrade. Their harbour, it was said, guarded by iron gates, could hold 360 ships at anchor. They were, legend insists, a unity – all booty was held in common, no man might absent himself for more than three days without special permission. They are supposed to have fought in a dozen different campaigns, a dozen different countries; one would like to believe unreservedly in their existence, their victories, their prowess, even in their double-dealing, such as the two-faced participation of their leader, Sigvaldi, in the downfall of Olaf Tryggvesson, but unfortunately we have little or no independent evidence to confirm the stories about them which have come down to us.

This uncertainty does not exist in the case of another, equally romantic, equally mercenary brotherhood far to the east – that of Byzantium's Varangian Guard. From the middle of the ninth century, Scandinavians were drawn eastward by tales of Mikligard and its gold, arriving finally within those stupendous walls, finding the legend turned to stone and flesh, to streets filled with a polyglot assembly, merchants come from Egypt, from Persia, from the mysterious lands beyond Kazakhstan, from every corner of the Byzantine Empire itself, the whole an intricate, brawling, over-decorated, mercenary, confused and confusing clutter of contradictions, perfumed and stinking, gustily profane and sickly religious, civilized and cruel, proudly Roman and subtly Oriental, a city of unimaginable luxury, of ostentatious piety, of implacable traditions, over which God, Mammon and history brooded in companionable trinity. What could a Scandinavian far from home and moneyless offer the rulers of such a place? Never one to be over-awed, the northern wanderer carried his answer ready to hand – he had his sword, his axe, the skills he had learned in a dozen skirmishes, a score of battles; he had his courage. Soon Byzantium could add to its other traditions the hiring of Viking mercenaries, Varangians come eastward to carve out wealth for themselves, or fame, or perhaps to do no more than pass a decade or so in testing adventure.

Some of these Varangians were soon to be drawn from closer to Constantinople than Sweden; the treaty of 911 between Oleg of Kiev and the Byzantine leadership gave Rus the express right to serve as mercenaries in the empire's forces. Seven hundred of their seamen took part that same year in a naval expedition led against Crete by an Admiral Himerius; their presence, however, seems to have brought the Byzantines no great success and the attack failed. They fought in Crete again some three decades later, they fought against the Arabs in Asia Minor, their ships were frequently recorded as an integral element in the empire's patrolling forces. It was when Vladimir of Kiev sent Basil II Bulgaroctonos the six thousand men he needed to defy rebellion in 988 that these perhaps makeshift and temporary arrangements first appear to have been regularized. It is more than probable that other groups of foreigners had long served in the Imperial Guard; now this detachment of Varangians, of Swedes and Rus, joined them, keeping within the corps their separate existence. The Varangian Guard was in being.

For the next hundred years, at least, other Northmen would be found on active service in the provinces and on the frontiers of the empire, while in Constantinople itself, the Guard watched over the emperor and his city. By and large, they seem to have kept themselves apart from the Greeks around them, partly because they did not speak their language, partly because they did not share their temperament. The Byzantine mixture of devious calculation and sybaritic self-indulgence, both only slightly modified by the booming, *basso profundo* certainties of the Orthodox Church, were not likely to make much appeal to forthright Scandinavian warriors whose highest pleasure was to pour down their throats the heavy wines of the Eastern Empire, whose highest rhetoric was the clumsy and unverifiable boast, whose highest virtue was reckless courage on the battlefield. One consequence was that the many labyrinthine plots by which the throne of Byzantium was threatened rarely, if ever, involved the Varangians. They did stage a mutiny against Nicephorus III Botaniates towards the end of the eleventh century, one reason perhaps for the anxiety of that emperor's successor when, in 1103, Eirik I of Denmark paid Constantinople a visit. It seems to have been felt that Eirik would somehow use the common language of the northern people to suborn, and incomprehensibly, these stout guardsmen, with who knew what disastrous result. Eirik, however, appears to have shared the Guard's own opinion of itself, telling the Varangians that they had achieved the highest honour open to a Northman, hoping that in virtue and sobriety they would prove equal to this, promising them bounty when they returned home, and taking on himself the burden of maintaining the families of any who might fall in Mikligard's exotic battles.

Each member of the Guard was given his quarters and his food free; in addition, he was paid between ten and fifteen golden *solidi* every month. There was also prize money to be won in war, and there were various grants; it was therefore not exactly for nothing that the Swedes and others came, in ones and twos or even in large contingents, to join their colleagues in the Byzantine service. However, an eleventh-century writer advised the emperor never to promote foreigners to high rank, nor to overpay them – if they served for no more than their clothing and bread, 'be assured that they will serve you loyally and wholeheartedly, looking to the bounty of your hands for trifling sums of money and for bread.' Given high rank, the author considered, a foreigner 'would then become disdainful and would not serve you well'. And he points out that none of a long list of 'emperors of blessed memory promoted a Frank or a Varangian' to any but the lower ranks of the military hierarchy: 'Yet all these served them for bread and clothing.' It seems to have been the case that it was always a Greek who commanded the Varangian Guard, although in the field one of their own aristocrats would lead them. The Greek officer, a Court official, was known as the *pansebastos* and *megalodiermeneutes*, and had administrative rather than military functions, acting as interpreter for the Northmen and as their principal liaison officer with the Byzantine authorities.

Mikligard was the magnet, then; the Varangian Guard provided the glamour of an elite, certifying with its own impeccable reputation the valour and worth of those it recruited. It thus drew to itself the best of those who came or had come eastward from Scandinavia, draining Russia to its detriment of the young, the courageous, the nobly-born and the ambitious. Beyond the Guard, the armies of Byzantium, too, were eager to use these 'axe-bearers' in their constantly embattled ranks. Sometimes, indeed, a northern warrior might shuttle from campaigns on the frontier to duties with the Guard inside the imperial palace itself. After 1066, English and Danes, ousted by Norman successes, began to alter the composition of the corps. By the end of the eleventh century, it was no longer principally a Scandinavian force. But for a hundred years before that, it had offered to Viking swords one of the last opportunities they would ever have to be unsheathed with all the ancient flourish. As the darkness of history closes in, we can see in the golden glow of Byzantium that familiar glitter of steel and hear through the gloom male voices raised in Viking song. And under the grey skies of Sweden, their memorials stand, the ancient rune stones, telling of their exploits or of deaths made glorious by distance. 'Ragnvald had these runes cut. He was in Greece. He was commander of a military unit.' The statement, in all its clarity of pride, rings undiminished down nine centuries.

The Vinland map, for long the centre of controversy, but now proved fraudulent. It cleverly brought together what was known of Viking exploration in North America with both the saga tradition and the established Norse settlements in Greenland. By showing America and even China, the map daringly went beyond what is believed to be the picture of the world held by medieval geographers.

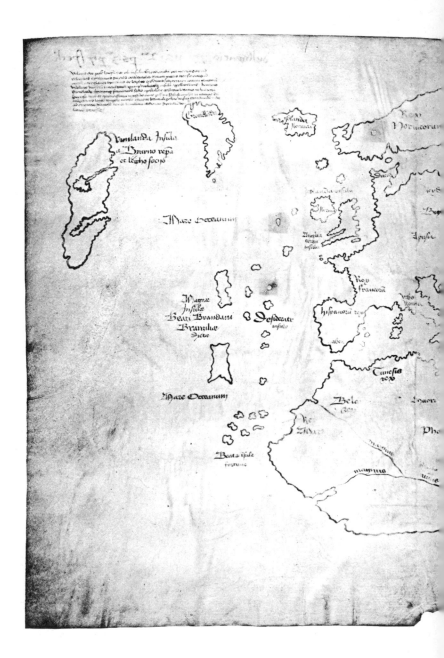

7 WESTWARD TO VINLAND

Westward from Norway. Nothing lies there, a man might think, staring out from some jutting cliff-top at the grey-green, heaving sea, the sky descending, dank and drab as a workhouse blanket, that far horizon lost in an uninviting mystery of spray and drizzle: water endlessly, and gloom, to the very edge of the world. Such panoramas would offer nothing but threat to European sailors, even the Portuguese navigators creeping half-timidly along the endless coast of Africa, until in the fifteenth century rumours of the earth's circularity would at last persuade them to strike, westwards too, out into the inscrutable ocean. Their self-congratulations on subsequent successes must have made Valhalla rock with contemptuous guffaws; those northern heroes, after all, had made such journeys four and five and six centuries before, the sea never for a moment an enemy, its paths never a secret, no hesitation in their minds as they launched their shallow-draught, clinker-built longships, pointed the tall figureheads, those glaring, ferocious masks, into the unknown and, hoisting sail, flung themselves before the wind out into a world they never doubted would show them wealth, adventure and an endless gallery of marvels.

Ahead of them was no one but a handful of anchorite hermits, mostly Irish, who had placed themselves at the disposal of God's gales. Dicuil, an Irish monk, wrote in 825 of 'islands in the ocean north of Britain', two full days' sailing away, some very small, on which, he claimed, 'hermits who have sailed from our Scotia (which is Ireland) have lived for roughly a hundred years.' Now, however, the holy men had gone, forced out by Norse pirates, and instead 'they are full of innumerable sheep and a great many different kinds of seafowl.' Thus shyly the Faroes sidle into human awareness, islands which before the arrival of the Irish hermits were, as Diciul pointed out, 'constantly uninhabited since the world's beginning'.

The first Scandinavian to settle there about whom there are any records is one Grim Kamban. He appears at the end of the ninth century, a man stripped of most attributes but hung with fame, whose stature in life persuaded those who remembered him after his death to make him the object of a curious worship; his spirit, it was said, could guarantee good seasons, if properly propitiated. Yet Grim was, perhaps, a Christian, his second name a corruption of the Irish 'Camman' and thus a possible indication of baptism. He probably sailed to the Faroes by way of Ireland; later settlers were to come directly from Norway, some

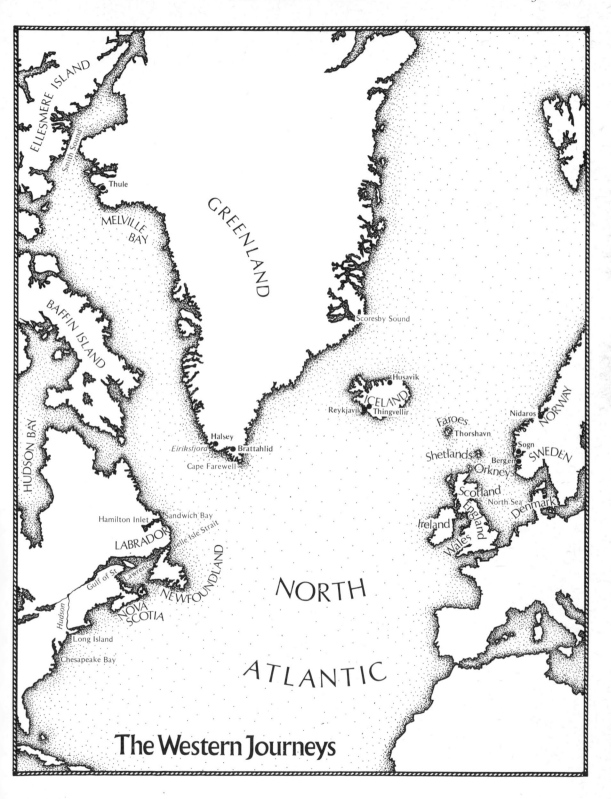

The Western Journeys

of them refugees from the heavy, kingdom-building hands of Harald Fairhair.

Harald – who was, according to Snorri Sturluson, 'a stout, strong and handsome man, both prudent and manly' – came to the throne of a kingdom already carved out by Halfdan the Black at some time between the years 860 and 880. He was only ten then; before the end of the century the pressure of his efforts to consolidate and extend his rule had created a confederacy of the disaffected, the disinherited and the affronted. These, coming out in armed alliance to assert their rights, found Harald more vigorous than they. At the great sea-battle of Hafrsfjord, kings fell like ripe plums. A mighty *berseker*, Tore Haklang, tried to take Harald's ship, lying alongside it, bellowing, but it was his own which was cleared of the living. Survivors fled, thistledown before the gales of dynasty. As Snorri puts it, in his straightforward way, 'After this battle King Harald met no opposition in Norway, for all his opponents and greatest enemies were cut off.'

Within Norway, Hafrsfjord made Harald Fairhair secure; outside Norway, its consequences undermined the security of thousands. For 'a great multitude fled out of the country', many of these the proud, born to command and to wealth, now stripped of title and denied their rights, their lands sequestered and their gold forfeited. Elsewhere, on foreign shores, were those who would have to pay these debts; many years of desperate raiding followed Harald's victory, and many innocent dead were offered in brutal compensation for that king's success.

Other Vikings, however, forced to seek new land, remembered stories of islands in the west and turned the prows of their ships in that direction. It is true that all the normal pressures which drove the Scandinavians to their great break-out were still operating and that because of these the Faroes, and Iceland beyond them, and so onward through the sunset Greenland and America, would probably have been reached in any case and just as vigorously colonized. But to the Icelandic historians it was Harald's victory which endowed that exodus with its especial energy and, given the known movements of Vikings and the dates on which they occurred, there seems no reason to doubt them. Naturally, the settlers were not all refugees from Harald's might; some, indeed, had been his allies. All the usual Viking rest-lessness and Viking greed had not been abruptly jettisoned. But Hafrsfjord seems the moment at which the light of history began to beam westward with a new and steady clarity.

The light it shines upon the Faroes shows us new settlements, chiefs lording it on their own detached small islands, a central *thing* established to pull the community together, the meeting place at Thorshavn, still today the islands' capital. Names appear – the Gateskeggs of Gata on Austrey, descendants of that Aud the Deep-minded who had once been queen in Dublin, but had later ventured westward, settling finally in Iceland but on the way bringing a grand-daughter to the Faroes, bride for the Gateskeggs' then newly-settled progenitor. From this family sprang two brothers, Breste and Beine, who ruled half the Faroes, Halfgrim, a chieftain on Sudrey, governing the other half. It was this division which created the tensions from which drama sprang, murder and armed confrontation, mercy and revenge – stuff for the sagas, which the poet did not ignore.

Halfgrim and the two brothers stern in rivalry, Thrond, a Gateskegg cousin, dour, large-muscled, red of hair and beard, a man of power, bringing out his faction on the side of the Sudrey chieftain; a murder, then, on uninhabited Dimon minni, when Breste and Beine were there, sheep their only concern, their followers elsewhere, only their two sons Sigmund and Thore at their sides, children aghast as three boat-loads of men sullen behind threatening steel came hurrying up from the restless surf; struggle, harsh defence, the boys perhaps in the thick of it, puny but determined, or else behind rock, staring white-faced from their scant safety, as their fathers, swords busy, struck uselessly for their lives, tumbling at last on the stained, sheep-cropped grass, the body of their enemy Halfgrim beside them; Thrond magnanimous, sparing the children's lives, going on to enforce his rule throughout the islands, then giving up to Össur, Halfgrim's son, the half which had been his father's domain. Then, years later, the boys grown men, their support coming from that *Jarl* Hakon whose regency helped to unite Norway, two ships under them for their voyage of revenge, arriving over the eastward horizon. Össur died behind his own thick walls; Sigmund Brestesson was his successful attacker. Thrond accepted the alterations of power – Hakon, he agreed, was overlord of the Faroes, Sigmund his immediate agent. In Norway, soon after, Olaf Tryggvesson raised Christianity's most bloody sword; among the souls he claimed was Sigmund's. Sigmund, King Olaf said, would bring to the Church the rest of those people whom he governed in the name and with the support of Norway's Crown. At the Thorshavn *thing* Sigmund set out his new evangelical message – to be howled down. The old gods, as the little town's name showed, were active in the Faroes; the people held to their ancient allegiance. And it was Thrond, crusty upholder of the rooted order, who was in the forefront of this vociferous resistance. Many Scandinavian leaders had fallen from power and popular support over this question of conversion; when they saw gods where their people saw none, the virtue of rulership went out of them. Kings were priests, too; it was proper – and politic – that they should worship at the altars their subjects recognized. Thrond, genuine in his unwavering devotion to Asgard, must also have realized how much this religious factionalism could help him to regain his previous position.

Sigmund, however, could see it too; elsewhere, a king with a finely-balanced temper awaited results. Abruptly, Sigmund appeared on Thrond's own Gata threshold and took him prisoner. Thus forcibly converted, Thrond was humiliatingly presented in place after place as an advertisement for the new faith, a threat of what might happen to those who would not accept it. Christianity triumphed, fear rather than conviction generating its success. Soon, however, Thrond counterattacked, and there followed a progress of foiled murder attempts, Sigmund each time surviving, even triumphing, on the last occasion Thrond and the others in water, Sigmund, boat-borne, above them, sword in hand – but Christian, generous, unable to cut down the defenceless. Saved, therefore, the pagan leader and his companions struck again, landing at dead of night in Sigmund's own isle, Skufey, and forcing him and his companions, after defence and flight and sudden counter-thrust, to swim for their lives. Three leaped into the water; only Sigmund landed on Sudrey, sodden, exhausted – to be killed there for the gold in his ring and the salt-stained clothes on his back. Much later, when Thrond was once more master of the Faroes, he learned of this killing and hanged the men responsible. His leadership of those loyal to the old religion kept that faction together; when he died, around the year 1030, paganism and the separatism it had given rise to could no longer hold out against Norwegian pressure. In 1105 there was a bishopric established, a see turbulent for those appointed to it, one of whom as late as the year 1308 was starved to death within the half-built walls of what would never now become his cathedral.

With the Faroes settlements thus rooted and nourished upon the usual Viking mixture of sea-water and blood, they provided stepping stones to the new nation building through those early years in Iceland. Dicuil knew of it, those adventurous holy men of Ireland having made their way west-nor'-west to its broken but un-expectedly hospitable shores. 'They deal in fallacies,' he pointed out, 'who have written that the sea round the island is frozen,' dismissing also rumours of seasons offering either perpetual day or perpetual night – 'for those sailing at an expected time of great cold have made their way thereto, and dwelling on the island enjoyed always alternate night and day save at the time of the solstice. But after one day's sailing from there to the north they found the frozen sea.'

Who first dared that reported cold, sailed under the coasts of so distant an island, landed, returned and reported it good? Perhaps Gardar Svarvasson, whirled there by storm, wintering at Husavik, returning to his native Sweden full of praise for his discovery; perhaps Naddodd, a Norwegian miscreant, on the high seas to avoid pursuers, who was also led there by gales, climbed Reydarfjall but saw no signs of human occupation in the land below, then sailed away before enveloping snow-storms, the mountain screened from his retreating sight, his name for the island in the compliments he would later give it therefore Snæland, Snowland; perhaps Floki, from Rogaland, who was actually the man who named it Iceland. He knew its direction; he used ravens to find its location. He let the first free once he had left the Faroes behind, but the bird knew better and flew back to them. The second came back to him, the ship its only haven. The third rose some time later, hung in the sky, then set a course and vanished, flying strongly. Floki followed; soon he was landing at Vatnsfjord, unloading his supplies, his livestock, his seeds. Seals were plentiful and too friendly for their own continued safety; fish curled and stretched in heavy nets, a constant silvered plenty. Then the cold came down, petrifying the world. Vikings should have been more provident. The animals died, for Floki had put aside no fodder. Winter lingered, undermining spring; from a peak, Floki saw ice in the southern arm of the fjord – it was with bitterness that he named the island. Gales brought him back to shore when he at last wanted to leave, and he was forced to endure yet another winter. Of the three pioneers, he was the only one who could find nothing good to say about the place when he finally returned to his native Norway, vowing never to return.

A decade passed. Then there sail into the sight of history cousins, foster-brothers: Ingolf and Leif. This pair, their estates forfeited as a result of a blood-feud which they had prosecuted with too sweeping a success, decided to carve out new lands for themselves on the island which had so repelled Floki. After a voyage of reconnaissance, they returned, laden with a settler's necessities. It was around the year 870, Norway was still the Æsirs' land, Ingolf one of their devout worshippers. Off the Iceland coast, he threw overboard the wooden pillars of his high-seat, vowing to build his house wherever Thor saw fit to bring them to land. Perhaps Leif (or Hjorleif now, Sword-Leif, his name a tribute to a sword he had taken from an Irish burial mound) had learned some sort of Christian contempt for Thor and his tribe; in any case, he made no vows, but insisted on his own choice. He landed, built his first walls, then found himself abruptly at the end of fortune, tricked by his Irish slaves, his death the price of their freedom; with what had been his women and his goods, his killers fled to a tall off-shore island. Searching for the still-missing pillars of the seat, Ingolf's men stumbled upon the scar-crossed dead. Ingolf, although he could not help sermonizing on the fate of these men who had refused to sacrifice to their fathers' gods, was not slow in tracking down the murderers. He killed every one of them, his vengeance as total as his duty demanded. Soon afterwards, his followers came across the place where Thor, through the carved pillars of the seat, had decreed Ingolf should make his settlement: today there is a city there, Iceland's capital, Reykjavik.

Thereafter, new settlers came in steady shiploads, in small flotillas, those in search of holdings denied them by birth or snatched from them by fortune, the harried, whether by Harald Fairhair or by those who, elsewhere in Europe, were now beginning to stand up to Viking depredations, were even beginning successfully to counter-attack. Perhaps some twenty thousand came, enough in the end to worry Norway's rulers, who levied a tax on all proposed Iceland voyages. Those who landed found an empty countryside, the lowlands fertile, green valleys curving about the long glitter of the fjords, dark mountains beyond, overlooking with a benign gloom these thousands of waiting, useful acres. Among those peaks and valleys, in the uplands which covered three-quarters of the island, glaciers wound, green-white, crevassed, spread like the waiting claws of winter. Torrential rivers, ice-cold, glaciers' spawn, roared dangerously to the sea. But the air was milder than the latitude suggested (the Gulf Stream alters the temperature of those seas) and soon wheat was growing, cattle walked the soggy lowland pastures, sheep flecked the long slopes of the upland moors. When the birch and juniper had been cleared, the soil began to erode, but too slowly for the early settlers to care. They had, in any case, taken vast areas for themselves, settling into their territories like the cattle barons of a later westward emigration, living as raw and wild and wealthy a life, indeed, as any Arizona rancher. From their estates, they began to send wool abroad, and woollen cloth; later, sulphur, easily gathered in this island of hot springs and deep volcanic grumbling, would add to their wealth.

Tenth-century bronze statuette of Thor, from
Eyrarland, Iceland.

Ingolf himself took territories about as large in extent as Norway's Vestfold, that square of land lying to the west of Oslofjord which was the basis of Harald Fairhair's power. When Aud the Deep-minded came, the estate she took for herself would later provide steadings for eighty prosperous farmers. It is clear that land-holders of such wealth, many of whom had learned both pride and a hair-trigger belligerence in the wars and raids with which the Viking world resounded, could become creatures of cruel whim, the single-minded prosecutors of blood-feuds, tyrants over those not strong enough to withstand their contingent might. On the other hand, in an island larger than Ireland, steadings and estates were widely scattered and men grew up in the arrogance of isolation. Under so wide a sky, freedom became an absolute. Nevertheless, some social organization was essential, and in every district a man or a family would soon emerge who had enough of the trust and respect of the others to assume some kind of leadership.

Such men, known as the *godar*, were usually heads of clans; as elsewhere, they combined chieftainship with a priestly function. One reason for this is that worship demands some centre, a meeting-place which can act as a temple, even if at lengthy intervals; only the rich and established could provide such a hall, and the food and drink which both worship and the worshippers demanded. It was Thor mainly, and his Asgard companions, who were offered sacrifice and tribute at these gatherings, for although a few settlers seem to have been Christian (a handful were Celtic, almost certainly from Christian Ireland, where others had spent some time before travelling further), almost all of them were adherents of the older religion, some as fervently as Thrond of the Faroes. The *godar*, therefore, instruments of temporal power and channels for the divine, soon became the arbiters of right and the analysts of custom for the whole island.

By about 930, all the available land had been taken; Iceland was settled. It needed government, now, a structure to consolidate what anarchic enterprise had created. Tradition says that the first *thing* was established at Kjalarnes, north of Reykjavik, at the instigation of Ingolf's son, Thorstein. Soon similar assemblies were gathering throughout the settled areas of the island, each presided over by the local *godi*. While such meetings could keep the peace and even, within limits, legislate, their jurisdiction was by their nature only local. Increasingly it was felt that Iceland needed a country-wide constitution, a system of law to which all men could adhere. At this point there came forward Ulfljot of Lon, a *godi* who had come originally from Hordaland, in Norway, with the suggestion that he be sent back to his homeland in order to study the legal and political structures being developed there. What most impressed him during that journey was the Gulathing Law by which men lived in western Norway – the three folks of Nordfjord, Sogn and Hordaland had learned to settle their differences by a single unifying legal system administered at one general legislative and juridical assembly, the Gulathing. It was because of its example and Ulfljot's report that, after his return, Iceland's *Althing* was formed, that national assembly now (though not unmodified) well into its second millennium. It was on the basis of Ulfljot's recommendations, too, that

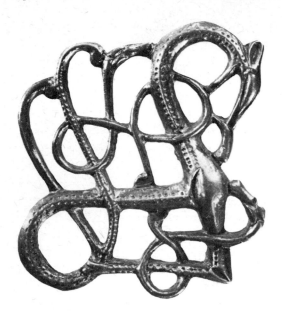

Eleventh-century silver brooch in the Urnes style, from Trollaskogi, Iceland.

the laws Iceland adopted and by which the *Althing* judged were finally drawn up. It is not now clear what exactly this code was, much of it having been lost and the rest probably rewritten two or three centuries later; its first provision seems to have been an injunction to sailors to remove their ships' figureheads within sight of the shore so that the 'gaping heads and yawning jaws' would not frighten 'the spirits of the land'.

The *Althing* would meet for a fortnight every summer, out in the open, on a plain thirty miles east of Reykjavik, the *Thingvellir*, river-loud, buttressed by lava and volcanic rock, its grass bright and level, a wide lake beside it, the water's surface inverting the grey or blue-white skies of the northern summer. Here there would gather the thirty-six *godar* of the *lögretta*, each with his two non-voting advisers, to debate the making of law at the foot of the Law-rock, the *lögberg*, while around them the people watched their discussions, approved or criticized their decisions. For the meeting of the *Althing* was also a gathering of the people of Iceland, a pro-longed feast, a fortnight-long fair, a reunion of old comrades, a revitalizing of family ties, a reiteration of unity. It was here too that men could bring their individual cases to judgment in the *domr*, where the judges, each a *godi*'s nominee, sat in attentive conclave.

After 965 Ulfljot's constitution was rendered more complex by the regulariza-tion of local assemblies, three each in the newly established East, South and West Quarters, four in the North. Each assembly met under the eyes of three *godar*, but since this would have given the North Quarter more of these powerful men to represent it in the *Althing*, each of the other Quarters appointed three extra *godar* who, although they had no local assemblies to attend, had a seat at the *Althing*. Thus political balance was maintained. Each Quarter set up its own court at the *Althing* gathering and it was to these that men locked in disagreement now brought their cases. Early in the eleventh century another court was set up, an appeal court made effective by allowing a simple majority to reach decisions – in the lower courts, the need for near-unanimity often produced unsatisfactory compromise or stalemate. At the local level, there also grew up a sort of co-operative institution called the *hreppr*, in which some twenty or more well-established farmers came together in order to regulate such matters as land-boundaries or the marks by which each man identified his animals, and above all to organize the annual sheep round-up, a complex business on the high moorlands requiring organization and unity of effort.

What all this interweaving of responsibilities omitted, however, probably because the temper of the people made it impossible, was the establishment of any central authority with the obligation and the executive power to keep the peace and uphold the law. It was perhaps the lack of such a focus which made the religious differences of the late tenth and early eleventh centuries so bitter. It was in Iceland, more perhaps than anywhere in the Viking world, that both Christians and pagans were prepared to see their whole society disintegrate rather than accept the allegiance of new gods or hold to the allegiance of old ones.

Christianity reached Iceland in a series of raids, each beaten back, each leading to a renewed attack; indirectly, there was also a seepage, as it were, from the outside world, a constant small accretion to the new, isolated congregations as travellers returned from the outside, and Christian, world. But it was missionaries who led those probing raiding parties – Thorvald Kodransson, preaching the gospel of Jesus, an Aaron for the would-be Moses of the Saxon bishop he had come home with, speaking up fatally at the *Althing*, being forced from the country then in 896; Stefni Thorgilsson, Icelandic too, but sent now from Olaf Tryggvesson's busy Court, rampaging about the country in the manner of his royal patron, anathematizing ancient gods, overturning their idols, destroying their sacred houses, until he too was forced away by the outraged islanders; Thangbrand, a German adventurer, a man both violent and determined, out of favour with Olaf of Norway and therefore sent to this remote outpost of the Church Militant as a mark of his disgrace, grimly pursuing the souls which would buy him the approval of the King and the gratitude of heaven, but brought to a halt at last, side-stepping death, finally forced to flee the island.

It was Thangbrand's mission, however, which had had the most success so far; two of his converts, men of wealth and influence, stemmed Olaf Tryggvesson's fury at being thwarted and diverted his plans for bloody reprisal by promising, while visiting his Court, to do their utmost to persuade their countrymen to accept the new religion. The *Althing* was their natural forum; arriving too late for diplomatic groundwork, for the ferreting work of jest, discussion, gift and surrender by which support is bought and faction built, they could do no more than present themselves and insist as well as they were able, a minority in a hostile place, that their case should be heard. The *Althing* split; the Christians here, the pagans there, declared their rivals to be outside the law. Swords usually settled such differences, and both

A modern view of Thingvellir, where the *godar*,
priest chieftains, met at the *Althing*.

sides were ready, a readiness which in itself led to further discussion; it was not the
Althing's function to cause or sanction civil war. Thus it was agreed that the
Christian case might be put, and for the first time the *lögberg* overlooked the
Christian cross, carried in its protagonists' solemn procession. When the advocates
of Jesus spoke, their numbers seemed less than adequate for their claims, but those
listening knew that it was the world which spoke to them. Beyond the seas which
hammered their eastern and southern shores, the new faith had won all its battles.
Norway, their fount and distant overseer, had turned to it; Ireland had accepted

it long before Viking memory; Danes had followed Saxons into the new religion in England; recent Normans had accepted the doctrines of long-established Franks on the continental mainland. These few local zealots, properly numbered, spoke with the voice of an enormous majority; it was Iceland which would be alone if it resisted, some sixty thousand isolated souls stubborn in their allegiance to Europe's spiritual discards.

The *Althing* had as its elected president the 'law-speaker', the *lögsögumadr*, a man who in himself stood for law and constitution and was thus the embodiment of national heritage, his influence vast, though his formal power was so limited as to be non-existent. When the *Althing* split, the Christians had elected a president of their own, Sidu-Hall Thorsteinsson, expecting him to set out a Christian law. He was, however, too wise a man for that, foreseeing that no community as small as Iceland's could survive the proclamation of two codes of law. He took the lead in stating the Christian case; it was the actual *lögsögumadr*, Thorgeir of Ljosavatn, who most prominently opposed him. Yet it was to Thorgeir that Sidu-Hall left the decision, the final speaking of the law. 'Thorgeir', the historians tell us, 'lay down and spread his cloak over him, and lay quiet all that day and the night following, and spoke never a word.' The next day, however, 24 June (the year 999 or perhaps 1000), he spoke to some purpose – and to the dismay of his own party. For his verdict was that since 'our affairs have come to a dangerous pass if we do not have one and the same law', everyone in Iceland should now have himself baptized, Christianity should be the country's public religion and the old temples, and the idols they housed, finally demolished. At the same time, he encouraged a compromising adherence to the old ways by suggesting that such ancient customs as the exposure of the newly born and the eating of horseflesh might be continued in secret.

In this way matters went on, the public split healed, Christianity the obvious religion of the state, but everywhere the old gods privately worshipped; yet not so privately that the practice did not scandalize the rest of the Viking world. Finally, Olaf the Stout, ruling in Norway and on his road to sanctity, brought pressure on the *Althing* to outlaw the old worship entirely and, when they had done so in 1016, celebrated this triumph by sending the timber with which a church might be built on the Thingvellir. Soon, the priests and bishops who serviced this and other churches were native Icelanders; Norwegian pressure and native intelligence had brought about a fundamental change.

The part played by the kings of Norway was also significant, a sign of how closely connected the two countries still were, despite all the islanders' fierce passion for independence. Indeed, it was that very passion, manifested in their private feuds, which was finally to lose it for them. Riven by disagreement, desperate for an impartial, central authority, it was to the Crown of Norway that they finally turned. It was internecine struggles in which the historian Snorri Sturluson was deeply involved which brought them to this pass, he against his brother Sighvat and his family, Snorri fleeing to Norway, returning to what might have been power, then overturned by Gizur Thorvaldsson and assassinated in 1241.

Made *jarl* by Norway's Hakon, Gizur used the islanders' delight in liberty as a weapon against his protector, while eroding their independence in its own power-ful name. But, long-headed, his compatriots saw through him. With over a thousand men behind him, he came to the *Althing* to make a stand for Iceland's freedom from Norway and thus his own continued arrogance and extortions, only to discover that in choosing between evils the people had decided that he was the greater. Hakon Hakonsson of Norway, they felt, would at least protect them from the power of upstarts essentially no better than themselves, men who set themselves up without legal claim and would not suffer the fair restrictions of the law. An astute man, Gizur at once made himself the spokesman for what was now the majority faction, a position which his role as Norway's representative made more plausible than it might have been otherwise. In 1262, therefore, Iceland and the Crown of Norway made a bond, a bargain Iceland would have many opportu-nities to regret, but which, inevitable at the time, survived until in 1814 the island began its Danish connection; this, modified, would continue into the twentieth century.

The Faroes, Iceland – but there was land still, on westward over those bleak seas, shores Vikings were bound to discover. Here as elsewhere, accident led them, Gunnbjörn Ulf-Krakason, a sailor from Norway, being flung by storm outwards from Ireland, to be the first who sighted the swelling meadows which lifted above the narrow fjords of Greenland. Then came Eirik the Red, a wild man, a stubborn fighter, blood on his hands three times over, exiled for that from Norway, then from Iceland, travelling in 982 to verify Gunnbjörn's story and delighted when Greenland's eastern coast, ice-bound but clearly within sight, proved the existence of this waiting land-mass. He coasted south, rounding at last what is today Cape Farewell; two summers he explored the further, western coast, marking for him-self and his men the site of homes and steadings, naming landmarks, noticing with delight a land rich with game, a sea heavy with fish. Three winters he survived in prepared quarters, as Northmen knew how to do, and then he sailed back to Iceland, his period of banishment over, but already firm in his conviction to settle this empty land he had explored: a land to which he gave its name, that 'Green-land' a message of hope and opportunity to Icelanders beset by famine and already pressed for holdings on an island where all the land had been apportioned fifty years before.

It was with fourteen ships, therefore – survivors of the twenty-five which had set out – that Eirik returned in 986, the colonizers staring upwards at the rock-walls of the fjords, exclaiming perhaps at the grey-green slopes beyond, their cattle lowing at their tethers, the women gathering themselves for the long home-making to come. Two settlements were established, the Western and the Eastern, the latter the older, centring on the founder, Eirik, the former some 170 miles to the north. They built farms, houses, soon established a *thing* on the Icelandic model, would have churches and even, so they insisted, a cathedral for their bishop, but Greenland's population never grew beyond that of a small country town: perhaps

Christianity in Iceland:
LEFT Birchwood figure of Christ from
Ufsir. FAR LEFT Upper roundel of the
carved church door from
Valthyofsstadir.

some three thousand inhabitants. These clung, it must have seemed to them, to a narrow possibility, survival a matter of the fifty miles separating the coast from the ice-cap which rolls northward from there to the turning axis of the globe. Their corn and most of their iron and timber had to be carried to them on trading vessels which would make the uncomfortable return run laden with furs and skins, wool, oil and walrus tusks.

They tried to stretch their little colony, exploring northwards along the shores of Baffin Bay, opening up new areas for diligent hunters to exploit. Traces of their voyaging have been discovered almost at the eightieth parallel, some seven hundred miles from the North Pole. The stability of Greenland's population came, however, from the Eastern Settlement, the most southerly, the fattest, some two hundred homesteads flourishing along its fjords or folded in its cool meadows, its focal point Gardar, where the *Althing* assembled, its deliberations the formal centre and necessary excuse for the population's periodic rediscovery of its communal reality.

In 999 tradition has Leif Eiriksson, heir to the colony's founder, making the long journey to Norway, a renewal of his roots, perhaps, and in the event the establishing of a new direction for Greenland. Olaf Tryggvesson was king in Norway and Leif a guest at his Court; and far to the west, Greenland was still unconverted. This concentration of circumstances could have only one outcome; when Leif returned home in the year 1000, it was as a Christian, a priest his companion and the alteration of Greenland's faith his reluctantly accepted responsibility. This new development very shortly split the new missionary's own family, for his mother, Thjodhild, was soon baptized, an acceptance of Jesus which led to rejection by her husband. Eirik the Red crustily stayed loyal to older convictions and banished his wife from his sight. One imagines that such disputes were not unusual; nevertheless when Adalbert was archbishop in Bremen during the middle years of the eleventh century, emissaries arrived there from Greenland asking that clergy be sent to them, so that it seems it took only three or four decades for Christianity to become the colony's dominant faith.

It may be that in those latitudes they needed the reassurance of a system less anarchic than Asgard offered, some certainty that the death which constantly threatened them and the poverty which bound them about were in themselves the beginnings of marvellously better things, respectively gateway to and guarantee of a rich and delightful eternity. As it was, even on a less transcendental plane, they needed the support of others, they needed a life-line connecting them with the European mainland and their past. It was, quite naturally, in Norway that the other end of that line was fixed, the country then dominant along the seaways of the North Sea and the North Atlantic and the homeland from which most Greenland families stemmed. In 1261, therefore, they shuffled off the burden of independence in exchange for that of taxation and turned their country into a colony of the Norwegian Crown. They hoped in this way to ensure that they would never be abandoned, that the connection between Greenland and Scandinavia would

Skeletons from the graveyard of Thjodhild at
Brattahlid, the settlement that Eric the Red
founded in Greenland.

remain unbroken, even strengthened. In such optimism they were to be deceived.

By then, however, they had made and seen collapse yet one more attempt to break through the bleak walls of sea, ice and mountain which contained them. North had failed them, so once again they had driven westward, continuing the logic of that Viking journey of which their own colony had become the spearhead. Not that the effort was ever planned or thought out – it began, as had Greenland's own discovery, by accident. But it seems likely that navigators of their experience, knowledgeable in the signs of cloud and bird flight, men who without qualm had made the leap between Iceland and Greenland, may well have known that some-where to the west of them there was more land. If Eirik and his companions had such suspicions, it was not long before they were confirmed.

In the summer of 986, Bjarni Herjólfsson arrived in Iceland, his ship laden, his intention to spend the winter in his father's house. To his dismay, it was strangers who met him – his father had sold his holdings and taken ship, one of Eirik the Red's colonizing followers, his ambition to found new estates in Greenland.

A Viking map showing Greenland,
Newfoundland and Labrador. It was drawn
before the discovery of America in 1492, but
shows Eskimo boats and figures.

Bjarni followed, bravely alone and with little guidance but hearsay; fog descended, all direction disappeared, for days the ship moved only at the demand of breeze and current. Finally, with sunshine and the mist unravelling, Bjarni could continue his journey, secure in his sightings. A day later, he saw a coastline – low hills, tree-covered, the curves of the country low and undramatic. This was not the Greenland of fjords and meadows and distant mountains which had been described to him. He swung to the north and coasted for two more days, past flatlands heavy with forest. Three days sailing more, and he found himself off an icy land, a place of crag and glacier. On this, Bjarni turned his back, setting a northerly course and holding it for four days. With the fortune of the imperturbable, he thus arrived at his destination, soon putting in at Herjolfsnes on the Eastern Settlement's Herjolfsfjord, these place-names witness of his father's presence.

Fifteen years later Eirik the Red's son Leif turned Bjarni's voyage upside-down. In the same ship and with some of the same men in his crew, he sailed southerly from Greenland; a few days later, he became the first European to stand on the soil of what would not be 'America' for another four centuries. It was a barren place, scrubbed bare by wind and ice, a place of stone overlooked by stark, glacier-seamed mountains. It was most probably the southern shore of Baffin Island, possibly even Labrador's stern eastern coast; he called it Helluland, Land of Flat Stones. He sailed on with his thirty-five companions until he came to a pleasanter landscape, low slopes falling gently to wide beaches, land edged with their brilliant white, the sand a contrast to the heavy woods beyond. Leif Eiriksson called it Markland, Land of Woods, but what do we call it? His position here to some extent determines his next, and the next has proved the stimulus to academic frenzy for many years. Was he as far south as Nova Scotia, or was he still coasting down the indented shores of Labrador, no further south than Hamilton Inlet at the most? Climates have altered in a millennium and it is difficult now to be precise. What is certain is that when he put ashore a third time, he called that place Vinland.

He had sailed in a generally southerly direction for two days to get there, a helpful nor'-easterly pushing him on. When he landed, he found rivers rich in salmon, fat pastures and even wild grapes, the plant from which he took the country's name. Today, no vines grow north of the forty-fifth parallel; did they then, when the climate was warmer? A sun sighting is mentioned, the duration of its appearance noted on winter's shortest day; this too has provoked attempts to settle Vinland's location definitively. It cannot be done. Warmth, a bountiful nature, lakes and rivers generous with fish – was this, as some have asserted, Chesapeake Bay, south of Long Island, in Maryland? Today, it is not thought likely, partly because salmon are never found south of the Hudson River and the Vikings seem to have found them in great profusion; more prosaically, it is the north coast of Newfoundland, where Belle Isle Strait divides it from the mainland, which is now considered the most probable site of Leif Eiriksson's Vinland. Certainly archaeology offers some confirmation of this, the remains of houses of the type used by Northmen having been found there.

Leif called his little winter-quarters Leifsbudir, Leif's Booths or huts; in the
spring, he sailed north again, returning to Greenland to find his father dead. He
announced his discoveries, praised the mildness of the climate and the fertility of
the soil, then settled to his new responsibilities as head of the community's most
influential clan. It was his brother Thorvald who took up the more glamorous
burden of exploration. It is likely that he sailed with some of Leif's crew; in any
case, he had no problems in reaching Leifsbudir. Having wintered there, he began
to reach out in wider exploration. Woods, islands, an empty land; one abandoned
hut, however, told of humans, the little structure unfamiliar, probably a sort of
wigwam, certainly built by men. Winter again, passed easily at Leifsbudir; then
an eastward exploration, a bright bay ringed with beauty, its delights a welcome,
but death their price. For the first time, Northmen came face to face with
Amerindians, the people they called *Skrälings* (probably 'screechers', perhaps
'ugly ones' or, more comprehensible to our chauvinism, 'savages'). They found
three canoes, nine Indians hiding under them; instantly, with Viking reaction,
they struck at them. Eight died, but one was allowed to flee, such fortuitous
survival always a murderers' hazard. That night, bitterly informed, the Indians
returned in force and bent upon revenge. Behind their longship's shield-wall, the
Northmen rode out the attack, warding off spear and arrow, beleaguered but by
no means overcome. They seem to have suffered only one loss, but that one crucial
– Thorvald himself, struck by an arrow which had crept between shield and gun-
wale. So his blood and body settled into that alien soil, while in the spring his crew
sailed back with a complex tale to tell those who awaited them.

Eirik the Red's third son, Thorstein, told of his brother's death, set out in 1007,
perhaps to fetch his body. He took his wife and twenty-five men, put forth bravely
but arrived nowhere, wind, fog and current keeping his ship at sea, his route
tortuous and not now to be made out, his final landfall nothing more than Greenland's own shore, Lysufjord in the Western Settlement. After this for more than a
decade the shores of the western continent were left unvisited. They were not forgotten, however; when around 1020 Thorfinn Karlsefni of Iceland brought two
ships laden with goods into Eiriksfjord to trade, he heard them much discussed.
This is less surprising when one learns that he wintered at Brattahlid, the home
Eirik the Red had built and which was now his surviving clan's focal point, the
place where, if anywhere, the deeds of Leif Eiriksson and his brothers would be
matter for conversation, praise and debate. Thorfinn, indeed, became himself a
member of that family, marrying Gudrid, who had been the wife and was now the
widow of that Thorstein who had failed in his one attempt to reach Vinland. Perhaps she wanted to repeat with greater success her earlier voyage, perhaps
Thorfinn saw trading opportunities in the new lands, perhaps he and his companions simply felt the stir of the old Viking curiosity, the sense that what could be
reached should be and that the sea was the Northman's natural highway. What
seems clear is that he intended this time no reconnaissance, but rather a prolonged
stay, one which would lay the foundation of a colony.

They landed at a place they called Straumfjord, which may be on the north coast of Newfoundland, like Leifsbudir, or may have been further south across the Gulf of St Lawrence. Autumn gave them food and their cattle provender; then winter foreclosed their mortgage on the land, the cold and ice withdrawing all the promises the earlier mildness had implied. The people struggled; Viking fashion, they withdrew to an island where the animals did fairly well, but the humans no better than before. A whale, unexpectedly stranded, provided them with sustenance, conjured up, it is said, by a disagreeable old heathen named Thorhall the Hunter who was trying to prove Thor superior to Jesus, this small miracle therefore an argument in the New World's first religious debate. The Christian counterargument, the illness of some of those who had eaten the flesh, somewhat diminished Thorhall's triumph. Perhaps because of this, perhaps because of his impatience with the new land, which did not seem to him as wonderful as reports had suggested, Thorhall with nine others left the main party and as soon as the ice had broken sufficiently, sailed back towards Greenland. According to *Eirik's Saga*, however, he was blown off course to Ireland, was made a slave and in that sad condition died.

The rest of the party sailed on south until they came to a land-locked bay and named the place after this configuration, *Hóp*; they found its waters crammed with fish, wild vines on the hillsides, self-seeded wheat, and pastures rich and rolling which seemed to have been created for their cattle. Here they decided to settle (although there is only dispute over how 'here' may actually be identified – is Hóp on the Newfoundland coast, on the banks of the St Lawrence estuary, in Novia Scotia, at the mouth of the Hudson River, on the shores of Maryland or even Virginia?). For a while, its little houses snugly built, hunting and agriculture imposing their own rhythms, the little colony seemed to be contentedly moving towards prosperity. *Skrälings* appeared, skittering across the water in their light canoes. By means of signals – the Indians waving staves, their motion that of the sun, the Vikings hanging up a white shield – the two peoples indicated that they wanted peace. The Indians came ashore and according to *Eirik's Saga* and the *Groenlendinga Saga* the Northmen were not impressed by their appearance – small, dark, broad-cheeked, with coarse hair. Having looked around, the Indians went away again, leaving the little settlement to face a winter which astonished them by its mildness; there was no snow and throughout the whole season their beasts could find their own fodder in the open.

In the spring, the Indians returned, a multitude of canoes springing into sight around the headland, the staves whirling again in the signal of peace. Soon they had landed and approached the Northmen, not empty-handed this time, but carrying skins and furs which they clearly intended for barter. In exchange, they wanted weapons, but this was a commerce Karlsefni would not allow. The Indians, however, proved equally delighted by some red cloth which the Greenlanders offered them, taking it a span at a time, giving a skin in return, then tying the cloth about their heads. As stocks of the material began to run short, the

A Viking saga dating from medieval times,
mentioning Vinland.

Vikings, traders for centuries, cut their spans more and more narrowly, until, we are told, the lengths of cloth were no wider than a finger. Still the *Skrälings* took them, happily giving a skin for a span, whatever its width.

The Indians' pleasure with what these aliens had brought to their shores did not last. There were incidents, it may be that one of the *Skrälings* was killed while trying to steal weapons, Karlsefni felt it necessary to build a defensive palisade and before long the settlement was under attack. When Spain and Portugal made their assault on the Americas, they brought with them guns, armour and horses; behind them, they had the resources of great kingdoms. These earlier settlers had no such advantages. Their weapons were, perhaps, more sophisticated than the Indians', but the margin of difference was nothing like as wide as that which would later be expressed in the terrifying roar of gunpowder. There is no record that they were supplied or reinforced from their home bases in Greenland; even if they had been, one cannot compare a wealthy European country like fifteenth-century Spain or Portugal with a scattered community of some three thousand people subsisting, sometimes desperately, at the northern edge of the known world. The Vinland colonists were, to all intents, on their own, and in such a situation they were too few and too exposed to survive. Hemmed in by the native Indians, they also began to bicker among themselves; there were women, but not enough, always a cause of dissent, and there was probably disagreement about whether to go or stay. After three winters, Karlsefni had realized that in a country already inhabited they would never be able to put down roots unhampered and that this would always outweigh the land's admitted advantages. So, after the early hopes and the long months of struggle, the Northmen turned their backs on this new continent, on the very extremity of which they had been perched, succumbing to the logic of history, which had decreed that for such a conquest time and technology would not be ready for another 450 years.

Not that Vinland and these western shores were to be forgotten. Indeed, there was, according to the records, yet another voyage made by one of Eirik's clan, this time by Freydis, his daughter, who had been on Karlsefni's expedition. She is said to have persuaded Thorvald, her husband, a man who, though rich, had long succumbed to her will, that their partners in the venture, two Icelandic brothers named Helgi and Finnbogi, had insulted her. Thorvald, therefore, led a murderous foray against the brothers' men and killed every one of them, Viking ferocity in feud spreading blood across this soil, too, as it had on that of every country where Northmen had set foot. Five women, the story insists, were spared – until Freydis, despairing of her men's soft-heartedness, took up an axe herself and split them, all five, broken-skulled into death.

Whether this melodramatic adventure ever occurred, or occurred there, or then, hardly matters now; it was, in any case, not the only voyage to be made in that direction. A hundred years later, a missionary bishop, Eirik Gnupsson, set off to preach the Word to the *Skrälings*, but if they heard it or paid any heed, it is not recorded; the bishop simply sails westward and disappears. It seems very likely,

however, that Greenland ships sailed to America successfully on more commercial
enterprises; the journey, after all, is shorter than the one between Denmark and
England, the rewards were cargoes of timber and furs, the former a desperate need
in Greenland, the latter a staple of the country's export trade. Furs sent from a
bishop in Greenland to his colleague in Bergen included pelts taken from animals
known in America but not in Greenland. As late as 1347 a ship, driven to Iceland
by storm, had been in this way diverted from her home port in Greenland, the
sailors aboard her on their way back from wooded Markland. It was always known
in Greenland that skins and walrus tusks and either fresh timber or driftwood
could be brought from those shores and it is unlikely, therefore, that contact with
the lands discovered by Leif Eiriksson was ever completely broken during the
centuries of the Greenland communities.

Contact, however, is not colonization. The flint arrow-head, of Amerindian
manufacture, found in the graveyard at Sandnes, in Greenland, spelled the death
of more than the single Viking in whose body it must have been brought back. The
ground-plans of Scandinavian buildings, etched into the soil of northern Newfoundland, mark the furthest stride westward of the Viking expansion. After this,
the tale is one of recoil as, throughout the world, the energy of the Northmen at last
ran out and, here in the north-west, conditions and circumstances turned against
them. As the twelfth century ended, the climate reversed. Ice crept southward, all
over Europe snow fell lower on the mountain slopes, upland trees died. Pack-ice
cluttered the coasts of Greenland, then tightened, an Arctic noose to strangle
movement. With the cold, the Eskimoes (whom the Greenlanders also called
Skrälings) began to move south, short men, squat in their furs, eyes glinting from
within their shaggy hoods, their culture and metabolism both better adapted to
these changed conditions.

Norway declined; Greenland, now its colony, suffered that decline's consequences. The Greenland trade was a monopoly of the Norwegian Crown, one
which was guarded with an energy which might have been better spent on
developing it. The incidence of royal ships, always infrequent, dwindled constantly. Bergen, the city in which the Greenland trade was vested, did not need it
in its prosperous years, having more than enough of its own; when Black Death
and the Hanseatic League made life more difficult, the island became too distant,
too hard to reach.

Slowly, then, Greenland became isolated. Occasionally, ships would call, some
brought involuntarily, by storm. The Western Settlement crumbled, the assault
from *Skrälings* and the cold too much for it. The Eastern Settlement survived;
rumours which the world believed – that it was heathen again, that it had thrown
its cultural lot in with that of the Eskimoes – were libels. Stubbornly, its people
clung to what they were. Their light was Christian, their traditions unbrokenly
Norse. The grim decades passed, poverty wrestled with them, overthrew them
with sickness, diminished their stature; their pride, it seems, remained. The last
royal carrier in the Greenland trade sank in 1369; the last bishop arrived in 1377;

Christian relics in Greenland: LEFT Crozier and ring found on the excavation sites of Viking settlements in Greenland. BELOW The ruins of Halsey Church.

carly in the fifteenth century, a party of Icelanders were driven there by chance and stayed for a clutch of years. But the darkness was coming down, was pressing down ceaselessly, a night which would take them all at last, the dark blizzard of time, merciless in its indifference. It hides from us the last decisions, whatever there was of agony, of struggle, hope, determination or acceptance; having encircled them, it has never let them go.

Around 1540 a German merchant ship, blown into these now inhospitable waters by gales, came cautiously up a Greenland fjord. Islands complicated it; on some, Eskimoes lived, and these the skipper, Jon, decided to ignore. He landed at last on an island heavy with the silence of solitude. Above the shore, however, he saw buildings, half-ruined but familiar, buildings like those he had seen often in Iceland: fish-sheds, drying houses for fish, dwellings for men. Before them, a man lay, the woollen hood on his head covering his features as he curled face-down in the dirt. Sealskin clothes, and woollen, covered him. A knife lay beside him, curved, the blade worn by years of use and sharpening. At the feet of these astonished sailors he rested there in the long inertia of the dead – they the last European visitors to Greenland's Viking colony, he the last Greenland Viking anyone would ever see.

The coast of southern Sweden, typical of the
lands from which the Vikings sailed.

8 THE LAST VIKING

The Viking passion was for freedom – one's own, at no matter whose expense. As a consequence, the Viking age more than any other is dominated by individuals, men who by their disproportionate ambition and the convulsive energy placed at ambition's disposal took hold of history as though it were a sack and shook it empty of its prizes. States were no more than the artifacts of those who had created them, personal possessions, insubstantial structures vanishing with the deaths of their colossal kings, each great monarch of the age a single-generation dynasty. The world was a dangerous maze stacked with riches, through which a series of muscular and overbearing egotists smashed and blundered, bloodying the soil and, with the stained tips of their swords, picking up the gold, the titles, the trinkets which would proclaim their heroic status. Poets, seconding such proclamations, told the stories of their lives in stressed lines stiff with the metaphoric compression of kennings, these *skálds* thus making immortal the ephemeral violence of piracy and conquest. If it was economic forces which first drove the young men into their insubstantial ships and out across the sea to wrench plunder and land from the nameless ones who owned them; if as the centuries turned, Viking liberties were slowly hemmed in by the coral-like growth of organized nations; if the spider, history, would at last bind them in the ten thousand strands of its web, necessity, it was nevertheless while freedom lasted the individuals of the Viking age, savagely criss-crossing their world, who for four hundred years dominated their times, their societies and their neighbours and sometimes, in their wild rage to succeed, altered almost single-handed the logic of a whole continent's development. It is right, therefore, to make such a man the climactic hero, the one man whose death can stand as the death of all, whose fall brings down the darkness on the Viking centuries, and whose departure clears the world for those who would inherit the ambition, the energy, the cruelty, but little of the gaiety, the poetry or the anarchic delight, of their northern predecessors.

Harald Hardradi appears, active and belligerent, in the midst of doom and the clash of high ambition, death, disaster and defeat about him, battle his stage. The field was Stiklarstadir, where in 1030 Harald's half-brother, Olaf of Norway, the mundane glitter of his crown snatched from him, the transcendental nimbus of sanctity not yet attained, was making his desperate assault on his old throne. Snorri names Harald 'the most distinguished man' among those who rallied to Olaf's cause, but he was not much more than a boy – 'fifteen years of age', but

The Viking warriors: BELOW Helmet found in
a grave at Vendel, Uppland, Sweden. RIGHT
The great axe found at Mammen, Jutland. On
it is a bird with limbs in the form of the
acanthus creeper and spiral-shaped thighs,
typical of the so-called Mammen style.

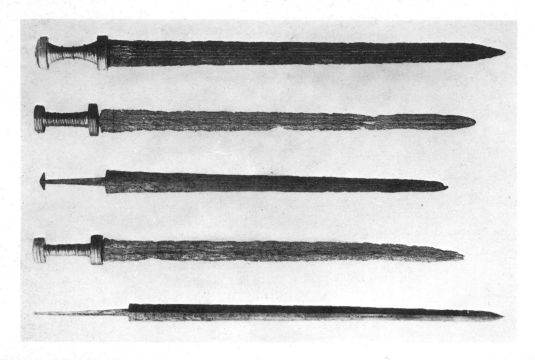

Weapons used by the Vikings: TOP Two-edged
swords found in a bog at Kragehul. BOTTOM
Ninth- and tenth-century Norse sword, spears
and axe-head.

'very stout, and manly of growth as if he were full-grown'. Olaf fell, to work his
miracles and become Norway's saint and *perpetuus rex*; Harald, either more or less
fortunate according to one's convictions, was wounded, hidden, healed and able
finally to flee 'east to King Jarisleif in Russia'.

In Kiev, Harald settled for a while to the service of the great Yaroslav, helping
him in his struggles to consolidate his territories in the north and west, becoming
the commander of his armies and fighting in the bitter campaign to enforce peace
on Russia's western borders with the Poles. He took Yaroslav as his patron and
protector; the great Prince eventually rewarded him by giving him his daughter
Elizabeth as wife. In 1034, however, as yet unmarried, Harald travelled on, his
journey that of many ambitious Vikings before him: with five hundred followers,
he sailed down the Dnieper to offer his skill and his courage in the lucrative
service of the Byzantine emperors.

Legend like a wreathing mist now alters and magnifies the already tremendous
outlines of fact. What is certain is that for nine years Harald remained in the
service of Byzantium, his sword at the disposal of three successive emperors.
Almost at once, it seems, he found himself fighting Arabs in Asia Minor and the
Levant. A year or so after his arrival in Constantinople, one hears of him harassing
the infidel on the banks of the Euphrates. He might have been the Christian commander who took Jerusalem into the keeping of Jesus's faithful, but Byzantium
would rarely fight when it could negotiate and he was recalled once the Caliph
had conceded the Christian right to visit holy places. Some two years later, Harald
appeared in Sicily, his enemies still Muslim, victory once more his theme. The
Greeks, mercenaries beside them – Normans, now, as well as Varangians – took
the eastern part of the island, and with it Syracuse and Messina. Then, as so often,
intrigue and ingratitude, meanness of the pocket and of the mind at the very
centre of affairs in Constantinople, worked to divide those who served Byzantium
and to alienate those who had been both faithful and successful. The disgruntled
Normans went away, the victorious commander was ordered home as though in
disgrace, the Varangians lost their natural zest for battle and the war swung
against the Eastern Empire.

When the Normans in southern Italy became a greater threat than Islam,
Harald was, however, among those who went to fight them there. By the autumn,
he was engaged against the Bulgars, who had proclaimed their own Tsar in

Belgrade and had subsequently struck deep into Thessaly. Checked outside
Thessalonika, the rebellion collapsed in disunity in 1041, the Bulgars for all their
Albanian and even Greek allies proving themselves unable to withstand the
Roman discipline of the Byzantine forces. There followed in Constantinople mis-
rule, violence, insurrection and death: Michael IV was succeeded by the cruel and
incompetent Michael V Calaphetes, whom after a few months the people turned
on, beset, pursued, searched out and dreadfully killed. Harald and his Varangians
were somewhere and vigorous in these bloody affairs, but it is hard to say in what
way – though Snorri tells us that it was Harald, the field commander of the
Varangian Guard, who was given the task of tearing out the eyes of both the
humbled Emperor and his unpleasant uncle.

Harald by now had been given the rank of *spatharocandidate*, the third level in the
hierarchy of courtiers, officers and administrators who surrounded the Throne
and perhaps under the new emperor, Constantine IX Monomachus, his career
might have continued to blossom, its fruit honour and wealth. But it may be that
recent events had shaken his faith in the firmness of Byzantine intentions or even
institutions; it may be, too, that far in the north he saw new and better opportunities. His nephew Magnus, son of the sainted Olaf, had left Russia as soon as
the great Knut had died. Svein, Knut's son, ruling Norway with the advice of his
rigid and avaricious mother, had soon proved unpopular. In 1035, he had been
forced to flee; in his place, the people had chosen Magnus. Now, when another of
Knut's sons, the equally incompetent Hordaknut, was newly dead in England,
Denmark had, without demur or bloodshed, accepted Magnus Olafsson's rule. It
may be that, with Magnus the king of two countries and Svein still lurking, disaffected, in the northern shadows, Harald could detect a brittleness in the political
situation which someone both ambitious and ruthless might exploit. The name by
which men called him, 'Hardradi', means 'Hard-Counsel' or, more loosely, 'the
Ruthless' – was it this ability to see and use possible weaknesses which earned it for
him? In any case, he seems to have been determined to leave Constantinople. His
decision to do so did not please the new emperor; there is a suggestion that he was
even thrown in prison (although that may have been because of Yaroslav's unhappy assault on Constantinople in 1043). If he was, he was soon released or, as
the story prefers, managed to escape. He took with him, according to *King
Harald's Saga*, the abducted niece of the Empress, but set her ashore unharmed as
proof that had he wanted to he might have married her. He then bounced his
galley over the chains protecting the Bosporus by having his men run first to the
stern and then to the bows, so lifting the ship on the barrier and then tilting her into
a slide to safety. In this way, he broke into the freedom of the Black Sea. It was now
that, back in Kiev after nearly a decade, he married the Russian Prince's daughter.
Shortly afterwards, he turned his back on the eastern world for ever; he had done
with serving royal masters – he wanted mastery for himself.

The reasoning behind his armed diplomacy in the north was simple – Magnus
was king of two countries because he was Olaf's son: should not some part of these

domains at least belong to Olaf's brother, a man who had nearly died at Stiklarstadir struggling to place Olaf back on the throne which now gave Magnus's rule legitimacy? For a while, Harald and Svein, the deposed son of Knut, worked together in an alliance largely meaningless because of their own implicit rivalry. They came marauding down the coast of Zealand, Harald demonstrating afresh his Viking energy. But it was Magnus who really held the cards and he split his enemies by the simple and magnanimous device of giving Harald what he asked for, a share in the Norwegian crown. For a while, late in 1046, early in 1047, this potentially uneasy situation seemed to be continuing remarkably comfortably; then, abruptly, death dissolved it. Magnus died, it is not clear where or how, although it does not seem to have been violence which dragged him under; Harald Hardradi was the undisputed king of Norway.

In true Viking fashion, he seems to have considered his new power as little more than a secure base from which he could make endless war. Heroes must write their histories in the blood of many corpses; monarchs must watch for rivals and jealously dispatch those who threaten, or might threaten, or might be thought to threaten, the stability of their reign. Thus great lords were lopped down or forced to flee, friends were treated as enemies, enemies were pursued and ferociously done to death. The power of the *jarls* of the north was restricted, undermined, sometimes demolished; it was because of this devastation however that Harald's line grew so strong, sons over several generations succeeding their fathers, establishing the kind of dynasty which other kings had been unable to found. The north was made secure for them by his campaigns, and the borders with Sweden were solidly established.

Denmark, in the meantime, had turned to Svein, and it is clear that this decision irked Harald and that he would have liked to reverse it, to wrench it aside by force of arms. Soon after his accession, therefore, there began years of raids, of sudden assaults, of skirmishes and indeterminate battles, his fleets busy about those waters, stinging at Svein's kingdom, hornets come in clouds to harass and torment an enemy. As at the beginning of the Viking years, smoke signalled destruction above the steadings and small towns which lined a coast, but this time the coast was that of a Viking country.

In 1049 this campaign, old-fashioned in its reliance upon swift descent, swift destruction and swift flight, reached its climax in the burning of the great trading town of Hedeby, which stood not far from Schleswig, not far from Eckernforde, in today's German *Land* of Schleswig-Holstein. Founded in the eighth century, the town was protected by a rampart on the three landward sides, its buildings wooden or of daub-and-wattle construction, with thatched roofs, the material usually reeds. Slaves stood in its market place, brought from the east, dragged miserably from their Slavonic homelands to find their way to their buyers' estates; from the west came glass and pottery, wine and weapons, from the north furs and skins; from Hedeby itself came complex artifacts, jewellery and cloth and carved bone, carefully manufactured in the quarter where the craftsmen lived and

Examples of Viking craftsmanship: RIGHT
Eleventh-century pendant found at Gråträsk,
Sweden, and tenth-century brooch with riveted
animal figures, from Torsta, Hälsingtuna.
FAR RIGHT A Viking head carved in elkhorn,
forming the top of a stick, from Sigtuna,
Sweden. OPPOSITE BELOW Decorated bridle
mount from Broa, Halla, Gotland.

worked. The town was rich enough to strike its own coinage; its smiths knew how
to work cunningly in iron and bronze. Upon this activity, this wealthy tumult,
Harald swooped with all the old, mindless Viking ferocity; his men rampaged past
those tall-roofed houses, their shouts rang down the stonepaved streets; flame in
their fists, they ran helter-skelter, destruction their delirium, death their attendant; screams lay about them on the air, cacophony of pain and fear, a music which
had for so many centuries riven the hearing in those lands which the Northmen
struck. Then fire arose, a whole town sitting under a firmament of sparks, the
laughing raiders happy at so brisk, so glittering a success. But Hedeby would
recover, if only briefly; and Svein would not be forced from Denmark's throne.

Harald's struggle to drag Denmark into Norway's, and his, domination, continued off and on for seventeen years. In 1060, there was a great sea-battle at
Nissa; Svein was defeated, some seventy of his ships lost, yet his hold on Denmark's
throne remained secure. Three years later, weary at last, Harald entered into
negotiations with his neighbour and in 1064 they met, to debate his ambition and
Svein's stubbornness face-to-face. Irresistible force, perhaps, and immovable
object; the result, in any case, was that as things were so they would remain,
frontiers should stand, neither land nor money should change hands, the kingdoms
should be frozen in their established shapes. Harald went back to the firm and
sometimes over-vigorous organization of his own fiefs, asserting his sovereignty
over the Upplanders, always in the past dangerous asserters of their own independence; he did so partly by the profitable expedient of extending the Crown's
properties through the forced forfeiture of private land. He cut down further the
power of his aristocracy; for a hundred years after his death no one would use the
old title of *jarl*. He asserted national authority, and therefore his own, in ecclesiastical affairs, Christianity being complicated in the country by the existence of
priests owing allegiance to the see of Bremen, of missionaries sent by the rival
Church in England, and of bearded practitioners of the Orthodox Church, come
from the east perhaps in Harald's own wake (though they were, naturally, to be
met with in Sweden, too, travelling along the trade routes which linked that
country with Russia and Byzantium).

It may have seemed that the old Viking Adam lay moribund in Harald's breast.
He had almost all he had ever wanted, he was nearly fifty years old, his name was
safely in the sagas, in the long roster of heroes. But such a flame as burned in him

never dies completely. He had fought under the blue-white skies, heat-heavy, of
the East; he had explored, so it was said, the far extremities of the northern seas,
stopped there by ice, it might be, or as Adam of Bremen preferred, by the vast
terror of the world-encompassing abyss; he had fought for and won a crown, and
had consolidated its power until it sat more firmly on his head than on that of any
king in Norway's history. Nevertheless, when new adventure called him and
another crown appeared like a mirage to trouble his ambition, he responded with
all the vigour of his youth.

It was England he wanted, his claim tenuous though not entirely without merit.
Custom in those days made a king's own declaration a crucial factor in his succession. In Germany, Konrad I had nominated as his heir the Duke of Saxony,
Henry the Fowler, a man with whom he had no blood ties – though from Henry
there had stemmed a great dynasty. It remained a fact, however, that even the
king could not pick anyone he fancied as his successor, for the new king had to
have either great power or a blood-claim to bring him the acceptance of his
country's magnates and aristocrats. Without such an acceptance, his reign was
likely to be troubled, bloody and short.

At one remove Harald Hardradi had, he insisted, received such a royal nomination: when Hordaknut left Scandinavia in 1038 to begin the journey which would
bring him to his father's throne in England, he and Magnus Olafsson of Norway
had made an arrangement by which each had named the other as the heir to his
crown. In this way Hordaknut had established the peace on his Danish frontiers
which had enabled him to make his English claims. Edward the Confessor had
come to power when Hordaknut died 'as he stood at drink' in 1042; Magnus had
been occupied in Jutland, threatened by an invasion of Wends. On the eve of
Michaelmas, 1043, he had smashed that, but had then had to cope with Svein.
Two years later, Harald himself had added to his preoccupations. Magnus had
therefore never been able to make more than a gesture towards the English succession which he maintained was his own. Now, however, there was a man of
Magnus's blood prepared to take up that cause and make all those suffer who
opposed it. This, of course, was the nub and only substance of Harald's claim; like
all true Vikings, he understood the logic of arms better than he did the subtleties of
succession. To make his right to the crown crystal-clear, he had only to enforce it –
the thinness of his arguments would be of no importance then. And that he could
enforce it, aware as he was of his reputation as the greatest warrior in the north and
perhaps in all Europe, he did not for a moment doubt.

The English, although they kept a wary eye on Harald and his Norwegian
mutterings, were perhaps more concerned about their nearer neighbour, William
of Normandy. Nomination was the basis of his claim, too; he, however, had been
named by Edward himself as his successor, the English king's leaning towards
Normandy made clearer by his appointment in 1051 of a Norman, Robert de
Jumièges, as Archbishop of Canterbury. When the great Godwin, the earl who
ruled the south and had helped both Edward and his predecessor to the crown,

tried to combat this foreign faction by raising an army, Edward exiled him; it was then that he confirmed (or in some accounts stated for the first time) his preference for William to succeed him. William, after all, had married Matilda, in whose veins, although she was daughter to the Count of Flanders, the blood of Alfred flowed.

Within a year, Godwin was back, as powerful as before. Perhaps even more so, for now he could dictate new terms to his king. At the height of this renaissance he died, but his son Harold was no weaker a man than he. He consolidated his strength and his position, until no one could challenge him as the first man in the kingdom under the king – and perhaps not even with that proviso, for he had become commander of the army. It became clear that when Edward died, his would be a formidable claim for the throne; he was the man practically in possession, in any case, he was English, and towards the end of his life it seems that Edward too considered him as his heir. The mysterious journey to Normandy and the enforced oath of allegiance to William, that curious episode laid out in the strip-cartoon sequences of the Bayeux Tapestry, did nothing to undermine his situation in English eyes, however much William felt it supported his own.

Edward weakened, sank; the English, contemplating their future, grew tense. Threatened from abroad, it seems that they rallied to their own champion, Harold, however they may have mistrusted or disliked the over-proud line of Godwin. Early in January 1066, Edward died, a holy man whose abbey at Westminster stands as his memorial nine centuries later. Only one day after his death, Harold was proclaimed the king of England, his status now confirmed by the clearly expressed wish of his predecessor that the throne should be his. Everyone wondered how William would respond. Uneasily, the country looked to its arms and gazed southwards, waiting for the dark shapes of a Norman fleet to punctuate the shining and unsteady skeins of the Channel waves. But it was, astonishingly, in the north-east that the beacons of alarm were lit, and it was Harald Hardradi of Norway and not William of Normandy who was the first to step on English soil, sword poised to catch a crown.

Circumstances and old rivalries had helped Harald to his decision to invade. In order to extend his power northwards, Godwin of Wessex had made Harold's brother Tostig Earl of Northumbria. Tostig, however, was not a man of Harold's calibre, nor one who understood how to win the affection of a people to whom Godwin and his sons had been little more than names. The Northumbrians had turned on their new earl in 1065, after a decade's hard experience of him, and Edward had replaced him with Morcar, grandson of that Leofric who had been earl in Knut's time. Embittered, Tostig had hoped for help from Harold, but his brother, a diplomatic and intelligent man with an eye on the crown, had been able, or willing, to do very little. Thus there was one powerful Englishman at least in that spring of 1066 clearly available for foreign intrigues.

In May, Tostig with a clutch of ships had appeared off the south-east coast, and Harold had had to drive him off. To the English it seemed that Tostig was in

A messenger brings news of Harold Godwinsson
to William the Conqueror: from the
Bayeux Tapestry.

league with William; Harold had called out the army and through that summer, increasingly impatient, increasingly burdened by the work not done on their own lands, the men had waited for the Norman attack. In Norway, meanwhile, egged on by emissaries from Tostig and from the Northmen of the Orkneys, Harald Hardradi had been assembling a fleet. In the early autumn, his ships had put to sea, travelling the old Viking sea-road, south-west to England's east coast. When the men of Orkney and Tostig's detachment had joined them, Harald had found himself the commander of three hundred ships, almost ten thousand men. With these, a Viking always, he now slashed at the little coastal towns – Cleveland, Scarborough – before swinging into the mouth of the Humber and then up the Ouse until, at Riccall, he came ashore at last. One sees him, this tall man, proud perhaps with the consciousness of legend, busy in the disembarkation, signalling the disposition of his destiny, marshalling the forces of his last ambition, confident, experience containing his excitement, aware that only what he understood best, battle and the dealing of death, stood between him and the rich throne he coveted.

Three miles from where his army stood, the River Wharfe flows into the Ouse; on its waters, at Tadcaster, lay the few English warships which his fleet had pushed along the coast before it. There would be little threat from them. Ten miles to the north stood York, that city both local nexus and national symbol. Guarding it, an English army, too hastily called together, too unprepared, waited under the command of Morcar and his brother Edwin, Earl of Mercia. Harald advanced upon them, Tostig openly beside him, anxious for the earldom his treachery might buy. Two miles from York, at Fulford, invaders and defenders came bloodily together. Despite English unpreparedness and Viking ferocity, the day was declining towards evening before Harald could be certain that once again battle had answered his demands. English ranks wavered, split, came together, split again; men seeped away, defeat as always the solvent for that corporate loyalty on which discipline is based; the army broke. Too many men had died, however; that day's honour had been bought at a price which, for both English and Norwegians, hopelessly mortgaged their future.

It would be Harald upon whom history would first foreclose. Not that he behaved badly now, or overplayed his hand. He spared York, did not even remain in the city. With the customary hostages, he retired to his camp at Riccall; he even asked the people to help him in his attempt on the crown. With victory behind him, he must have felt an easy certainty that the road south to glory and success lay open, that all he had to do now was march down it. He had forgotten or had never learned that Harold still stood in the south-east at the head of an assembled and impatient army – had stood in the south-east, but was now in huge forced marches striding up the length of England, furiously intent on repairing the damage done at Fulford.

Now Harald made the Viking's supreme gesture of confidence – he left his ships, moving the main body of his army twelve miles away to Stamfordbridge, a small town on the Derwent. It was seventeen miles from Tadcaster, where the English ships still lay – and where, abruptly, Harold Godwinsson appeared, having miraculously brought his army to join them. It was 24 September; Fulford had been fought only four days before. So swift had Harold's movements been that the Norwegian king, although only a few miles from him, had no suspicion of his presence. It was, however, soon to be made evident.

Monday, 25 September, the Viking army half-relaxed, it seems, and on the east bank of the Derwent, the bridge protecting them inadequately guarded, Harald it may be still leisurely in his expectation of satisfied ambition; then, abruptly marching down from York, eight miles away, the grim columns of the English army, those men tense from the empty months of waiting, angry at this unexpected assault, eager for action, for revenge, for the repulse of the Norwegian and the downfall of the traitor, Tostig. They had already covered the seventeen miles from Tadcaster, but they were prepared, keyed-up, and they could see that they had surprised their enemies. Such an awareness may have nullified whatever nervousness they felt at facing this redoubtable and world-famous warrior; their king had caught him unprepared, after all, had brought him unexpectedly about, had out-manœuvred him and trapped him. Yet the armies were well-matched, not unequal in numbers or equipment; the day would be hard, and its ending would see a crown usurped or a crown confirmed.

At this point, facts recede; there are legends, snatches of unlikely conversation, magnificent quotations not now to be traced back to those to whom they were later attributed. Harold's promise that the Norwegian invader should have seven feet of English soil, the grave's length of a large man, 'or as much more as he may be taller than other men'; Harald Hardradi on horseback, his black horse ominously stumbling, the English king remarking, 'I think his luck has left him'; the two kings vying as poets as they extemporized warlike verses, Thjodolf Arnorsson of Iceland capping them both; Harold Godwinsson's offers of peace and quarter to his brother, rejected by Tostig out of loyalty to Norwegian Harald – all these, poets' inventions, Snorri's additions, folk memories, the romance of *King Harald's Saga*, are overtaken by the metallic clatter of honed edge on helmet and chain mail, by the nervous snorting of horses, by battle cry and frantic order, by the overwhelming, rotten-fruit thudding of the suddenly-dead bodies on the trampled grass. 'The Englishmen made a hot assault upon the Northmen, who sustained it bravely,' Snorri tells us, his account two centuries too late for accuracy. But he gives us, plausibly, an even battle until the Vikings, enticed by some fancied weakness in their opponents, broke their order of battle and, advancing, found the English crushing upon them from three sides.

Then Harald 'went into the fray where the greatest crash of weapons was'; he 'was in a rage, and ran out in front of the array, and hewed down with both hands, so that neither helmet nor armour could withstand him, and all who were nearest gave way before him.' One sees him, the seven fearsome feet of him, his helmet tall above those quaking before his strength, the nearest turning to flee against the

The silver Gundestrup bowl, from Himmerland, Jutland. This is Celtic work of the second or first century BC and harks back to the victory rites of the Danish Cimbri, who cut the throats of their captives and let their blood flow into a huge bronze cauldron.

press of their comrades, the earth beneath their feet dark and slippery with the blood of those already riven by the great warrior's sword, the whole line beginning to give way, to bend before the black fury of his desperation – for, says Snorri, 'It was then very near with the English that they had taken to flight.' But there was to be an ending, now, to the violent saga of his days. An arrow hit him, so Snorri recounts, in the wind-pipe, 'and that was his death-wound'. So, after all, his height was humbled, his great estate was snatched from him, the darkness came to cut him off from the glittering demands of his ambition. His truth ended, and the wonderful lies of his legend began.

Tostig died also, and rank after harried rank of the Norwegian soldiers. The twelve miles between Stamfordbridge and the Viking ships were marked by the empty bodies of the dead; blood streaked those valleys, dark signal for the carrion crows. Olaf, Harald's son, was allowed to depart by the English king, a magnanimity establishing a stable dynasty in Norway which would make a sad contrast with Harold Godwinsson's own curtailed line; but only twenty-four ships sailed with the new young king back to the fjords and harbours from which more than two hundred had set sail, and for a generation Norway would lack the young men necessary to enforce policy or support aggression outside its borders.

In retrospect, the fall of that enormous figure, the blood frothing from the gashed neck, the eyes staring as the lungs clogged and life withdrew, seems like the final thunder-clap of some tremendous storm. His name is the last in that gallery of warriors, bandits, pirates, butchers and usurpers who had, sword in one hand and blazing torch in the other, carved out for themselves what insubstantial realms they could, taking all that fell to them and burning what did not. Halfdan the Black, Turgeis, Hastein, Eirik the Red and Leif, his son, Olaf Tryggvesson – it was with such men that Harald Hardradi would be ranked. But he would be the last. With his death, that roster closed for ever. A new breed, sprung from Northmen's blood, but bleaker, narrower, would from now on trouble Europe with their restless lust for conquest. Two days after Harald's death, William of Normandy set sail across the Channel.

A representation of Vikings sailing over a
mermaid-infested sea.

9 THE LEGACY

We like to trace the history of Europe through the brilliance of Greece, the great opulence of Rome; the Renaissance on which our modern culture rests is a rebirth of what were thought of as their artistic and spiritual values. It was a knowledge of their languages which was for centuries the single unimpeachable evidence of a person's education, it was familiarity with their pantheon which was the necessary stock-in-trade of every poet and rhetorician anxious for the attention of his world. Greek philosophy, Roman discipline – this was the combination upon which the only good and viable society might be built. And as our ancestors conversed and postured in the reflection of that even, classical light, that glow of splendour from the south-east, they hardly noticed the lightning-fractured gloom behind them, the jagged waves and implacable cliffs of the sea-girdled lands to the north from which so many of their customs, laws and political institutions had been brought by their shaggy-bearded, red-cloaked, axe-wielding and evil-smelling forebears.

There were, first, the demographic and political divisions of Europe, many of them the direct consequences of those great sweeps of Viking raiders, bandits and colonizers across the Western world. To the east, there lay mysterious Russia, a land difficult of access and unutterably foreign, yet founded by Swedes who had held open the trade-routes to Byzantium with the blades of their swords. Novgorod (originally Holmgard), Kiev, Rostov, Vladimir – few people realized that such alien names described cities built by the cousins of those who had first thrown up walls, earthen or timbered, about the captured towns of eastern England. It was the injection of Scandinavian energy which promoted that turbulence in the Dnieper Valley from which arose the might and grandeur of the early Russian principality. It was the blood of Vikings in the veins of Vladimir and Yaroslav which made them so bold and so decisive in their struggles for Russia and the Christian religion. As late as the eleventh century, the chronicler Thietmar of Merseburg could describe the people of Kiev as 'Danes' – here a blanket-word for Scandinavians. In the twelfth century, Swedish merchants still maintained a guild-house in Novgorod. Only after that, with the trade routes to the east cut and the Slavonic language and culture overwhelming the traditional Scandinavian, did Russia begin to become that separate and disturbing entity, that strange, inaccessible country brooding at the edges of European awareness, with which no real contact would be made again by the West until Elizabeth I sat on the throne of England.

A hoard of silver objects – coins, rings, bracelets
and other ornaments – found at Birka, Sweden.

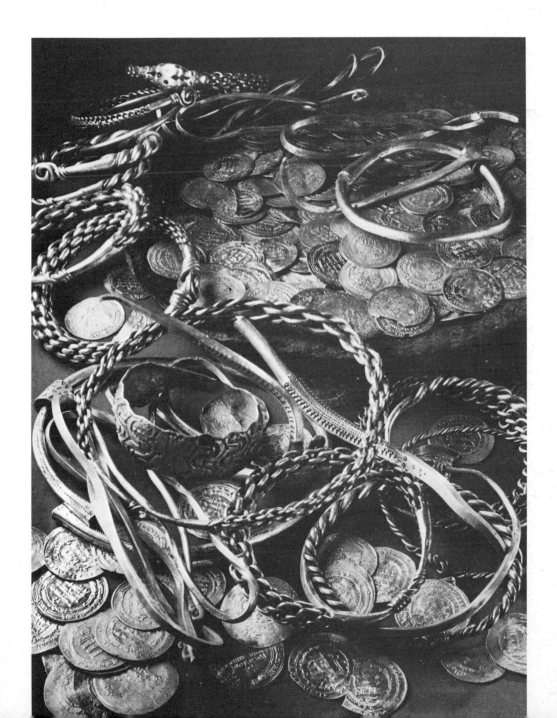

The Jelling cup, found in a royal grave at
Jelling. This tenth-century silver cup bears a
remarkable double-contoured animal motif
typical of what is now called the Jelling style.

For Ireland, the Viking invasions had been like a thunder-storm awakening
some deep dreamer long asleep. Sitting on the seaward edge of Europe, swathed in
its Celtic culture, separate, self-absorbed, its struggles internecine, its Christianity
special to itself, the country seems hardly to have been aware of the world beyond
its shores. Then, with the vigorous arrival of that famous first 'Turgeis', Irish
history was suddenly dragged into the ordinary currents, floods and tides by which
its contemporary world was being altered. War was nothing new to Ireland, but
invasion was; so was the consequence of invasion, the addition of another genetic
element to its people's heritage. The new outward-looking aspect of the country
was exemplified in the sea-ports which the Vikings now established – Vikingalo,
Veigsfjördr, Hlymrekr, which we still know as Wicklow, Wexford and Limerick.
Dublin, where Nordic kings held Court, was their own city, and it was their
presence which made it known elsewhere in Europe. 'Go south then to Dublin,' the
Norwegian noble Brynhjolf told his son. 'That is now the most praiseworthy
voyage.' Ireland, a staging-post on the sea-routes, for both traders and raiders, had
been grappled to the body of Europe. The very invasion of Normans which led to
its long and disastrous connection with its neighbouring island was a direct consequence of the Viking presence and of the Irish struggle, unrelenting and in the end
successful, against it. After that, there was no longer any possibility that Ireland
would slip away from western consciousness, to lie, green, rounded, fertile, in its
endless mists and swirling rains, a pleasant legend nobody needed to verify. It
remained strange and its people wild, thirsty for song, unpredictable – but it
remained within European reach, one country among others. It was Viking
determination which had dragged it there from its once-remote Atlantic
anchorage.

To the west, Iceland lay, a country which owes its whole being to Viking
enterprise. The few Irish settlers who had made their way, gale-borne, to those
rumpled shores had never been enough to found more than a hermitage or two.
It was Northmen, land-hungry, easy on distant seas, who came tumbling up
those craggy headlands, those rocky beaches, to establish a state there,
simulacrum of those they had left behind. The institutions, the language, the
blood-line of the inhabitants, all have their roots in Scandinavia, roots fertilized
by the blood and sweat of the early adventurers. For a long time, distant Greenland mirrored the Icelandic condition. Even when, in the end, the altered climate

and Scandinavian indifference brought to starvation and death the few impoverished settlers who had survived, the island remained in memory, a fact which in itself kept open the eventually fertile idea of some bourne far to the west. Nearer to the centres of European life the Faroes, too, were peopled by the same eager Vikings, who thus for all time extended, even if only by a little, the area of the known and habitable world.

Within the body politic of France Normandy had settled, rooted so deeply that later generations never thought about its people's Scandinavian origins. It is, indeed, sometimes difficult to see in those hard-faced defenders of towering and multiple castle walls, those grim exactors of every last feudal due, the lineaments of their brawling, careless, peripatetic ancestors. But the energy which drove them deep into the Mediterranean basin on their campaigns of conquest was doubtless the same as that which had carried the Vikings across the oceans and along the river-valleys of the Western world. For that reason the alterations to the maps and cultures of Europe for which the Normans were responsible is a part of that complex legacy which the Northmen left behind them. Had their clamouring raids up the Seine Valley not resulted in Rollo's founding of his dukedom, nothing of what followed, from England to the Levant, would have happened in the way it did.

Christendom itself, once heavily beset by the Vikings, whose marauding ships robbed monasteries and churches with a pagan exuberance, ended in the sea-farers' debt. Northmen became ferocious missionaries, but although they preached with sword-edge rather than Bible, with mundane threat rather than heavenly promise, they made their converts. Olaf Tryggvesson in Norway, Sigmund Brestesson in the Faroes, Vladimir in Kiev – such men ordered baptism as other rulers did military service or some outrageous tax; after their time, how-ever, Christianity was the established religion of their peoples. Whether this was always a good thing may be debated; that it had its consequence in the creation of Europe as a continent dominated by a single faith is clear. The very restlessness of Scandinavian voyagers, their endless flitting to and fro before the various winds of their years, helped to carry this new message about the world. From having torn at the borders of Christianity's realm, they became one of the many complex elements which tied it into a ramshackle, sometimes rickety yet always very real unity. That centuries later Christianity was no longer under threat, that Christian gentlemen from the Renaissance on could regard with a pleasant, scholarly detachment the pagan antics of Olympian deities, was due in part to Viking work in pegging the canopy of their faith securely to the very edges of the navigable world.

If it is difficult to assess the precise contribution the Vikings finally made to the spreading of the Christian faith, it is even harder to decide what their effect was on the development of the social institutions which we now prize so highly. It is customary, for example, to look into that dazzle of genius which is Periclean Athens for the model of our own version of democracy. But our connection with the world of Greece is finally an indirect one; it comes filtered through the authori-tarian Roman experience, culled from works rescued by Arabic translation, or from the rediscovered writings of ancient sages which so excited the fifteenth and sixteenth centuries. Finally, it has been modified by the narrow certainties of the Christian Fathers and the commentaries of Schoolmen. What most of Europe knew directly was the weight and insatiable demand of the Roman Empire. The Romans conquered, and they expected their conquests to be of value to them; in return, they gave their subject peoples system and order. Democracy they kept for themselves. Yet even for the Roman citizen such democracy, based on the magis-terial *rogatio*, permitted nothing but a simple positive or negative response. There was no real question in that forum of debate, the raising of grievances, the discus-sion of alternatives, the tidal movements of party, faction or opinion. Neatness was all; power lay in the hands of those who framed the questions. The only alterna-tive, frequently resorted to, was popular violence.

Where, in that case, have their erstwhile subject races, their former colonies, learned to value democracy so highly? If it was from Rome, then it could have been no more than by hearsay – democracy in the Empire was a matter of report, the property of privilege. It seems more likely that our passion for this kind of participatory government, which is so strongly rooted in north-west Europe, has its beginnings in those institutions, northern institutions, which lie in our direct historical experience. If that were to be conceded, we would be forced to consider the Vikings as something more than romantically blood-thirsty brigands, for it was they as much as anyone who spread those institutions through their scattered settlements, and thus throughout precisely those parts of Europe where democracy appears most central to the functions of the state.

The instrument of Viking democracy was, of course, the *thing*. Its function was fundamentally legislative and juridical; it decided the limits of freedom, then maintained those delineated freedoms in its judgments. Since law to be effective covers all our social life, the *thing* became an assembly prepared to discuss any matter of public concern. Organized on a local level, it worked in a fashion similar to the meetings of freemen in the Greek city states, and for the same reason – the numbers involved were small, they knew each other personally or by easily verifiable repute, and they were able to consider their problems at length because slavery gave them the leisure to do so. Called on a national basis, the *thing* was perhaps too unwieldy to be effective, its operations often diminishing into little more than that simple agreement or disagreement which authority permitted the citizens of Rome. Even within those limits, however, its power was not negligible – it was the voice which frequently decided whether peace or war lay before the people and one of its functions was the election of the king (although often a royal accession had to be ratified by a whole series of regional *things*, a tedious process, but necessary for the consolidation of a royal personage's individual power).

The yeomen householders, petty farmers inheriting the freehold of the land they worked who made up the bulk of those assembling for a *thing*, were above all jealous of any encroachment on their freedom; often this made them a nuisance to the king and his noblemen, sometimes it thwarted policies demonstrably better than the traditions which they so bitterly defended. In the end, in any case, the political and economic logic of the new nation-states overwhelmed them – but not before the freedoms to which they had so stubbornly clung had become, as it were, a popular heritage, a legend and a hope, leading to an endless, deep expectation which had to be given shape again as new institutions developed.

It was not the Scandinavians alone, of course, who governed their affairs and settled their differences by such assemblies. In England, the Saxon institution of the *folk-moot* and the *shire-moot* played the same role. There was even an approximation to a national Parliament in the *Witanagemot*, the assembly of the wise; it had no legislative role, but it was a kind of supreme court, it was the collective overseer of public appointments and the apportionment of public lands, and it played its part in the election of kings. Once kings had placed themselves securely on the throne, the *Witangemot* could act as a council, a committee of ealdormen, bishops, warriors and notables (categories, of course, largely overlapping) which could modify, if it could not over-rule, the royal whim.

Eleventh-century Anglo-Saxon manuscript
showing the *Witanagemot*, presided over by the
king. This council was equivalent to the
Viking *Thing*.

The arrival of large clusters of busy Danes and their establishing of settlements in eastern England did nothing to undermine this ancient system. It merely added an alternative version to that by which the Saxons lived. It is therefore not surprising that this stream in English life, forced underground by the heavy and newly deposited stratum of Norman feudalism, should begin to surface again in the thirteenth century, when Simon de Montfort, for his own revolutionary purposes, called his succession of Parliaments, gushing springs from which, eventually, a vast river, part mud, part silver clarity, would roll with grave exuberance along the centuries.

It seems to me no coincidence that it was in England and in those countries in which Vikings were predominant that Parliaments should either never have disappeared, or reappeared very swiftly when done away with. Denmark, for example, had a powerful council of nobles, the *Raad*, in the twelfth century; a hundred years later, a much more widely-based Parliament, the *Danehof*, was forced on the king. Even the *Rigsraad*, composed as it was of members of the leading families, was able because of its elective power in the dynastic succession to restrain Danish kings in a manner unknown to Habsburgs or Bourbons. Sweden held its first *Riksdag*, an assembly including representatives of clergy, burghers and peasants as well as aristocrats, in 1435, after a rebellion led by Engelbrekt Engelbrektsson; that Parliament has been in existence ever since. The free men of Iceland have had their say through the *Althing* since the tenth century. Even the tiny Isle of Man has been able, through its *Tynwald*, to keep alive its own tradition of freedom, one founded by its Viking settlers nearly ten centuries ago, thus holding at bay the administrative greed of English bureaucracy. While these assemblies were giving a voice to at least some of the people, elsewhere in Europe autocrats ruled, dismissing or ignoring at will such Parliaments as existed, their haphazard despotism enjoyed or endured by their subjects with no more than an occasional sullen and almost always doomed uprising of the desperate, such abrupt violence no substitute for the reasoned debate which in the northern countries could at times modify the exercise of absolute power.

Thus the English Revolution of the 1640s was less the beginning of a new political consciousness than it was the culmination of an inexorable popular movement which sprang out of traditions inherited from the country's Saxon and Viking founders. Westminster was far from being the Mother of Parliaments; indeed, it took that convulsive seventeenth-century leap for it to overtake those assemblies, already established in northern Europe, which had long been at the business of defining and defending a people's ordinary freedoms. In contrast to these, the new constitutions which were to be written in the United States of America and in France some 150 years later seem artificial constructions, models made of words, of ink and paper, the careful theories of philosophers, concerned with balance, hierarchy and the distribution of power. It is in those countries where a man's liberty was long guaranteed by access to the *thing* or recourse to the sword, where Vikings forced on authority a recognition of individual existence and where no ruler could long survive popular disapproval, that freedom became an organic matter, growing under the pressure of its own inner necessity and made manifest in the flesh and blood of powerful assemblies.

Some of the most solidly-established democracies of the modern world can thus trace their direct development back to such Scandinavian and Germanic roots, however much that development has been modified by the ideas and the vocabulary of ancient Greece. It seems also to be true that the legal systems which support those democracies and which enshrine the individual liberties of which they are so proud have their beginnings in the same local and regional assemblies by whose decisions the northern communities regulated their existence. The Greeks certainly knew a jury system and expected to be judged not only by committees of their peers but even by judges essentially amateur; these were elected for a period, rarely arriving at eminence through either aristocratic influence or scholastic application. The Athenian jury, however, numbering hundreds and sometimes even thousands, was picked to stand for the people as a whole, a representative assembly in which might be found all the elements which made up the social strata of the free citizens. (Foreigners, slaves and women, of course, were not considered fit to perform such duties.) Those involved in law suits were expected to represent themselves, thus completing the caste of ordinary citizens appearing on the crowded, over-populated stages of the courts. By Roman times, however, there was no longer any question of a jury system. Law was administered by public officers, the evidence being collected by investigating magistrates. Thus our direct connection with Greek freedom was, in this sphere as in the political, cut by the authoritarian practices of the intervening Roman Empire.

Roman law did, it is true, allow for the practical acceptance of the everyday in provisions equivalent to those of the Common Law of England. But in essence it was an imperial system imposed from above. Ordinary people had no access to the legislative process, nor did they play any part in reaching juridical decisions. It was the Scandinavian *thing* and the Anglo-Saxon *moot* which, in the north European experience, allowed a man to put his case before an assembly of his equals. It is with these that our past is directly connected, rather than with the porticoed and pillared courts of Greece, noisy with the rhetoric and passionate logic of litigants busy in the causes of an entirely alien society. It is to the Saxons and above all the Vikings, it seems to me, that the peoples of north-west Europe are truly indebted, and it is their stubborn conviction that the personal liberty of each free man is sacred which underlies our own.

In England, the jury system even survived the autocracies of Norman feudalism. The local knowledge of a 'hundred meeting' was itself the repository and register of both precedent and tenure, though guilt was frequently arrived at through trial by ordeal rather than any particular eloquence, or even proofs. It was in the twelfth century, when Henry II tried to attract men with differences to settle to the law rather than the field of combat, that juries of twelve first sat in Assize Courts. Called to adjudicate between rival claimants, particularly in land-tenure cases,

Viking jewellery: TOP Brooch from Valla,
Klinte, Sweden. BOTTOM Silver and niello
ring-headed brooch from Birka. OPPOSITE,
ABOVE Necklet of silver-gilt. BELOW Gold
brooch and ring, from Hornelund, Denmark.

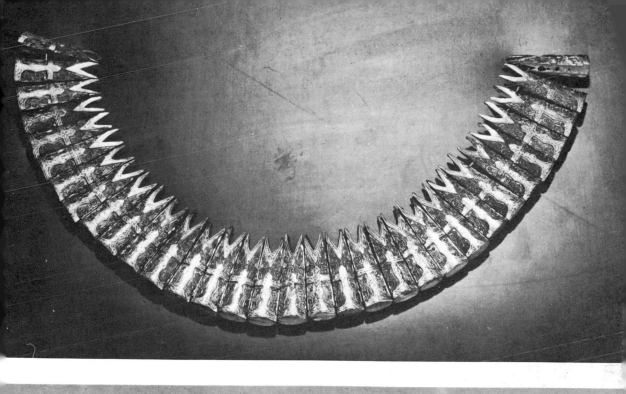

twelve knights with local knowledge were required to arrive at a verdict in the matter. In a modified way, law had been given back to at least some of the people, no longer remaining simply one of the instruments of authority. A consequence of this has been that the judiciary has never been totally controlled by governmental decree, a separation of functions upon which all liberty must rest.

The fact that there were twelve jurymen on these twelfth-century panels, as there have been ever since, is perhaps of some significance. In Viking as in Saxon days, the innocence of a defendant could at times be upheld by the swearing of a solemn oath. This was normally supported by the opinion, equally sworn, of others; such voicing of public conviction was the function of those called in as 'oath-helpers'. Oaths of this sort had been used in pagan times to ask the gods to show their benign or unpleasant aspects according to the truth or falsehood of what had been stated; after the arrival of Christianity they proved their own vigour by transferring from the authority of Asgard to that of the Bible. It was no longer the sacred arm-ring upon which a witness swore, it was upon holy relics. Although there was no set number of these 'oath-helpers', twelve was a very common number (in fiercely contested suits, however, oath would be flung against oath in barrage and counter-barrage of the sworn and the forsworn).

At first, an accused man naturally sought his oath-helpers from among his own family and kin; there was in those days rarely a shortage of willing cousins within reach. Since blood-ties were on the whole closer and more compelling than those between man and God, these easily-acquired supporters were soon considered of little real value. In various parts of Scandinavia, therefore, there arose the use of an independent panel from which some at least of the oath-helpers had to be chosen. In both Norway and Denmark, the panel from which those who would swear might be chosen numbered twelve. In Denmark and Sweden, this independent panel after a while quite naturally took upon itself the burden of arriving at some decisions about the guilt of the accused before consolidating his protestations with their own; no kin of his, they felt no duty to support him simply because he had asked them to. Noting these echoes and connections, one cannot help suspecting that our jury system, like that of representative assemblies, has its roots in northern Europe rather than the Mediterranean. Consolidating such suspicions, an ordinance passed by Æthelred in 997 commands twelve thegns to sit with the reeve in each *wapentake* of the Danelaw, their function the giving of information, on oath, about suspected criminals, thus connecting Saxon command with Scandinavian practice.

If freedom is indivisible, so are the institutions of freedom. The assembly of free men was an institution widespread in northern Europe; the freedom it guaranteed was reinforced by the right of an accused to stand before a group of his equals and put to them the question of his guilt or innocence. Just as Parliament arose by direct evolution from the *things* and *moots* of northern peoples, so did juries. In England, it may be, the main influence was Saxon – but though half of England was modified by the conventions of the Danelaw, this aspect of life did not change.

The fact is that Viking and Saxon both took it for granted that freedom came in these forms; when Norman brutality and arrogance seemed to have crushed the previous society, these convictions proved resilient; when the right moment came, the old institutions surfaced to offer at least a version of the ancient liberties to a recently-oppressed people. Once they had appeared again, they were difficult to suppress, and though Crown and privilege attempted such suppression, they flourished nevertheless. Eventually they became so accepted a part of every man's expectation that it seemed no incongruity to turn to ancient Greece for liberty's rationale. There philosophers could be found to explain the nature and proper extent of freedom (though also the necessity for authority and order); it was from further north, however, that the actual structures of freedom were inherited.

Equality in freedom can sometimes make for vulnerability, even for anarchy. The English word 'fellow' comes from the Norse word *felag*, which means 'partnership'. The *félagar* were those who freely combined, sometimes permanently, sometimes only for the period of a specific venture, in order to support each other in enterprise. Working the land, trading, owning ships, raiding – all these were best conducted by groups of men pledged to some kind of active interconnection. Such associations became formalized eventually in the guilds which grew up in Scandinavia, the earliest apparently of merchants, later those of craftsmen, others then developing with a more generally social rather than a narrowly practical purpose. These friendlier groupings were more clubs than guilds, including women and children, celebrating their existence in feasts to which all contributed and cementing their amity with prayer – such guilds were often formed in the name of some saint. In this way there was established a principle which, one feels, never totally disappeared from common awareness – that it may be necessary voluntarily to surrender some aspects of freedom in order to safeguard its essence.

The guilds of the Northmen were brought about not by coercion but by an awareness that a freely-given allegiance to a group will give that group coherence and strength. Not that the guilds' purpose was defensive; it was positive, active, enterprising. But their effect was to give everyone who joined them support and protection, an authority alternative to that of the state on the one hand, the family on the other; they offered a set of rules which, forced on no one, was accepted by everyone as the price of their special unity. The very existence of the guilds seems to prove the depth and maturity of Scandinavian liberty, maintained through the centuries when royal power grew, an alternative to the hierarchies of feudalism, founding a tradition kept sinewy and supple even until today.

Certainly the world needs such traditions. The press of population, the complexities of industrial economies, the inter-dependence of states, the new worldwide groupings of both nations and enormous private enterprises, the increased and increasing responsibilities accepted by governments for the welfare of their citizens, all threaten the fragile liberties of which human dignity are woven. There are whole political philosophies which accept that their success depends on tearing this gossamer cloak off mankind's shoulders. Human welfare involves for them a reduction in human significance which they do not even regret. Throughout the world, value becomes a matter of price. Governments bribe whole populations, paying for their power by increasing their supporters' standard of living. Such increases are in turn paid for by the people, whose taxes rise and whose freedoms diminish. Both expediency and necessity everywhere dictate measures which only a complex and expanding bureaucracy can administer. And everywhere bureaucracy, perhaps by its nature, encroaches further and further on human activity. Its highest good is a vision of total order; then paper will flow through the arteries of the world's societies, a pallid life-blood fit for communities of zombies. No ideology will save us then – the tendency is universal, forced on by the logic of the birth statistics, seized as eagerly by the servants of democracy as of tyranny, of communism as of capitalism, of left-wing people's republic as of right-wing military junta, of rich industrialized states as of poor and under-developed ones.

The pressure is universal; how is it to be resisted? In many different places the answer seems to be by returning to older traditions, by remembering a different past. Throughout Europe, Basques and Bretons, Scots, Ukrainians and Welsh struggle against absorption, fight to maintain their local singularity. For those who have no such roots to sustain them, however, the searing winds of coerced order seem to be creating irresistible deserts. As we stumble into these, perhaps we shall find in our own past the springs to nourish the cool oases which may even, carefully tended, turn back the deserts themselves.

If one function of history is to show how things have become as they are, another is to demonstrate that they need not be so. In Greece, where we imagine we can discern those examples upon which our own freedoms have been modelled, the seeds of our present regimentation can in fact be found. It is not the spirit of that ten-thousand-headed *demos* which animates our masters, but the arid and precise ideas of Plato and his successors. For them, the example of Athens lies not in the liberty of its citizens, but in the death of Socrates. Yet if we are to survive under our present pressures, where shall we look for the support of history? Only the tradition of an inherited wildness, a desperate recalcitrance, may save us.

It is here, perhaps, that the Viking saga may yet have its main importance. Romanticized, made sanitary, deodorized and certified hygienic, it remains nevertheless a story based on savagery, on restlessness, on a vigorous dissatisfaction with conditions as they were, on a search for self-assertion; it is a long statement made over centuries of man's courage and individual significance, in a period always turbulent, often violent and sometimes vile, but brightened by a pride and a dauntlessness which flutter in its smoke-heavy gloom with the grandeur of banners. In this way, it may lurk at the edges of our consciousness, a fog blurring the clarity of directive and decree, a cold, northern sleet, its discomfort a refreshment, through which we can discern, if we choose to look, the heavy-shouldered, helmeted figures of these cruel adventurers, swords black with blood, braceleted arms tight about screaming women and plundered gold, but in their eyes a conviction of freedom which we may yet use to sustain our own.

One of the ends of a tenth-century horse-collar from Søllested, Denmark. It has gilded bronze mounts, and each end has the head of a predatory beast, while the rest is decorated with human masks.

It is perhaps necessary that beyond conformity there should be a mental area given over to anarchy, to a strutting assertion of individual importance, even a sort of wilderness of the imagination in which war-cry, scream and dying groan mingle in a cacophony of violence, in which primitive strength makes statements no central authority can prevent or even deny, in which a man's birthright is no more than his name, the ambition to make it immortal and the skill with sword and sail to try for that ambition's fulfilment. Such an area of the mind becomes a repository of alternative values, not all of them admirable, but most of them essential if we are not to be rendered nameless, impotent and dull by the watchful ordinances of governments which know by instinct that blandness is all, that a people lulled is more easily managed than a people coerced.

Some fifty years ago, ghosts walked on a Jutland hill, on the island of Als. A clergyman with oak stake and hammer slammed them into silence, driving his wooden post into a spot he had mysteriously chosen. Four decades later, an official from the museum at Sønderborg Castle, digging in that place, found the stake had riven the breast of a skeleton, the strong bones of a Viking warrior, buried there a thousand years before and long forgotten. The authority of an organized church had beaten back the wildness of an earlier time; for the clergy-man's flock the reward was security. Perhaps the price they paid for it was higher than its worth. Perhaps it is time that we developed some ancient part of our own sensibilities, kept open some keen awareness of the psyche, so that when our Vikings too walk towards us through the mists of the dead, their message an ancient liberty, we will outwit our protectors and welcome them.

The Frankish Empire

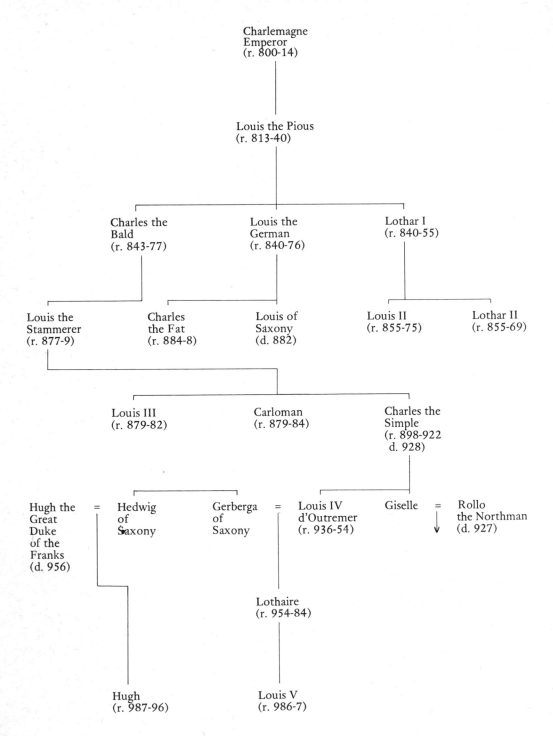

Charlemagne
Emperor
(r. 800-14)

Louis the Pious
(r. 813-40)

Charles the
Bald
(r. 843-77)

Louis the
German
(r. 840-76)

Lothar I
(r. 840-55)

Louis the
Stammerer
(r. 877-9)

Charles
the Fat
(r. 884-8)

Louis of
Saxony
(d. 882)

Louis II
(r. 855-75)

Lothar II
(r. 855-69)

Louis III
(r. 879-82)

Carloman
(r. 879-84)

Charles the
Simple
(r. 898-922
d. 928)

Hugh the
Great
Duke
of the
Franks
(d. 956)

=

Hedwig
of
Saxony

Gerberga
of
Saxony

=

Louis IV
d'Outremer
(r. 936-54)

Giselle

=

Rollo
the Northman
(d. 927)

Lothaire
(r. 954-84)

Hugh
(r. 987-96)

Louis V
(r. 986-7)

The Anglo-Saxon Kings

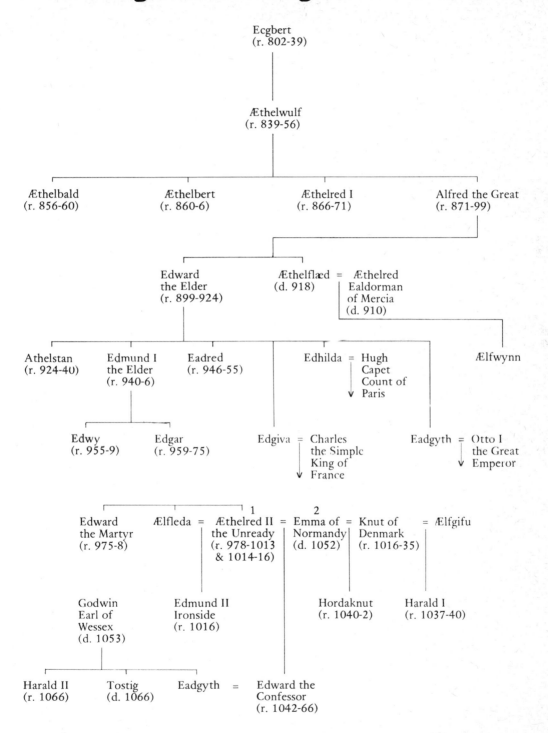

The Byzantine Empire

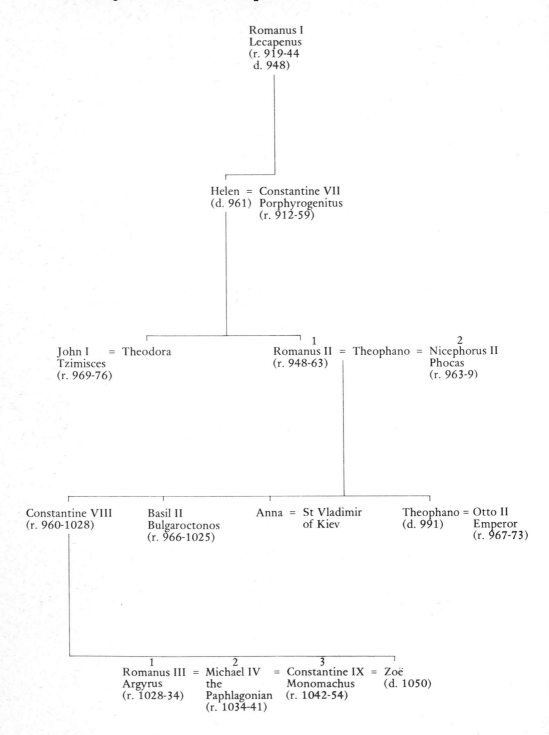

Romanus I
Lecapenus
(r. 919-44
d. 948)

Helen = Constantine VII
(d. 961) Porphyrogenitus
(r. 912-59)

John I = Theodora 1 Romanus II = Theophano = Nicephorus II 2
Tzimisces (r. 948-63) Phocas
(r. 969-76) (r. 963-9)

Constantine VIII Basil II Anna = St Vladimir Theophano = Otto II
(r. 960-1028) Bulgaroctonos of Kiev (d. 991) Emperor
(r. 966-1025) (r. 967-73)

1 2 3
Romanus III = Michael IV = Constantine IX = Zoë
Argyrus the Monomachus (d. 1050)
(r. 1028-34) Paphlagonian (r. 1042-54)
(r. 1034-41)

Russia (Kiev-Novgorod)

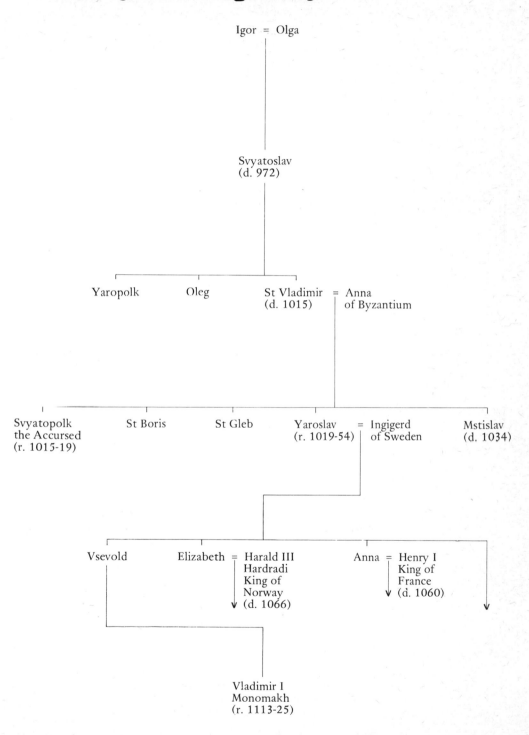

Igor = Olga

Svyatoslav
(d. 972)

Yaropolk   Oleg   St Vladimir = Anna
(d. 1015)   of Byzantium

Svyatopolk   St Boris   St Gleb   Yaroslav = Ingigerd   Mstislav
the Accursed   (r. 1019-54) of Sweden   (d. 1034)
(r. 1015-19)

Vsevold   Elizabeth = Harald III   Anna = Henry I
               Hardradi   King of
               King of   France
               Norway   (d. 1060)
               (d. 1066)

Vladimir I
Monomakh
(r. 1113-25)

The Scandinavian Kingdoms

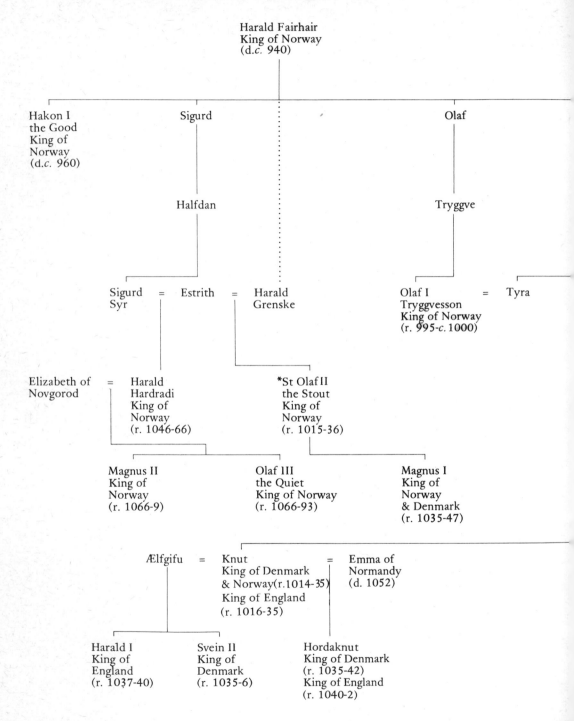

Harald Fairhair
King of Norway
(d.c. 940)

Hakon I
the Good
King of
Norway
(d.c. 960)

Sigurd

Olaf

Halfdan

Tryggve

Sigurd   =   Estrith   =   Harald
Syr   Grenske

Olaf I   =   Tyra
Tryggvesson
King of Norway
(r. 995-c. 1000)

Elizabeth of   =   Harald
Novgorod   Hardradi
                   King of
                   Norway
                   (r. 1046-66)

*St Olaf II
the Stout
King of
Norway
(r. 1015-36)

Magnus II
King of
Norway
(r. 1066-9)

Olaf III
the Quiet
King of Norway
(r. 1066-93)

Magnus I
King of
Norway
& Denmark
(r. 1035-47)

Ælfgifu   =   Knut   =   Emma of
              King of Denmark   Normandy
              & Norway(r.1014-35)   (d. 1052)
              King of England
              (r. 1016-35)

Harald I
King of
England
(r. 1037-40)

Svein II
King of
Denmark
(r. 1035-6)

Hordaknut
King of Denmark
(r. 1035-42)
King of England
(r. 1040-2)

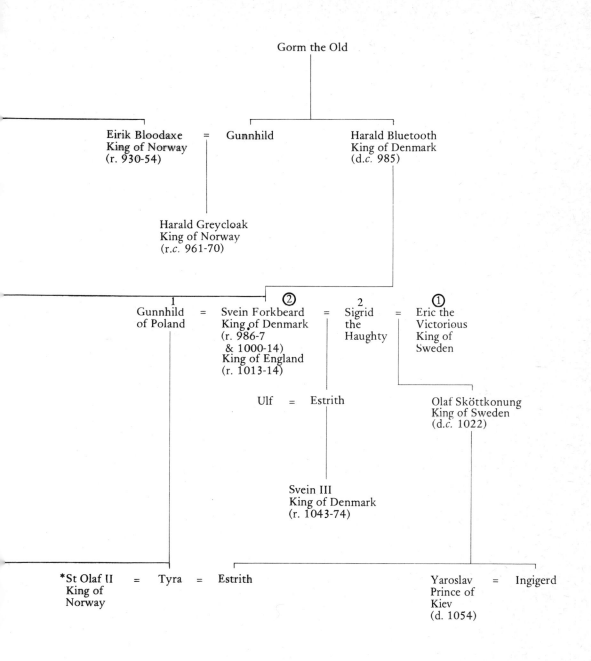

Gorm the Old

Eirik Bloodaxe
King of Norway
(r. 930-54)
= Gunnhild

Harald Bluetooth
King of Denmark
(d.c. 985)

Harald Greycloak
King of Norway
(r.c. 961-70)

1
Gunnhild
of Poland
= Svein Forkbeard
King of Denmark
(r. 986-7
& 1000-14)
King of England
(r. 1013-14)
② = 2
Sigrid
the
Haughty
= ①
Eric the
Victorious
King of
Sweden

Ulf = Estrith

Olaf Sköttkonung
King of Sweden
(d.c. 1022)

Svein III
King of Denmark
(r. 1043-74)

*St Olaf II
King of
Norway
= Tyra = Estrith

Yaroslav
Prince of
Kiev
(d. 1054)
= Ingigerd

: denotes generations of
: names unknown (i.e. Harald
: Grenske is descendant of
: Harald Fairhair)

BIBLIOGRAPHY

The author would like to acknowledge the especial usefulness to me in my retelling of the Viking story of *A History of the Vikings* by Gwyn Jones (Oxford University Press, 1968) and *A History of the Vikings* by T.D.Kendrick (Methuen, 1930).

Other books useful to the interested reader include the following:

Branston, Brian, *Gods of the North* (Thames & Hudson, 1955).

Brøndsted, Johannes, *The Vikings* (Penguin, 1965).

Davidson, H.R.E., *Gods and Myths of Northern Europe* (Penguin, 1964).

Foote, P.G., & Wilson, D.M., *The Viking Achievement* (Sidgwick & Jackson, 1970).

Klindt-Jensen, Ole, *The World of the Vikings* (Allen & Unwin, 1970).

Obolensky, Dimitri, *The Byzantine Commonwealth* (Weidenfeld & Nicolson, 1971).

Oxenstierna, Eric, *The World of the Norsemen* (Weidenfeld & Nicolson, 1967).

Sawyer, P.H., *The Age of the Vikings* (Edward Arnold, 1971).

Stenton, F.M., *Anglo-Saxon England* (Oxford University Press, 1943).

Wilson, David, *The Vikings and their Origins* (Thames and Hudson, 1970).

There are many of the Icelandic sagas available in translation, many of them the work of Gwyn Jones, notably Egil's Saga and the Saga of Eirik the Red, included in his *The Norse Atlantic Sagas* (Oxford University Press, 1964). Snorri Sturluson's 'Heimskringla', translated by Samuel Laing, is available in three volumes from the Everyman's Library.

Translations of Anglo-Saxon poetry have been taken from *Earliest English Poems* by Michael Alexander (Penguin, 1966).

INDEX